W9-BEY-939

GREAT GAA RIVALRIES

UNFORGETTABLE SHOWDOWNS

JOHN SCALLY

BLACK & WHITE PUBLISHING

First published 2019
This edition first published 2020
by Black & White Publishing Ltd
Nautical House, 104 Commercial Street
Edinburgh, EH6 6NF

1 3 5 7 9 10 8 6 4 2   20 21 22 23

ISBN: 978 1 78530 292 3

The publisher has made every reasonable effort to contact copyright holders
of images in the picture section. Any errors are inadvertent and anyone who for
any reason has not been contacted is invited to write to the publisher so that
a full acknowledgment can be made in subsequent editions of this work.

A CIP catalogue record for this book is available from the British Library.

Typeset by Iolaire Typesetting, Newtonmore
Printed and bound by CPI Group (UK) Ltd, Croydon, CR0 4YY

'*I love me county.*'
(John Mullane)

'*We are no longer the whipping boys of Munster.*'
(Anthony Daly)

'*We didn't underestimate them.
They were just much better than we thought.*'
(Pat Spillane, on Kerry v. Offaly, 1992)

David Hickey: '*Welcome to Hell.*'
Páidí Ó'Sé: '*True, but meet the Devil.*'
(Before Dublin played Kerry, 1975)

'*Rivalries are the lifeblood of the GAA.*'
(Eugene McGee)

To Ashling Reynolds

*A Flame that Sparkles Brightly
and an Enduring Inspiration*

CONTENTS

PART III: A TOWN CALLED MALICE

PART IV: EVERYBODY NEEDS BAD NEIGHBOURS

PART V: WHEN TWO TRIBES GO TO WAR

FOREWORD

by Donal Ryan

A cursory online search of the word 'rivalry' offers 'competition for the same objective or for superiority in the same field' as a definition. Slightly farther down the page is a more involved explanation: 'A rivalry is the state of two people or groups engaging in a lasting competitive relationship. Rivalry is the "against each other" spirit between two competing sides.'

The 'against each other' spirit is as close as it gets to a perfect parsing into words of the power and energy generated by the desire for victory in sport. The spirit that drives men and women to push their bodies and minds beyond the ordinary limits of endurance, to develop their skills to superhuman levels, to fight on when all seems lost, when victory seems a distant, impossible goal. It's the spirit of rivalry – that 'against each other spirit' – that forms us fans into armies great and small, coloured, bedecked, marching behind our heroes, feeling ourselves to be somehow pitched on match day in a battle for the honour and pride and very soul of our club or county or country. There are few sounds in life as sweet as the sound of the final whistle when things have gone your way; few sounds as terrible as the sound of your rivals' cheers of joy when they haven't.

I was 11 years old in 1987 when Galway beat Tipperary 3-20 to 2-17 in the All-Ireland hurling semi-final. It was the first time I'd felt the full power of the spirit of rivalry. Until that day I'd been a semi-interested observer of hurling, never playing it properly, only getting excited or upset when my home club of Burgess, and later Éire Óg Nenagh, were playing against their neighbours Portroe or Toomevara, because proximity breeds sporting rivalry like no other element. Neighbouring clubs go at it with all the pent-up frustration and resentment and desire for superiority of siblings close in age, and of course, like most siblings, return to being friends when the fire of battle goes out. But that day in Croke Park, watching Galway score 1-4 in the opening minutes, something ignited inside me that has never been quenched, a kind of madness, a burning away of reason. We were within four points of them at half-time.

'We'll do it alright, lads,' my father said.

'We will,' Tony agreed. 'We have them on the run.'

I could hardly speak: the excitement was almost too much to bear. The sides went to war in the second half. Pat Fox burst through from midfield with 15 minutes to go and scored a goal that put us a point ahead. I remember seeing flashes of red and bursting stars before my eyes as I screamed for joy, hoisted into the air by my six-foot-two cousin. Nicky English followed Pat's goal with a beautiful point and it seemed like we would pull away, put these Tribesmen to the sword.

But it slipped away from us. Noel Lane sealed it with a goal for Galway and our Tipperary hearts were broken. I'll never forget the desperate sadness I felt as the whistle went, the look of disappointment on my father's face, the ferocity of my feelings towards the Galway supporters as they celebrated. There was a sway in the crowd as we exited the Hill that threatened to become a crush and my father lost his grip on my hand as I was knocked from my feet. A giant bear of a Galway man lifted me up and carried me through the melee to the steps, and to my father's arms, and he and my father and Tony laughed and shook hands and we all walked together towards Jones's Road.

The next year Galway beat us in the final, and the year after that we met in a bloody, bad-tempered semi-final, Tipp winning by three. In 1991, Tipp won well against Galway in the final, and the mad intensity between the counties eased, for a few years at least. Rivalries like that can smoulder for years, for generations even, without ever really conflagrating, until circumstances and personalities and events line themselves up to be fed to exponential, uncontrollable growth. Simultaneous comings-of-age of promising players, serendipitous fixture draws, repeatedly convergent paths to semi-finals and finals: all sorts of factors lead to certain teams at certain times seeming to be the absolute embodiment of the 'against each other spirit' that makes sport so exciting, that makes victory so beautiful, and defeat so utterly devastating.

When the great Clare hurling team of the mid-1990s ended an 81-year search for All-Ireland glory against Offaly in 1995 we were largely congratulatory in Tipperary. Four years later we lined out against Clare in the Munster final and I walked up the steps of the Blackrock end into a Páirc Uí Chaoimh packed to bursting, the air humming and crackling with tension. Insults were flying across the grass from terrace to terrace and stand to stand: nothing mattered in the world in that moment to any man, woman or child in that place but victory. This nascent enmity between the counties had become superheated over the previous few years, had spun and spiralled outwards, gaining density and mass until it collapsed back under its own weight into a black hole of ambition and passion and wounded pride that sucked in and destroyed all reason, all logic, all reserve. Davy Fitzgerald ran from his goalmouth to take a penalty in the game's dying moments and the Tipperary fans were concomitant in censure. As Davy ran back after scoring the equalising goal that would lead to a replay, and an easy win for Clare, we coalesced into a single screaming pulsating body of rage and despair and thwarted hope.

Sporting rivalries are fuelled by the passion of players and supporters alike, by the fact that it can seem sometimes like nothing else matters but what happens on the field of play, that nothing can come to any good unless your team does well. Ancient battles won and lost, memories of joy and misery, of grudges and slights and all kinds of perceived injustices are taken down from history's high cabinets, dusted off and given pride of place in our consciousness, used to ratchet the tension between the opposing cohorts to almost unbearable levels. It's part of the joy of sport, part of the reason it can occupy us so completely, can seize us body and mind. For a sporting occasion to be wholly and gloriously immersive, for us to be able to put aside all of our cares and worries and stresses and surrender ourselves fully to the joy of competition, for our team's victory to become the object and measure on that day of all of our hopes and dreams, there has to be a sense of us and them, of absolute and total polarisation. We have to think of the people walking beside us to the same place to watch the same game with the same hope and expectation and sense of excitement and anticipation as being on that day completely different to us, by way of simple geography and its resultant allegiance to a very similar but very separate tribe. All the while knowing deep down that, of course, we're all in the same family, all our sporting hearts beat as one.

When Tipperary prevented an unprecedented five All-Irelands in a row for the seemingly unstoppable titans Kilkenny in 2010, all the pain of the preceding years was washed away, all seemed right with the world. When Bubbles O'Dwyer charged towards the Kilkenny goal from the left wing in 2016, I was three rows from the goalmouth in the Davin Stand. I saw the truth in Bubbles' eyes of what was about to happen. I saw the net shaking before he even struck the ball. John McGrath shook the net again shortly afterwards. 'Lord save us, Do,' my father roared beside me. 'I think we're going to do it!' And we did do it, and my father put his arms around me just as he had in that same stadium nearly three decades previously, and we laughed as we walked towards Jones's Road.

I'm sure we embraced again before he died but that's the last one I remember. I have one of the great GAA rivalries of all time to thank for that memory of a perfect moment shared with my father at his last All-Ireland final. But there have been many such rivalries throughout the decades, and John Scally will navigate you through them as only he can, with great insight and knowledge and an unrivalled love for our native games.

Donal Ryan

INTRODUCTION

A rather timid kind of man was in Glasgow on a visit and got an opportunity to attend a Rangers v. Celtic match. Mindful of the potential for violence on such occasions, rooted in the Catholic/Protestant antagonism, he decided that discretion was the better part of valour and resolved to play it safe and keep his head down and display no emotion whatsoever. Rangers scored and the man on his right went into a frenzy of cheering, shouting and singing. The man remained stoically passive. A short time later Celtic scored and the supporter on his left went completely wild with joy. But still the man remained indifferent. At which point he was hit by a bottle from behind as someone roared at him, 'You bloody atheist!'

One of the great sagas in Irish sport came during 2018–19. For a seeming eternity the soccer world got itself into a tizzy about whether West Ham's rising star Declan Rice would declare for Ireland or England. Finally, after a journey that lasted longer than a transatlantic ocean liner, Rice declared for England in February 2019. An indication of the rivalry between the two countries came in the comment of one Irish fan: 'The f**king English. They took all our potatoes away from us during the Great Famine. Now they have taken our bloody Rice as well.'

These two humorous anecdotes indicate the intensity of some of the most ferocious rivalries in the history of sport. For its part, the GAA has created some remarkable rivalries. This book celebrates many of them.

Of course, rivalries have a positive dimension. They push teams and individuals to become better versions of themselves. Would Roger Federer have become the tennis player he is without his rivalry with Rafael Nadal? Would Mick O'Dwyer's Dublin have hit the dizzy heights they did without Heffo's Army?

Our teams are part of our 'us'. But Gaelic games flourishes, at least in part, because for every 'us' and our circle of trust there is, in the unique dialect of the GAA tribe, a 'them' – our great rivals. Our GAA teams cause us to care, but our rivalries make us *feel* in a more intense way; they heighten our emotions, raise our motivational impulses to win, cause our blood to heat, and to appreciate the reward of the victory when it is against *them*. 'Them' is embedded deep in our language. It resonates with 'us' because the 'them' strengthens our collective bond in this battle of wrong and right. We lavish love on our teams and are thrilled in those electrified moments when they put one over on our rivals. When 'they' do the unthinkable and beat us it creates a uniquely GAA version of post-traumatic stress disorder and a medical condition called 'anhedonia' – the inability to feel pleasure in normally pleasurable activities – not to mention bitter rancour. We are like trees that have been severed from their roots.

Our rivals, like our teams, are part of our identity, our sense of being part of something larger. They are part of a history so thick that we can choke on it, although we often rewrite it to fit our own narrative. Here we play fast and loose with the real truth because our felt truths are much more powerful, persuasive and pervasive, and the inconvenient truths like 'We were beaten by a better team' do not fit our narrative.

In this obsessive reality every match becomes a battle in a war that has been the result of one side seeking to avenge the remembered calamity, a matter of death and life, inflicted upon it by another.

In many areas of life Google has made the need for memory redundant, but not in the GAA. This insult to our collective pride in their cacophony of voices may have been real or exaggerated or no insult at all, but no matter, it is the 'memory' of that snub that calls us to take up arms against 'them'. We hate them because we 'remember' what they did, and so we must act in the name of that memory. Defeat to them cuts deeply because we lose our sense of who we are and we seek – no, *demand* – that the loss be avenged with the intensity of a spurned lover calling up to the bedroom from the street below. In this target-rich environment we imagine their fans as stiff-shirted, buttoned-down old men badly in need of an irony infusion, preening like bigwigs, with smiles as bright and false as fool's gold.

There are 50 shades of GAA rivalries. Given the volume of rivalries in the GAA at intercounty level, still so evident in both the Munster hurling championship and the Ulster football championship in particular, and so thrillingly encapsulated in the Leinster hurling championship in 2019, no one book can go close to adequately documenting all of them. Given the constraints of space, this book captures the rivalry between counties in the main using snapshots – so that the microcosm represents the macrocosm. I have opted for many of the obvious ones but also wanted to include some less obvious ones. I could only touch briefly on club, college and provincial rivalries. I did not dwell on the rivalries in squads, e.g. in recent years there has been an enthralling rivalry between David Clarke and Rob Hennelly for the goalkeeper position on the Mayo team.

One of my favourite people of all time is Seán Boylan. I have never spoken to anybody who has ever met him and not loved him. The irony is that in my lifetime I have never seen any team which has generated the same intense reaction as his Meath side. Likewise, I have never seen a hurling team induce such a visceral response as Ger Loughnane's Banner brigade.

Those at college level, intervarsity level, club level and provincial level would each deserve a book on their own. Hope is the limo GAA fans drive for free. So too is humour. Like before the 2019 All-Ireland final former Dublin star Keith Barr said to Kerry legend Oige Moran: 'May the best team win.'

Oige replied: 'Jaysus I hope not.'

NO SHOW JOE

The classic Dublin–Kerry rivalry spawned an unexpected controversy in 2019. After his comments about the referee in the All-Ireland final Joe Brolly was 'dropped' from the RTÉ panel for the replay. Joe's response was phlegmatic: 'If anyone has a spare ticket for the replay I've just been let down.'

Dublin actor Gabriel Byrne's most famous role is in the classic film *The Usual Suspects*. Had he taken Brolly's place for the replay he would have used a line from the film and said, 'You only got one shot to kill the devil.' Kerry missed theirs the first day and Dublin completed their unique drive for five. A historic outcome from a historic rivalry in a hotbed of great rivalries.

This volume gives some representative examples of them.

PART I
Pride and Prejudice

There are many facets to Gaelic games. League finals Sunday 2019 illustrated a number of them. There was skill in the way Limerick copperfastened their status at the hurling summit by becoming the first team outside Kilkenny since Galway in 1989 to win a league immediately after winning an All-Ireland. There was grace in defeat in Kilkenny coach Ann Downey's generous comments after Galway beat them in the camogie final. There was drama in the way Robbie Hennelly made a point-blank save from David Clifford to give Mayo victory over Kerry in the football final. There was sentiment in the Saw Doctors blaring 'The Green and Red and Mayo' over the PA system after the match. There was controversy about the denial of the injured Tom Parsons to the pitch afterwards to join in with the Mayo celebrations. There was the renewal of an old rivalry between Kerry and Mayo.

GAA rivalries are the ultimate tales of pride and prejudice. An integral part of the rich experience of Gaelic games is its rivalries and their associated myriad of marvellous myths and fiery fables. This section is a microcosm of the macrocosm and gives a taster of the good, the bad and the glad.

1

THE BRAWL

Meath v. Mayo

It was like a pantomime with no jokes.

It was the summer when a rivalry blossomed between two counties, like tropical flowers.

In 2006 a friend of mine went for a weekend away to County Mayo. She immediately fell madly in love with the stunning beauty of the landscape and the hospitality and warmth of the people. All was going swimmingly until on the Saturday evening in the pub she announced in a matter-of-fact voice to the assembled gathering that she was from Meath. An eerie silence invaded the hostelry. She was startled by the sudden change of atmosphere. A crowd gathered around her, moving slowly as if they were not sure what they would do when they got there, but somehow they were needed nonetheless as the tension ratcheted up. She did not initially understand what had happened to cause the friction and was shocked to discover that it was because of a taut, twisty football match between the two counties ten years previously and that its aftershocks would rattle on for a decade. In the GAA there are some wounds that never heal.

Most rivalries in the GAA take years to germinate, but the Mayo–Meath rivalry was unusual because it took only one explosive match to electrify it, and with the inevitability of sunrise, that one match would define the relationship between the counties for a generation.

STRANGE DECISIONS
In fact, there had been a gentle rivalry between the counties 50 years earlier. In 1949 Meath surprisingly beat Mayo by 3-10 to 1-10 in the All-Ireland semi-final. Mayo's full-back on that team was Paddy Prendergast. His conversation draws you to him like a warm fire in a blizzard.

'In 1949 the belief was that we would win the All-Ireland semi-final by ten points. After 24 minutes Seán Flanagan and I had a chat about how much we were going to win by. Then inexplicably the county selectors took two of our half-backs and replaced them with two forwards. The Meath half-forwards started to waltz through them. The incompetence of the county board knew no bounds. Their madness cost us an All-Ireland that year. If it was today, we wouldn't have accepted it.'

Prendergast believes that the ineptitude of the selectors almost cost Mayo the All-Ireland in 1950.

'We had probably the best goalkeeper in the country at the time in Seán Wynne and he was in excellent form for us all year. Then for some crazy reason he was dropped for the All-Ireland final against Louth and Billy Durkin was brought in for him. Understandably Billy was very nervous and the first ball he handled he dropped it. Seán Flanagan knew we were in trouble and pulled Billy aside. He signalled to the sideline that Billy was injured and Wynne came in for him. Only for Seán doing that we would have probably lost that All-Ireland.

'I remember the joy was unconfined after the game. People

8

don't realise how different Ireland was back then. We were on our knees in economic terms. The GAA made an awful difference to people at such a black time. The bonfires that blazed after we won were a sign that people could still have hope.'

In 1951 in front of an attendance of 78,210 Mayo beat the Royal County by 2-8 to 0-9 to retain their All-Ireland title. A disappointing game was lit up by one performance. When it comes to forward firepower, the big battalions of Gaelic football experts are in agreement that in any speculation about the greatest forwards available, the late Pádraig Carney's name would have to feature prominently. The capacity of the Flying Doctor (a medic based in America who flew home for big games) to amass epic performances while remaining stylishly fluent, apparently immune to the exhaustion engulfing others, must have been transmitted through his genes. In attack he had verve and inventiveness, and there were times it seemed that his determination would be sufficient in itself to guarantee Mayo a triumph.

Paddy Prendergast recalls the contribution of another forward that day, Tom Langan, with undisguised affection.

'Tom was one of the best footballers I've ever seen. Above all he was one of the original thinking footballers. He won many games for us, but he was very badly done by the Mayo selectors in the early years. Our whole history is peppered with stories like that. I could think of a litany of them. Our centre half-back Henry Dixon was the same. He was nearly over the hill when he was brought on to the team.

'Tom was all knees and bones and was very shy at times. He was from Ballycastle, and there we are not allowed to be too forward! As a garda he was more inclined to give people a warning than apply the full rigour of the law. He was very special. One of my clearest memories of him was when we played Kerry in the drawn game in the 1951 All-Ireland semi-final. We were four points down but Eamonn Mongey gave Tom the ball and he flashed it into the net.

'My abiding memory of him, though, was the night before we played Meath in the 1951 All-Ireland final. He was in the lobby of the hotel and he had one of the lads pretending to be the Meath full-back Paddy O'Brien, who of course was chosen as full-back on the team of the century, who was as tough a marker as you could get. Tom would do a sidestep to the left and a sidestep to the right with the ball and I remember at one stage he went crashing into a chair. When the game began, the first ball that came into him, he sidestepped Paddy O'Brien and stuck the ball into the net.

'We would like to think that we brought something new to the game and we had some very thoughtful people, especially Seán Flanagan and Eamonn Mongey. Crucial to our gameplan was to get the opposition full-back line on the back foot by the way we employed Tom Langan. Only Seán Purcell was ever able to handle him. That's a big tribute both to Tom and an even bigger one to Seán. Once Tom got going you could sense the fear in the opposition.'

With apologies to John Donne, all family is a volume. When a father dies all the pages are not tossed aside but translated into a new language. In the fullness of time God's hand will bind our scattered leaves into that library where every book will lay open to one another. Dermot Flanagan is the curator of his father's memories. It is immediately apparent in conversation with him that he has intimate knowledge of the innermost workings of his father's mind and his thoughts on the team. He is prey to the secrets of its success.

'Eamonn Mongey did everything to a very high standard and had a single-minded approach. Paddy Prendergast mightn't have been the tallest full-back, but he had a spring in his step like Willie Joe Padden and could soar in the air. Mongey and Pádraig Carney had a tremendous partnership. The entire team were great players individually who would all be superstars today, and collectively they were a wonderful unit. When the going got tough they had the ability to come through really difficult games. They never knew when they were beaten. For them it wasn't just about football. Times were tough. They really wanted to do something that transcended the harshness of life and give Mayo people something they could never get in ordinary life.'

Likewise, Dermot is keenly aware of his father's place in the drama.

'He was part of a great-full-back unit. Mongey and my dad were very big on strategy and tactics. Dad was always thinking ahead. Before the 1951 All-Ireland, for some reason the Meath players had to walk through the Mayo dressing-room in Croke Park. Dad had warned his players that none of them were to make eye contact with the Meath lads because he wanted to make a statement that Mayo meant business.'

Paddy Prendergast's happy reminiscing about his Mayo teammates comes to an abrupt end when he is asked about the recent Mayo visits to Croke Park.

'Since I retired, I look at the failures of Mayo as my personal via dolorosa. At the moment I hardly want to see them play. It pains me to see them lose games they should have won like the All-Ireland against Meath in '96. I am tired looking at their failures and their lack of determination. You won't win All-Irelands unless you have courage and determination.'

FATHER AND SON
The link between the Mayo teams in 1951 and 1996 is their All-Star corner-back Dermot Flanagan, whose father Seán had captained

11

Mayo to back-to-back All-Irelands. In the 1980s the rivalry had made a brief reappearance. In 1985 Mayo reached the All-Ireland semi-final against Dublin. Dermot Flanagan's background was to prove a mixed blessing in the run-up to the match.

'There was a lot of media attention on me before the game because I was the only link to the '50 and '51 teams, and that drained me. In the first half of the first game I was feeling the effects.'

Nonetheless his performance on Barney Rock in the replay, keeping him scoreless from play, helped Flanagan to win the first of his two All-Stars that year. His next semi-final against Meath in 1988 was at once memorable and unremembered.

'It was a very physical game and I was knocked unconscious. I swallowed my tongue and was a little perturbed to find out afterwards that I could have died.'

For Mayo's All-Star midfielder T.J. Kilgallon, Meath's capacity to play mind games was something of a culture shock.

'When John O'Mahony came in to manage us he was a confident man who believed in his own ability. He brought new ways and new ideas. Meath beat us in the All-Ireland semi-final in '88 but we ran them close and that gave us hope that better things were coming.

'Gerry McEntee would always stand nearer the opposing free-taker than he was supposed to and would try and put the kicker off by saying something like, "You're going to miss." He would tell you that you would put it to the right or the left but never over the bar. Colm O'Rourke was not shy on the field. He would always be passing a smart comment to you. Some of the lads thought he might have been trying to get you irked enough to punch him so that you would be sent off. He was certainly trying to distract you and put you off your game.'

Martin Carney also played for Mayo that day.

'I loved playing Meath. They were a fierce, manly and honest team, though if it was needed they would rearrange your features!'

AH REF

John Maughan's appointment as Mayo manager would usher in a new era for Mayo football. Having recovered from a major operation, Dermot Flanagan was happy to know he was not forgotten in 1996.

'I really wanted to get involved again not just because of John but because of his backroom team of Peter Ford and Tommy O'Malley. Peter rang to invite me back. I told him I was going on holiday for two weeks in Portugal. I told my wife I was going back to play for Mayo so I spent the two weeks running up and down sand dunes. It was a huge psychological challenge for me. I was 34 and in the winter of my career. I knew the media scrutiny of me would be much greater to see if I had become a "has-been". I played in a challenge game against Donegal and Peter told me I had done fine. I was then selected to play against Galway in the League and that night Peter rang me to say that people had come to bury me but I had proved them wrong. I knew, though, that there would be ongoing questioning of whether I was the weak link on the Mayo team.'

It is clear from the tone of his voice that Flanagan still nurses a sense of frustration at one aspect of the events of 1996.

'Not winning the All-Ireland against Meath that year remains the big disappointment of my career. I am convinced that we were hard done by and I'm not just talking about the sending off of Liam McHale. Pat McEneaney (the referee) had come down to us before the final and had talked about what might happen if there was a shemozzle. I found his comments very strange and was convinced that there could be a very serious incident in the game. People may think this is sour grapes, but I still believe that the referee's decisions influenced the outcome of the game.'

HOLDING THE FORD

Dermot Flanagan's frustration was shared by Peter Ford. Shortly after his retirement from playing, Ford soon found himself back in Mayo football when John Maughan made him one of his selectors. The big chance of glory came in the 1996 All-Ireland final, a pure nail-biter.

'With 15 minutes to go I could only see one result. Mayo had a comfortable lead but we tried to defend it and pushed back too far and allowed Meath to pick off their points.'

It is very evident that Ford feels a strong grievance about the replay.

'The sending offs were a complete mismatch. Liam McHale was our best player, and while Colm Coyle was a fine player his loss to Meath in no way compared with the loss of Liam to us. I've heard it back since from informed sources, shall we say, that the referee had intended to send off one of the Meath midfielders but the umpire intervened and told him he had to send Coyle off because of his role in the melee. When we played against the breeze Liam would have been ideal for that. Nonetheless we struggled on and only lost by a point.'

THE 'GREAT' FANS

Mayo's then manager John Maughan still feels the pain of the two games in 1996 as if an ache deep in his soul continues to throb.

'There is no doubt the worst moment came when we surrendered a lead to allow Meath to draw with us in the 1996 All-Ireland final. I had been absolutely convinced we were going to win. I told punters that they were safe to back us against the bookies. So that game really hurt. I was physically sick after the game. I rushed to empty myself in the cubicle and then I had to go pick the team up for the replay two weeks later. I think we did that very well.'

The replay was marred by an ugly melee after just five minutes, involving most players on the pitch. Maughan has no interest in rehashing the controversy again. 'It's all water under the bridge.'

Although he does not share the hostility many in Mayo felt towards Meath he can understand it. He has been astounded by the behaviour of fans in general. His own controversial tenure with Roscommon came to a fractious end in 2008 after he was subjected to verbal abuse from a vocal minority of county fans.

'Football management is no easy ride. When I started with Clare back in 1990, it was fun but not any more. You keep going only because of the incredible buzz you get when you win. Abuse is now a regular part of being a county manager. Most people will recall the abuse Tommy Lyons took when he was manager of Dublin. In 2004 Mayo beat Tyrone in Omagh in a League match. It was one of those days when things went well for us, but Mickey Harte got dog's abuse for having picked a close relative on the team. I had an empty feeling coming away from that match. It was an ugly day.

'You do get abuse shouted at you when you are on the sideline. I particularly recall a game when Ciarán McDonald, who was such a brilliant player for Mayo, was having an off day with his frees and I thought I recognised the most vocal critic's voice. Sure enough, when I turned around it was one of the most prominent Mayo supporters in Dublin. Ciarán had walked away from Mayo football for a year and a half because of the abuse his family was getting, but this guy was lacerating him. After we beat Tyrone in 2004 in the All-Ireland quarter-final that same supporter came up to me that evening and threw his arms around me. I got my own back at his hypocrisy and reminded him of the incident with Ciarán and told him exactly what I thought of him.'

IN THE THICK OF IT

Mayo's towering midfielder Liam McHale is the name most associated with the 1996 All-Ireland final replay. He still feels sore about it.

'I had given some thought to retiring because I was working my socks off and tired of us always falling short before John Maughan took over the Mayo job in 1995. I played with and against John and I really admired what he achieved in Clare. I thought he would make things happen and he was very unlucky not to have won an All-Ireland. At that stage I had developed into a leader of the team. I did a lot of directing of the team and was used to barking out orders from basketball. It suited John Maughan to have someone like that around.'

It was a case of so near and so far for McHale.

'It was my greatest year and my worst year, 1996. They say you make your own luck but we were unlucky.'

The old wound must be re-opened and the interview cannot progress without reference to his sending off in the All-Ireland final replay.

'I will never get over that. I felt I had no choice but to get involved. Fellas on my team were getting hit with haymakers and I was their leader and had a big bond with those guys. There was no way I could just stand back and watch and leave them to their own devices. If I had done nothing, I would not have been able to live with myself. If I was presented with those circumstances again, I would still do the same thing. I have a clear conscience because I didn't shirk my responsibility.'

Then silence fell between us. It was like a blanket that covered us both as I wondered if he would carry those scars around with him forever. McHale's regret about the sending off is tied in with his view of the way that game unfolded.

'Well, I believe the outcome would have been different if Meath had had a midfielder sent off. When I went off, we had to get another midfielder on, which meant that we had to take Ray Dempsey off. Ray had scored 1-2 in the All-Ireland semi-final and was in great form, so losing him was a blow. You have to remember we could only use three subs then. If Meath had lost a midfielder too, we wouldn't have had to replace Ray.'

Many people were surprised when McHale stated that getting sent off was akin to hearing that your mother had died.

'Losing an All-Ireland final is far worse than losing any other game. When you get that far and lose, especially to lose by a point in those circumstances, was sickening. We put in an astronomical effort, working very hard, but had nothing to show for it.'

Meath manager Seán Boylan was less convinced about the impact of McHale's dismissal.

'I have heard so many Mayo people saying that down the years that it has become accepted as gospel. I don't agree with that at all. If you look back at a recording of the game, you will see that Liam McHale was having little or no impact. We had instructed Jimmy McGuinness to mark him like glue and that every time the ball came their way Jimmy was to punch the ball away so that McHale couldn't get his fingers to it. Jimmy carried out his instructions to the letter and as a result Liam McHale had little meaningful influence on the game. You will see if you watch a recording that McHale was getting more and more frustrated because the game was passing him by. The first real mark he made on the game was in the brawl.'

STANDING ON THE SHOULDERS OF GIANTS

Boylan has a fascinating background. His father, the man he still calls 'the Boss', was steeped in the Irish War of Independence and the Civil War and was a friend of Michael Collins – though he never spoke about it.

As Meath manager, Gaelic games provided Boylan with an ideal context in which to express his combination of cerebral gifts and extreme competitiveness. The football field was an exhilarating arena where he could pit his abilities and his nerve against those of everyone else – and only the best-equipped would survive. He wanted a theatre and here was one ready-made for him, with all the elements for testing himself already created and marvellously varied and endlessly fascinating characters.

From the beginning there was no doubt that here was a man with an obsession loose in the psyche. All champions are dedicated. All new managers come in saying they will give it their best shot. But few ever had quite such a sense of destiny as Boylan. Right from the start it was clear that here was a commitment quite daunting in its intensity. Spend an evening in Boylan's company as he recalls his managerial career and it is impossible to escape a sense that his mind often travels in a land uninhabited by the rest of us. He believed that the team would gain strength from time together, from laughter, from joy and from tears.

'One thing I strongly believed in was in having a small squad. There was no point in carrying players who knew they were never going to make it. How could you expect them to have the commitment we needed?'

The best person to appraise Boylan's success as a manager is the person who knows him best – his wife Tina.

'His secret was that he made ordinary players believe that not only were they extraordinary but that they were the best player on the pitch.

'The other thing is that he is a great judge of character. People told him he was mad when he made Graham Geraghty captain because Graham had been in so many scrapes. But Graham was an inspired choice because he was such a brilliant leader.'

I CAN SEE CLEARLY NOW

At times the great manager requires a touch delicate enough to catch butterflies without damaging their wings. Other times, less sophistication is called for. Boylan's profound enthusiasm for Gaelic football has been constant through the years, but as a manger the fruits of his happy commitment showed in a capacity to blend mastery of the classic fundamentals with soaringly imaginative improvisations.

'As always we went for a little limbering up session the morning of the replay against Mayo. Because of the traffic situation that year it happened to be in Trinity College. I noticed that one of the lads was off a bit. His head was not in the right space. On a human level it was a hard thing to have to do but I decided not to start him in the final. It was tough on him, and it was tough on me too, but I had to do what was best for the team.'

Croke Park on a September afternoon separates the strong, the enduring and, above all, the brave from the rest. It is a licence to thrill and be thrilled. In full flight in countless training sessions Boylan's team were something to behold and those recorded demonstrations of their talents implanted the thought that on a Sunday in September they would be just about unbeatable.

Many a team had arrived for a final with unlimited potential, but Croke Park had ruthlessly exposed its flaws. Would all the endless training sessions prove justified? Would a momentary lapse of concentration get a great team beaten? Again. Maybe the team was more vulnerable than its most fervent admirers would admit. The questions dried the throat and brought a sharpness of anxiety that had nothing to do with mere All-Ireland medals.

Teams win games but managers win replays. Boylan rose to the occasion in 1996.

'In the drawn All-Ireland final I could not believe my eyes because I saw fellas who would never kick a ball away. Then I realised that two of our lads were colour blind and they were confused by the fact that the two sets of jerseys were so similar. I made the decision that we would wear the alternate strip for the replay but I told nobody about it except the management team, and I instructed them to tell nobody because I didn't want the media to get the story. We didn't even want Colm O'Rourke to know because, although he would never print it, we were afraid that he might inadvertently mention it to someone and it would get out. In fact, when he saw the team come out he said on the television that he had no idea that we were wearing our second strip. I only told the players on the morning of the match. It was a small thing but it made a big difference.'

A late point from a difficult angle by Brendan Reilly sealed a 2-9 to 1-11 victory for Meath.

A GOOD NEWS STORY

Seán Boylan sees the rivalry that developed between Meath and Mayo that year as a positive for the GAA. The point was so clear to him, so transparent in its truth, his eyes were shining with its brightness.

'We had always enjoyed our rivalry with Dublin – and I use the word "enjoyed" deliberately. Things did get very hot and heavy between us and Mayo that year, but from the teams' point of view it was over and done with quickly. The Mayo fans were sore afterwards, and in their eyes it was "the one that got away". Undoubtedly when those situations arise there will be some who hold on to a grudge, but a new rivalry like the one that developed with Mayo and ourselves breathes new energy into the GAA and provides lots of talking points for people. It helps bring the GAA more into the mainstream of Irish life. It is more than sport. It is a central part of people's lives. Do some people take it too far from time to time? Yes. But when people are more fired up by our games that can only be a good thing for Irish life as a whole.'

POSTSCRIPT

The replay won, Boylan thought he could relax. Yet, there was to be a further twist in the tale. Furrows briefly slice across Boylan's smooth forehead as he recalls a duty that had to be covered, just like the safety briefing on an aircraft.

'Back then the GAA hosted a lunch for the day after the final for both teams. It was a nice idea in theory, but not very enjoyable if you were the losing team. So that day I walked to the door with Tommy O'Dowd and waited to be let in. There were two security men at the door and they refused to let us in. We didn't have official passes and they claimed not to recognise us. We calmly tried to persuade them at first, but they kept point-blank refusing us. So, things got heated. Eventually someone from on high in the GAA heard about the fracas outside and much, much later than we ever expected we were let in. It certainly killed the mood of celebration, I can tell you.

'The story was carried on the RTÉ news that night. I believe the GAA phonelines were jammed for the next week with people complaining about the way we were treated. I think it might not have been the GAA's finest hour from a PR perspective.'

POSTSCRIPT: THE SEQUEL

As a teenager Boylan had wanted to be a Cistercian monk. So, it was no surprise that he and his wife sought some serenity after the dramatic events.

'After all the hassle Tina and I decided we needed a break for a few days. With all the media frenzy after the game the problem was that there was no place where we would be able to go where people would not be hassling us and talking about the match. Eventually we decided to go away for the weekend to Howth. At first, we didn't have much intrusion but that all changed when we went to Mass on the Sunday and all these elderly women came up to talk to us. Every single one of them was an expert on Gaelic football!'

2

THE NEW AVENGERS

Clare v. Tipperary

If the need is for a little philosophical justification of the irrational enthusiasms that keep Ger Loughnane in thrall to hurling, or of the romantic resilience that sustains him, then I must concede defeat from the outset. What is certain is that his appetite for the game was whetted by Clare's intense rivalry with Tipperary.

Not everyone sees the rivalry as positively as he does, particularly after the Munster under-21 final in 1999 when a brawl broke out between the Premier County and Clare camps. Neutrals reported that rivalry between the two counties had given way to hate.

In spring 2000 the *Clare Champion* attached such weight to the issue that it devoted an editorial to it. It referred to a Harty Cup match in 1999 where supporters of Nenagh CBS were alleged to have chanted, 'Go home, you Banner bast*rds' to their opponents, St Joseph's of Tulla. Their main focus, though, was on the booing of Jamesie O'Connor by a section of the Templemore CBS contingent at the 2000 Harty Cup final. They speculated that Jamesie was a talent 'far too rich' for their Tipp rivals. They went on to apportion blame, suggesting that up to three years previously a healthy rivalry existed between the counties, but it was based on the premise that Tipperary were, and always would be, a vastly superior force, while Clare, after their 'flash in the pan win of 1995', would inevitably retreat to the land of no-hopers whence they came. 'Since that script changed, the bitterness has crept in.'

For the first century in the history of the GAA Tipperary were part of the three superpowers of hurling and Clare were seldom a threat to their dominance in Munster. That was all to change in the 1990s, when Clare moved from the basement to the penthouse. However, in the early years of the decade the old order ruled OK.

SMILEGATE

Munster finals for so long had remained the most enchanting of torture chambers for the Banner county, leaving its fans wailing in operatic misery. Apart from the magnitude of Clare's defeat, the 1993 Munster final is best remembered for an incident when Nicky English was alleged to have insulted the Clare fans. Fact or fiction? Ger Loughnane gives the inside story.

'I marked Nicky English a few times. I thought he was a really fantastic player. Sometimes, though, Nicky's too honest and too open. There is no deviousness about him. What happened in '93 was something I used subsequently to motivate Clare.

'I went to see Clare beat Limerick in the League in April 2001 as an ordinary fan with my son, Barry. On the way in he asked, "Do you remember the last Clare match we went to together?" It was the '93 Munster final. Barry was only 11, but he remembered it as well as could be. It shows how much the trouncing we got that day was on the mind of every Clare person. It wasn't just a trouncing. It was a total and utter embarrassment.

'Walking out after the match, I saw Seán Cleary just ahead of me. He was the principal in the school that I had been teaching in and his son, Eoin, was playing that day. I didn't want to catch up with him. I didn't want to have to talk to him because what could I say? The whole thing was a disaster. Clare were beaten out of sight.

'Tipperary had effectively beaten us after ten minutes. I decided to stay on until the end of the game. English scored a point and he went out and had the "high fives" with Pat Fox and had this big smile across his face. It wasn't that English was laughing at Clare but it encapsulated the whole scene of what was wrong with Clare. They were nothing. These guys didn't matter.

'Why do I still remember where I was sitting in the stand that day? Why would Barry still remember that day? Why would all Clare supporters remember that day? They all remember the trouncing by Tipp but what left an indelible memory on their mind was Nicky English's gumshield. I can still see it – years later. It was unfair to say it was English; it was the total annihilation. But what symbolised it was English's gumshield and that was the thing that really hurt. Every Clare person felt that "snub" keenly. English didn't mean it in that way. That defeat had to be avenged. That was what drove us all on.'

THE HOT SEAT

That defeat was instrumental in Loughnane's appointment as Clare manager. He came back into the fold but only on the condition that he would become manager the next time the post became vacant.

'After Clare were trounced in the Munster final Len Gaynor, who of course is a legend of Tipperary hurling, came to me and asked if I would return as selector and I said immediately,

"No way." He went off and tried to get further selectors, but he found it very hard to get them.

'He visited my home one night and asked, "Will you come back?"

'I said, "I'll come back on one condition. When you pull out as manager of Clare, I will succeed you."

'"How will we arrange that?" he asked.

'Brendan Vaughan was chairman of the county board, so Len went to Brendan and put the case to him, explaining the problem of getting selectors. Clare had been hammered by Tipperary in the Munster final. Brendan talked to me and again raised the problem of getting it through. I told him, "Brendan, the only way you'll get it through is if you launch it on them like a shot and have a decision made straight away."

'When Brendan raised it with them a few speakers spoke against, including the future chairman, Fr. Michael McNamara – though I never held it against him. They were trying to play for time but selectors were crucial for Len, so it got through. The last person many of them wanted was me. Ultimately it got through because of the shrewd tactics that Vaughan used. He wouldn't tolerate having the decision postponed. To many officers on the county board I couldn't do much damage until they would clip my wings for me.

'Len was happy to go along with the arrangement that I would replace him. In fairness he did everything possible. Whatever he's involved in, he'll give it his best. He did tremendous work here. He's the most genuine person you could meet. In my last year with him, he let me do a lot of the coaching of the Clare team. We got on tremendously well together. I think he did a great service to Clare while he was here. I don't think he'd ever have won with Clare if he was there for a long time but he definitely did an awful lot to bridge the gap between the total chaos of the previous era and the great organisation that came later on. He turned the corner but I don't think he'd ever have taken Clare across the finishing line.'

In fact, Loughnane's admiration and friendship for Gaynor would later cast a shadow across one of his greatest days.

'Before the final whistle was blown in the '97 All-Ireland, after Davy Fitzgerald saved from John Leahy, Len came over and shook hands with me and said, "Ye have it now." It took some of the good out of winning the All-Ireland for me because I was with him in Clare and I knew the pain losing was going to cause him and what the consequences of losing were going to be for him. He was going to get the blame for Tipp's defeat.

'I really liked him and fully appreciated what he had done for Clare. While the game was on, I'd have done anything for us to win, but when the final whistle blew and the human situation kicked in I knew how difficult it was going to be for Len. I remember thinking to myself, "It's great to win and beat Tipp but I wish somebody else was in charge." He had given everything of himself in his time with Clare and had an incredible passion for Clare to win.'

PAYBACK

For Clare hurling '93 had been a year of ignominy because of the scale of the defeat to Tipperary. The following year, 1994, was payback time for the Clare team. Loughnane was shocked by the person who made that point most forcefully.

'It was something that was born out of a tragedy. Playing for Clare in the '93 Munster final was a man called John Moroney. He had a cousin playing as well called John Russell. Later that year John Moroney was killed just outside Croom, coming back to Ennis from work. He was one of those quiet, really respected players and his one ambition was to play for Clare against

Tipperary the following year to avenge the defeat. He had made this statement to everybody; Anthony Daly, who was very friendly with John, and the other players were very conscious of that. The next year I was a selector and it was a huge motivational force for all of us to beat Tipp and avenge the defeat.

'Coming up to the championship in '94 the Clare minors were playing in Limerick. Len decided we'd go to watch them and have a team meeting afterwards to discuss our plans for the championship. We met in the Clare Inn. Seánie McMahon had just come on to the panel that year. At the time I would have seen Seánie as one of those quiet lads who plays away and never says anything but who wouldn't be half-aggressive enough for inter-county hurling. The meeting was nearly over and Seánie got up. Well, you could hear a pin drop. Here was a young lad of 20 years of age and he gave a speech of such viciousness that it left everybody absolutely stunned! The gist of it was: look at what those Tipp f**kers have done to Clare and by Jesus this year we're going to put them down. When he was finished, I said to Len, "Stop it now." There was no need to say another word.

'We beat Tipp. They were missing a lot of players, like English and Leahy. It wasn't the real thing but it was still great. The real thing was to come later on!'

When Len Gaynor retired Loughnane got the job by default. There was no ringing endorsement from the powers that be.

'When Len stepped down in '94 the job was there. A lot of people tried to persuade him to stay on, largely because they didn't want me! Before the county board met, I went on Clare FM with Alan Cantwell and declared that I was Clare manager because of what had happened before. He asked me, "What can you do for Clare that Len Gaynor hasn't done?" I turned it back on him and I said, "When Len Gaynor was here he did everything he possibly could for Clare to win and that's what I'll be doing as well."

'The county board met and they were really lukewarm. I sat at the back of the room. Michael Daly, from Feakle, said Ger Loughnane had to be manager of the Clare team because the thing had been fixed and he wished me well, but he was the only one who spoke apart from myself. There was no enthusiasm and no round of applause when I finished.

'It was a coup. Of all my difficulties as Clare manager, the biggest one I had was getting appointed in the first place.'

BREAKTHROUGH

Players cannot leave their characters in the dressing-room. They go out on the field with them. If genuine stellar talents could not be found, lesser performers were processed to become the part. But did they have the mental toughness to be champions? In Loughnane's playing days when the big games came along the Clare players had already surrendered. They had grown comfortable with the idea of being a 'nearly' team. Although many of the players were exceptionally skilful, more than capable of bringing a touch of élan to the proceedings, they were guilty of flitting in and out of big matches, rarely taking them by the throat. Loughnane created a different culture.

'We met Tipperary in the league in '95 in Ennis and it was a watershed game. Tipperary had their full team, including English, Pat Fox, Aidan Ryan, Declan Ryan and all the stars that had demolished Clare in '93. We had won all the matches in the league up to that. We had started off by just scraping wins over Antrim, Galway and Kilkenny and then it came to Tipperary. I said to them in the dressing-room, "This is the day you have to stand up to them. We have to make a statement. They've come with all their big guns and today we've to put them down."

'Not alone was it a hurling battle; it was a verbal battle as well. The message was sent out loud and clear: you might have demolished us two years ago but you'll never do that again while we're here. That's what they told them up to their faces. We might have got a reputation later for dishing it out but we really dished it out that day! Clare really stood up to Tipp. It was a terrific game and our lads saw that for the first time they could outhurl them. The Tipp lads really wanted to win. I saw Nicky English after the game and he was really disappointed. We beat them and after that we felt something big was going to happen.'

It was a watershed moment for Loughnane.

'People say that the league isn't important but some games at some times are vital. That was the crucial day for us. Cyril Lyons missed a free from 30 yards out and I belted the wire behind me. We knew everything was at stake that day. It's very hard to make progress when teams are shattered and the least thing can cause a psychological meltdown. It's like someone who has a phobia: when you meet the something that is causing the phobia, that's the only test whether you can overcome it or not. I rate that Tipperary team of the '80s and early '90s as the side with the most exciting forward line I've seen, but our lads drove them back every way: physically, verbally and hurling wise. Every team that's going to go places needs to make a statement. You can afford to even take a step back after that. That was the really vital day.'

LAYING DOWN A MARKER

In the old days, win or die was the code, arousing the players' anger. That kind of approach, though it often gets the blood boiling, interferes with concentration and may ultimately back-fire. Loughnane appreciated the fine line between playing hard and playing angry. When individual players were matched up against someone with superior skills, the message was: 'We'll give you any help but you're going to have to be the door that doesn't open.' Sometimes a few words like that were all that was needed for Loughnane.

'Clare played Tipperary in a league match in May 1997. It was the kind of game you rarely get to see. The game had to be put back 15 minutes so that everyone could get in. I went in to tell the ref that the match was delayed. He was actually shaking in the dressing-room. Everyone was caught up in the tension because it was in Ennis and it was Len Gaynor's first match against the team he had trained. When the game started it was the toughest match I ever saw. Everybody knew the chances were that we would most likely meet in the championship later on. There was a lot of "sorting out" going on by both sides.

'Tipperary had this young corner-forward who was supposed to be a player of the future and had played a great game shortly before against Kilkenny. He was marking "Hallo", Michael O'Halloran. After about ten minutes, this young Tipp player gave a bit of "attention" to Hallo. The next thing we heard O'Halloran giving his response. We didn't see it but we actually heard the thump of timber on flesh. The Tipp player was substituted later. Hallo got the reputation then of being a "hard man". He didn't deserve it really, because he got hit first and he was settling the score in this highly charged atmosphere – where there were unreal physical exchanges all over the field.

'It was a brilliant hurling game. John Leahy came on in the last 20 minutes and Tipperary won narrowly. I went into the Tipperary dressing-room afterwards and they were absolutely delighted. It was as if they had won the Munster final. Len came into our dressing-room and he could see how disappointed everyone was. It was like a funeral scene.'

A few months later Loughnane created a postscript to this incident.

'It came to pass that Tipperary met Clare in the Munster final, and surprise, surprise this time Tipperary had a new corner-forward. Just before the national anthem I saw Len Gaynor calling him over to the sideline and he started to adjust his helmet. Hallo followed him all the way onto the sideline. When I saw this, I was immediately suspicious. I could be wrong but I thought that Len was worried that Hallo was going to strike his man, before, during or after the anthem. Len was looking straight at Hallo. I went up beside them and immediately the national anthem started. The Tipp player was right beside me and I sang the anthem as loud as I possibly could into his ear. He looked as if he was going to turn into absolute jelly! Not a word though was exchanged between any of us. Then when the anthem was finished, I let out an almighty roar to Hallo. O'Halloran hardly gave his man a puck of the ball and the Tipp forward was taken off. He would have been a lot better off if he had stayed where he was before the anthem!'

PEAK PERFORMANCE

Given the enormity of the '95 All-Ireland victory to Clare fans, it would be reasonable to assume that it was Loughnane's proudest moment. Reasonable, but inaccurate.

'I'll never forget our most thrilling victory. It was against Tipperary in Pairc Uí Chaoimh in 1997. We had set our sights on winning the All-Ireland in '97. We had great days in '95; beating Cork in the championship in '97 was wonderful; but from a purely hurling point of view, because of their great tradition and well-deserved reputation, to beat Tipperary was the day of days.

'It was a beautiful, sunny day. We had gone into the '95 All-Ireland in a relaxed frame of mind but there was no relaxation that day. We went to Cork with a sense of going on a mission that was only recaptured when we played Waterford in the

Munster final replay the following year. Everybody was totally up for it. When we met the bus outside the Shamrock Hotel, Frank Lohan was dancing from foot to foot. When Fitzy arrived, he was pale. There was none of the usual chatter. This was *the* day. There was an awful lot at stake.

'As usual the team went to bed after breakfast and the mentors and I went for a walk in the grounds of UCC. It was the first time I had been there and it's a really beautiful place, but all the time the thought was flashing in our minds: this is the day.

'We went for a puckout in the Mardyke. Afterwards I called on the players and told them that they had done so much for Clare already but today we wanted a really special effort. I said in a soft voice, "Everything we've achieved is at stake today. Our entire reputation rests on the match." We went onto the coach and really the bus didn't need an engine to power it. Everybody was totally geared up.

'My last words to them were "Everything depends on today. Make every second of every minute count."'

As he talks, Loughnane relives every moment of the match.

'I can't remember everything before the two All-Irelands, but I can remember every second of that day. As soon as we went we could feel the tension that was in the air. It wasn't a tension that drained you, it was a tension that enlivened you. For the first time when the names of each of the Clare players were read out there was a massive cheer. The crowd was really up for it. There was an incredible sense of oneness between the team and the fans.

'When the game started we were playing at 90 miles an hour. We made a brilliant start and led by 0-13 to 0-8 at the interval. Barely seven minutes after the re-start Tipperary were level and playing with the wind. The Tipp supporters started singing "*Sliabh Na mBan*". I immediately leapt to my feet and shouted to each of the players, "Is that the sound you want ringing in your ears all the way home?" Clare lifted their game and regained the lead almost immediately when Seánie [McMahon] scored a point from a free. Suddenly the tide had turned in our favour again. We brought on David Forde and he scored a wonder goal.

'Clare were seemingly going to be beaten, after enjoying a huge lead. Then we came back, to lead again, with a magic goal. We were winning by three points. Then John Leahy broke through and Tipp almost scored a goal in the last minute to tie the match.

'When the final whistle blew, I just lost the head. I leapt out of the dugout and got a belt of a flag and my face was bleeding. Some lady jumped on me. I was ecstatic.'

I HAVE A DREAM

For Loughnane this game was the stuff of dreams.

'We won two All-Irelands and they were brilliant but this was unique. People outside Clare would find it very difficult to understand just how much it mattered. This was the dream for every Clare person for decades – to beat Tipperary in a Munster final. Forget about All-Irelands. Had we won six All-Irelands and hadn't beaten Tipp in a Munster final it wouldn't have been as good, but to win that day and go into the dressing-room was sheer bliss.

'I made sure, though, the dressing-room was locked. The atmosphere inside was one of total and absolute contentment. We're not supposed to feel it in this lifetime. There was no need for a word to be said between each other. The downside was you knew that there never would be a day like that again, but it is a feeling that will last forever.

'You didn't even want to go out among the crowd afterwards. You wanted no patting on the back. We had all that when we won the All-Ireland in '95. We just wanted to sit back and share that among ourselves. We didn't want to leave the dressing-room because the magic was inside. It was great going out and meeting our relatives and everyone else in Clare, but even though the fans felt brilliantly they just hadn't felt what we felt in the dressing-room. Only those who were in there could ever understand what it was like. You just couldn't get it anywhere else and that was the magic that was Clare.'

For Loughnane this match was akin to a religious experience.

'The '97 Munster final is the treasure of all treasures. You ask yourself did it ever really happen? Everything that day was just bliss. It wasn't the All-Ireland final, but the Munster final was more important to us than the All-Ireland. That's what people don't understand. Munster is magic because of the local rivalries. Whatever changes are made in hurling the Munster championship must stay. You look at the Munster champion-ship and see the passion it generates. Croke Park is business. There is something spiritual about the Munster championship.

'It took us four hours to get home that night. All the towns we went through, like Charleville and Buttevant, were thronged with Clare people and Limerick fans delighted for Clare. It was such a pleasure. No night coming home from any All-Ireland final could match it. The only night that matched it was coming home from the Munster final in '95. We felt we really had arrived as a major hurling power.'

TIPPING POINT

Loughnane and his mentors insisted that his team be inoculated against the possibility of letting their standards slip. He spoke with unmistakable conviction that complacency in hurling is not an enemy that attacks head-on but an invidiously slith-ering infiltrator of attitudes. To do this he had no peers when it came to finding new persecution complexes to motivate his team and was able to tap into that psyche superbly and use it to fuel his players with extraordinary determination. Yet he knew too that if you send out a team with tears in their eyes they will not even see the ball. He tells a story which illustrates this point.

In the build-up to the 1997 All-Ireland final the rivalry between Clare and Tipperary was, to put it at its kindest, 'intense'. In this classic case of nouveau riche versus old money Clare were four points down at half-time. Instead of shouting at his team, the Clare boss told them that they were playing badly but could win if everyone took responsibility. He was the last man out of the dressing-room and as he walked out the Tipperary team passed him by. He was called every name under the sun.

'I knew at that moment that Clare were going to win because the Tipp lads were in too much of a frenzy. In my mind I said, "Continue on like that, lads." The bigger the rage they were in, the better I liked it.

'I always believe that the best thing to do is to whip up the opposition into a total frenzy. Before that All-Ireland that's what I did. Deep down I really feared that Tipp would pull one over on us. I knew the way Len operated. He's an emotional man and I knew he'd go absolutely ballistic over some things. I put out the story that Tipperary thought nothing of Clare and that Len Gaynor told us that when he was with us.

'A singer from Ennis, Ciarán McDermott, brought out a song coming up to the match and one line was: "We'll stop in Nenagh to really rub it in."

'Before the final, Des Cahill came down to interview me and he asked me something. I paid no attention to the question but I brought up the issue of how Nicky English had insulted Clare in '93 and how that was really motivating me to manage Clare and to really sock it to Tipperary. The whole thing blew up again and it was driving Tipperary mad!'

NOT TIPP TOP

Clare's win came at a cost for Loughnane.

'I look at photos of myself after the '97 All-Ireland and I think that I look absolutely terrible. I appear thin and drawn. That All-Ireland, especially because it was against Tipperary, took an enormous psychological and emotional toll on me. It took a massive effort to keep driving the team. We beat them in the Munster final. To come back and defeat them a second time was going to be very difficult.

'Everybody in Clare was afraid of their lives that we were going to lose to Tipperary. Earlier that year Babs Keating had written an article about the backdoor system and had used an example to illustrate it: supposing Clare beat Tipp in the Munster final, then Tipperary could beat them in the All-Ireland "when it really mattered". For months that comment about "when it really mattered" was really playing on my mind.

'Then there had been a lot of controversy over Anthony Daly's "No longer the whipping boys of Munster" speech after the Munster final. Then came the controversy about me alleg-edly accusing Wexford of "roughhouse tactics". It was the first time I had really encountered controversy.

'Coping with all that and at the same time managing the team was very draining. Then the All-Ireland itself was such a knife-edge affair and I was pulling every trick in the book to win it, which really wiped me out. I have never been more focused going into a game and it took me days to recover from it.

'The day after the game we were going along in the bus and Anthony Daly was beside me and he said, "I suppose this is the end for you now."

'I answered, "Definitely."

'Not long after Jamesie, Brian Lohan and a few others came down to me and they asked me to stay on for another year, as

37

they were looking forward to the new year already – '97 hadn't taken as much out of them as '95 had.'

Jamesie O'Connor gives an interesting perspective on the win.

'Winning the 1995 All-Ireland was great and it meant so much to the county, but in many ways for the team the second All-Ireland was more important because it showed that we were no flash in the pan and that Clare were a force to be reckoned with. The first win was for the county, the second one was for the team.'

TOUGH LOVE

Part of the joy for some Loughnane watchers was to observe if his style ceased to be intriguingly unorthodox and became a recipe for vulnerability. Yet when his players failed to perform, he had no difficulty telling them they had let him down.

'After the draw against Tipperary in the Munster semi-final in '99 I took the players into the dressing-room in Cusack Park during a training session and said, "If I took the 20 people I most admired in all the world, at least 12 of them are right here. To let yourselves down like ye did last Sunday is so disappointing."'

The resourcefulness which enabled Loughnane to find reha-bilitation from what was once a tragic history would reassert itself. If you can rescue a county from 81 years of losing, winning a replay is much less daunting. The soft-spoken put-down that day was more effective than a fire-and-brimstone speech. The results were to be seen in the near-perfect display Clare produced to win the replay by 1-21 to 1-11. The importance of this match to Loughnane is revealed when he is asked about watching the videos of his glory days.

'Not alone did I never watch the videos when Clare were playing, I haven't since I retired. Other managers spend lots of time watching videos of their games. I didn't do that. I've seen bits of games, but the only game I've ever seen in its entirety on video was the '95 final. I feel uneasy watching them, and I think if I did I'd only be looking out for mistakes the players made and I wouldn't enjoy watching them. The one game I wanted to see was the replay of the Tipperary game in 1999 and by chance a friend of mine got it and he hasn't given it back to me since. In that sense I have no nostalgia whatsoever.'

Loughnane, having engendered an era that was often spell-binding and gratifying, always wore his heart on his sleeve. Enthusiasm for hurling still shines naturally in his eyes and, not surprisingly, the glint intensifies when victories over Tipperary surface in conversation. There was one Clare–Tipp contest that was a sight to put a permanent tingle in the blood.

'In the Munster semi-final replay in Páirc Uí Chaoimh in 1999 against Tipperary we gave the most perfect performance the team ever gave. I always longed for the day that the team would give a display I'd be totally and utterly satisfied with. That was the display. It was so commanding: we overpowered them, outwitted them and were more skilful. Every aspect you could possibly judge a good performance on, that one had. Afterwards there was a great feeling that this was the ultimate collective performance.

'One of the smartest managers I've seen was Nicky English and he came into the dressing-room after Clare had beaten Tipperary in the replay and said, "Ye could win the All-Ireland this year if today hasn't taken too much out of ye." He was dead right. It had taken too much out of us.

'We were too satisfied afterwards. If the first day we had beaten Tipp by a point and everybody had said, "Ye no more deserved that", which we wouldn't have done, we might have won the All-Ireland. Everybody was too satisfied about beating Tipp. Now, whether you would swap winning an All-Ireland for giving Tipp a good trouncing is another thing!'

Enjoyment is the most well-remembered and treasured aspect of the experience. Ultimately for Loughnane it is how much we enjoy rather than how many trophies a team accumulates that really matters.

'Winning is not everything. Your goal is to get the very best out of players, and when you achieve this goal you are in right trouble. In '99 people said it was tiredness. It had nothing to do with that. We produced the perfect display in '99. There was no hill to climb after that, even for me. It enhanced it because it was against Tipperary, but the performance was everything I strove for since I first trained a junior team. Once you do get to the pinnacle there's no place else to go. Even when you win there are always flaws, but not that day. It's a lot better than winning an All-Ireland because you can win an All-Ireland and play badly.

'The whole thing left me with a treasure trove of memories. The thrill of it all is that when you are sitting down somewhere and the memory of a match like that comes back to you – that's what made it all worthwhile. But it was deadly draining.'

TIME TO SAY GOODBYE

An amateur with a professional approach, Loughnane had piloted the Clare ship through many stormy waters. Having gone through an emotional roller-coaster ride for six years, it would be Tipperary who would end his tenure as manager.

'I'm one of these people that when I'm in something I give it 100 per cent and when I'm out I just leave it. In 2000 I had been involved for such a long time that the thing had gone a bit dreary, a bit dead. When we were beaten by Tipperary in the championship, instead of being disappointed I was just relieved. The day you feel relieved to be beaten is the time to give it up. It was time to take a break from it.'

3

OBSERVE THE SONS OF ULSTER MARCHING ON

Armagh v. Tyrone

Probably the only thing that has united Armagh and Tyrone fans in the last generation has been a shared antipathy for Pat Spillane. In Armagh they take offence from his infamous comments at half-time on *The Sunday Game* during the 2002 All-Ireland final when he dismissed their chances of beating Kerry, especially his comment that although his mother had arthritis, she was still faster than the Armagh full-back line. A year later he infuriated Tyrone fans when he accused them of playing 'puke football' when they beat Kerry in the All-Ireland semi-final.

THE ORANGE REVOLUTION
One of Ireland's leading sports psychologists, Enda McNulty, was crucial to the 'orange revolution'. He feels that it was a variety of factors coming together like converging lines that paved the way for the team's ultimate success.

'I believe sport is the kaleidoscope of a whole range of small things made perfect. I think that is the road Armagh went down.

'In 2002 Armagh started to get more of all the small things right than all the other teams. We got some unbelievable guys in from a mental sessions point of view. We worked on team cohesion and did some good bonding sessions. The other thing we did was to bring in Darren Campbell from basketball for statistical analysis – which was on a different level because of his basketball background. I remember him handing me a sheet before we played Tyrone in the 2002 Ulster champion-ship with a diagram showing me where exactly Peter Canavan had received every ball on the pitch in the previous five games. From a mental preparation point of view that was great for me. Not only was it pinpointing to me when he liked to get the balls in those positions – so as the game went on, did he like to move out or in? That was invaluable. Then we went on a training week in the sun – which was very innovative then, though everybody does it now. Apart from the bonding it was a very serious trip. Not only was there no alcohol or nights out, there wasn't even a discussion about nights out or alcohol. It was very tough training and the mental resolve that trip gave us was important.

'We were walking up the hill in Clones like an army before the Tyrone game in the Ulster championship. Everyone knew we had been on the trip to the sun and one of the Tyrone fans shouted at us, "I don't see any suntan, lads." When Joe [Kernan] got us in the dressing-room he used that incident and said, "We'll show them a f**king suntan before the end of the match." That was the spark we needed.

'There were numerous small things. A nutritionist was brought in. Physical conditioning was brought to a new level, which probably reflected how driven the lads were. Joe brought a good team all around him. Every little detail was sorted out and that is why we won the All-Ireland in 2002.'

TYRONE'S TRIUMPH

The glory of 2002 was not to be repeated the following year for Enda McNulty.

'There's a lot of regrets about 2003. Probably on reflection we played better football in 2003 than we did in 2002, but we made a big mistake. Two weeks before the All-Ireland final we changed a few critical things. We changed from the way we'd played the whole year, which was a critical mistake. We picked some players in different positions, which was a big mistake in hindsight. Not only the gameplan and the positional changes, and I have spoken to Kieran [McGeeney] about this many times, but even more important was the change in our attitude.

'In all the games up to the final we had a "take no sh*t" attitude. We got stuck in and used our physical capacities, not in any dirty way, but harnessed the physical strength of the team: Francie Bellew, Kieran, the McEntees, Paul McGrane. In the run-up to the final there were a lot of articles in the press saying that not only were Armagh a dirty team but over-the-top dirty. One of the articles stated that somebody was going to be left in a wheelchair because of the way we played. I remember reading that article, which was written by a Fermanagh player, and thinking to myself, "Oh dear, what's going to happen if some of our players are affected by this?" We probably subconsciously decided not to be as physical as we were in the previous games, which was an absolute disaster. Armagh's game was built on our physical nature and in a lot of games in 2002 we crushed teams just by our physical exertions; we were so well-conditioned we could easily deal with anyone else in that respect. Against Tyrone in 2003 we decided we were going to show the whole country that we could win by playing nice football. We tried to play less tough football and more champagne football. We needed to marry the skills with the physical dimension. We could also have been more intelligent on the day on the pitch – I'm not talking about management. For example, I was marking Canavan and he wasn't fit to walk, and I marked him man to man. I should have come out in front of him and covered off Eoin Mulligan as well. So I am taking the blame for my own performance.

'The player I always knew I had to be unbelievably focused on when I was marking him was Peter Canavan. You knew you had to be incredibly switched on for every single ball because if you even blinked he would stick the ball in the net. We must all shoulder the blame. I wouldn't blame the management for any of our defeats.'

Pat Spillane puts Tyrone's victory in more positive terms.

'With three All-Irelands won in 2003, '05 and '08 Mickey Harte's position as one of the greatest managers of the game is secured. While I would not always agree with his methods, Harte has earned my respect. He raised the bar, which forced teams like my beloved Kerry to follow them and ensured that they raised their standards of preparation and professionalism.'

A RESPECTFUL RIVALRY

Enda McNulty embraced the rivalry with the Red Hand county.

'We don't despise Tyrone, though we have a great rivalry with them. You have to respect any team that wins three All-Irelands in the one decade. They were probably smarter than us in the games they beat us. I think the media have not picked up on the fact that winning Ulster so often has been a big disadvantage. We won way more Ulsters, but Tyrone won more All-Irelands. Playing in the qualifiers gave them more games and, above all, the opportunity to iron out their weaknesses when they lost. When we lost, we were knocked out and learned our weaknesses too late. It's not the only reason Tyrone have won more All-Irelands, but it has been an advantage to them. I would say the rivalry has been a positive thing for football.'

Pat Spillane, though, was displeased about one aspect of their rivalry in the early noughties.

'There is no doubt that the intense rivalry between Armagh and Tyrone back in the noughties was good for both counties – because it spurred them on to be the best they could be to beat each other. When Armagh won the All-Ireland in 2002, they started wearing arm bracelets to keep them focused; started using inspirational speeches from other sports, like Al Pacino in *Any Given Sunday* speaking to his team before the play-offs. But the big thing everyone else aped was their idea of going on a trip abroad to a training camp.

'The following year everyone was looking at the formula Mickey Harte used, such as having no challenge games, which quickly became de rigueur for everybody else, but had Armagh got a goal near the end of the 2003 All-Ireland final, when Steve McDonnell was clean through only for his shot to be blocked down by Conor Gormley, nobody would be talking about Mickey Harte's brilliant and innovative training methods.'

4

ROUGH STUFF

Clonbullogue v. Bracknagh

A great oak fell in the forest of Westmeath football in March 2019 with the passing of Mick Carley, perhaps the Lake County's most distinguished footballer. He gave me a revealing insight into the intensity of club rivalries in the GAA which confirmed why they really are 'the toughest'.

'I once was playing a club match in Offaly against Walsh Island, a club most people will know about because of Matt Connor. After the game was over, I togged in and was about to go home when a fella called me over and told me I should stay for a junior match between Clonbullogue and Bracknagh.

'I didn't really want to but he was adamant that I should stay. I agreed to stay for five minutes. There was nothing special for the first couple of minutes and suddenly a fracas developed and all hell broke loose. Everyone was swinging and punching. I found out later that they were all inter-married and there was a lot of history there. It took about five minutes for the referee to sort things out and get order back. He sent one of the lads off, but your man didn't do the usual thing and go back to the dressing-room and take a shower. Instead he stood on the sideline waiting for things to boil over again so he could get back into the thick of the fighting. He didn't have long to wait!

'Another melee broke out and they went at it again, only twice as hard. The referee finally restored order. But almost as soon as he threw the ball back in another scrap broke out. I swear that there was no more than five minutes' football in the first half. In fact, things were so bad that at half-time the priests from the two parishes went in to try and calm things down. Things went fine for the first 20 minutes of the second half and then another scrap broke out. I thought the fights in the first half were bad, but this one was really, really bad and the match had to be abandoned. Obviously, the man who told me to stay knew what to expect. My only regret is that nobody made a video of the game. I would love to watch the match again. It would have made a great comedy.'

5

JERSEY BOYS

Kilkenny v. Galway

If there really is a spirit of the times, hurling captures it best. Who will ever forget the 2018 hurling championship? Who will ever forget the unrestrained joy when Eddie Brennan's Laois shocked Dublin to qualify for the All-Ireland quarter-final in 2019?

After suffering a heavy defeat to Tipperary in the 1979 National League hurling final, a shake-up of the Galway team was necessary. Noel Lane was one of the casualties and was dropped from the panel. Breaking the news sensitively to him was not a priority for the Galway management.

'I got a letter in an envelope, which was handed to me in the dressing-room in a club game. I smelled a rat. No reason was giving for my omission. It was just: "We regret to inform you …" I felt it was severe to drop me like that.'

The opportunity for redemption came quickly.

'Babs Keating was training Galway at the time. He spear-headed a delegation that came down to see me to ask me back. I replied: "Not a chance." I was just playing hard-to-get. I was the first one in Athenry for training that evening.

'Babs was an excellent manager. As I was moved into full-forward he gave me a lot of his time and attention, coaching me on how to approach forward play and working on my solo and my passing. He gave me a lot of confidence in my own game. I really admired him as a player for Tipp. We had thought of ourselves as inferior to the big powers like Cork, Tipperary and especially Kilkenny, but he was one of them and I suppose to our surprise he was a normal guy. He gave us a lot of confidence. Babs was "let go" after we lost the 1979 All-Ireland to Kilkenny but I believe the belief he gave us was a significant factor in our breakthrough the following year. Although we weren't good enough to win against Kilkenny that year, the rivalry we had with them drove us on to become better.'

ONE OF A KIND

The most famous quote in the hurling vernacular is Mícheál Ó Muircheartaigh's observation: 'A mighty poc from the hurl of Seán Óg O'Halpín ... his father was from Fermanagh, his mother from Fiji, neither a hurling stronghold.'

However, a good contender for runner-up is another of his classics: 'Sylvie Linnane: the man who drives a JCB on a Monday and turns into one on a Sunday.'

Sylvie's fire-and-brimstone approach to the game was legendary and his clashes with opponents were like gladiatorial combats in Ancient Rome: 'For me the colour of a jersey, especially the Kilkenny one, was all I needed to get up for a game. I always had a passion for beating them. Everyone likes to take their scalp. I was never one to say anything to an opponent but I did believe they should know I was there. One time we were playing Kilkenny I received an uppercut from one of their forwards before the national anthem. I couldn't see after it, but I still let fly at him.'

6

AMONGST WOMEN

Cork v. Dublin

In the rich history of the GAA the Cork ladies' team of the noughties and beyond are the greatest team of all time. From never having won a senior title to winning ten All-Irelands in eleven years, nine league titles and ten Munster titles, their record is simply breath taking. They made household names of players such as Valerie Mulcahy and were led magnificently by the peerless Juliet Murphy, who ranks with Cora Staunton as one of the GAA Immortals. Famously in 2013 Murphy came out of retirement to lead Cork to another All-Ireland. Driving that team like a mighty engine was one of Ireland's most distinguished and decorated sports personalities of all time, Rena Buckley.

The manager of the Cork team, Eamon Ryan, was not prepared to accept the old ways. His message was: 'As a team we were feared by everyone out there, but we don't believe in ourselves. The dream can become a reality if we want it bad enough, but we need to believe.'

He told the players to realise the sacrifices needed to get to the top. They had to be more committed, loyal to their teammates and play with pride in the jersey. There were to be no cliques, no gossip, and what was said in the dressing-room stayed in the dressing-room. Three times they beat Dublin in All-Ireland finals, including the never-to-be-forgotten 2014 final, when Dublin led by ten points with just 16 minutes to go. In 2018 the Dubs finally beat Cork in a final to win their second consecutive All-Ireland. Then, in August 2019, Dublin reaffirmed their dominance with a seven-point victory over Cork in the All-Ireland semi-final.

The emergence of a charismatic Cork team, their thrilling rivalry with Dublin and the soaring attendances have seen ladies' football enjoy a much higher profile than camogie in recent years. The great rivalry that has developed between Cork and Dublin has had an unintended consequence. In autumn 2017, RTÉ television transmitted a documentary *Blues Sisters*, which gave the inside account of Dublin's incredible All-Ireland-winning season that year. Former Galway goalkeeper Pat Comer, who created the famous GAA documentary *A Year Til Sunday*, was part of the *Blues Sisters* production team and he became a regular at Dublin's training sessions and games throughout the season. One of the stars of the programme was Dublin's All-Star forward Nicole Owens, who courageously shared her own story of her battle with depression. Her interview in particular generated exceptional interest and Nicole has gone on to become a leading mental health campaigner on the national stage. It is as if she lives by the motto 'If you live without making a difference, what difference does it make that you lived?' At a conference in Trinity College in November 2018 she returned to her *alma mater* and spoke of her experiences and her philosophy.

BREAKING THE GENDER BARRIER

As a girl Owens literally stood out on the playing field. 'I used to play against the boys. Running out, spectators would be laughing and pointing at the guy marking me. Big mistake. It only put pressure on him, especially when I started playing well, but these comments were unwise as they fuelled my desire to play better. My opponent was the nearest victim. I was ten.'

To misquote Bob Dylan in the context of ladies' football, 'the times are a changing'.

'Gaelic football is the fastest-growing female sport in Ireland. There are hundreds of girls down at the nursery in my club, St Sylvester's, every weekend – which is great – but the value I got from playing against boys up to under-12s, when I was redirected towards the Dublin girls development team, has me split on gender segregation. I benefited from playing with boys. The coaching was way more advanced. The skills gap remains, but that is slowly changing. My generation of players have a role to play in this.'

MIND GAMES

She then turned to address her emotional space and her struggles in that area.

'I wasn't ashamed to be suffering from depression, but when I was struggling to figure out all these feelings in my own head it was difficult for me to articulate the situation to others.'

Nicole opened up about her depression to two of her teammates initially.

'People sort of see it as like a weakness or something negative. If you break your leg, it's something tangible and people can see it, whereas this isn't a tangible thing. I would have spoken to my friends about it – that it's hard to be in that place and understand it. There's no physical appearance of it, so it's hard to verbalise the feelings.'

So, when and how did her condition manifest itself?

'It was part of my story growing up. Another part was the silence I carried around. As a teenager, struggling with my sexuality, depression manifested because I didn't have a way to verbalise those feelings. To speak about them to anyone meant I'd need to address what was fuelling the problem.

'My way of handling it was to spend periods of time alone when I'd be very upset. This only happened every couple of months, so I could manage. Eventually, it got to a stage where every day I was waking up with instant dread. When I got really upset over something completely innocuous in college, people began to notice, so I had to open up. I turned to my mum. She's a pathologist, so it's hardly her area of expertise, but she had a lot of resources to draw upon.'

A major concern for Nicole is to speak out so that she might be able to help young women who find themselves in a similar situation.

'There are certainly more visible gay female athletes. Actual role models. Sport in Ireland, particularly GAA, does not have any visible gay male players and that's a real shame. My teenage years were a constant struggle to cope with who I am. Imagine how that feels. Looking back, I wish I'd spoken about it sooner. There were so many years of worry. Since I opened up, the reaction from friends and family, strangers even, has only been positive.

'It's been normalised in my circle of friends, but when age 15, 16, I held it all in. Someone would make a flippant comment about this or that being "so gay" and it felt like a punch in the heart. I carried that pain around far too long. The cure is simple: honestly, just say who you are. That's why the day of celebration is called "Pride". It's liberating. Frightening at first, but liberating afterwards.

'When I stared down my problems it wasn't as terrifying as

I presumed. Turns out the real terror was doing nothing at all, until it became too much to handle.'

Then came the watershed moment. Negative thoughts had entered her head and she needed help.

'One day it kind of came to a point where I broke down in a lecture and my poor mam had to leave work and bring me home. At the time I had been kind of having dangerous and really negative thoughts, and I realised I needed to talk to someone. It's something that people don't really … I didn't really have the classic signs in terms of I still loved playing football, but at the same time [I was] deeply, deeply unhappy.'

She had to confront her own preconceptions.

'At the start, my attitude to medication was "no way". I went to a clinical psychologist, but I was resistant to pills. It was an ignorant view to the role they play, but therapy alone could not bring me to a good place, so I went back to my GP and I've only had positive experiences since taking regular medication these past years.

'These are my experiences. Therapy can feel like a very "touchy-feely" method of dealing with depression, whereas I'm a very logical person who likes to employ actions to tangibly address a problem. Cognitive Behavioural Therapy (CBT) is a way of breaking down triggers, looking at what has me feeling down.'

LIVING IN THE NOW
Some conditions do not have a past tense.

'I've suffered from depression my entire adult life, it's always been something that has come and gone, but I've also had two major depressive episodes, age 21 and 24, that shaped the way I think about my depression and how I deal with it. The second time, in 2017, was when I really committed to CBT. You address your negative voice, that inner critic. Initially I presumed it was coming out of nowhere, but that isn't the case at all. I've learned to feel when a cloud is coming on. I deal with it by telling my girlfriend and we try to talk our way out of it.

'I need to practise this more, to keep up CBT, so I identify negative thoughts and challenge them, as by challenging them you can dismiss them. Don't personalise or turn everything into a catastrophe, the aim is to control your mental health.'

There were times, though, when things crowded in on her.

'It just became too much. I found myself cycling to training, to an environment I absolutely adore, yet thinking, "This is the last place I want to be tonight." Life away from training and games can weigh heavily on us all. Sometimes you can't leave your troubles behind. It could be the stress of work or an argument with a loved one or sometimes you are just having a bad day.

'Sport has a lovely way of lifting your mood. The girls rally around you and, unless it's been an awful week, the buzz snaps you out of your own head for a few hours. Exercise in general is hugely important for coping with depressive tendencies. Yet during that claustrophobic period I began to dread training. I needed to tell Mick [the Dublin manager, Mick Bohan]. His support and that of my family, friends and teammates was huge in ensuring I remained part of the All-Ireland-winning team. Weirdly, 2017 produced this dichotomy, as football-wise I've never had a better season, yet from a mental health perspective it felt like I was drowning.

'Mick stuck with me when it really mattered. In the All-Ireland semi-final against Kerry my performance would have prompted another manager to whip me off, but at half-time there was a quiet word of encouragement. Mick, being fully aware of my problems, had taken me aside on the Friday to see if I was able to start and in the second half he gave me a chance. I scored 1-1.'

HOME THOUGHTS FROM ABROAD

Nicole Owens is the living proof that absence does make the heart grow fonder.

'In the second year of my degree, sociology and Spanish, I went to Granada on Erasmus and took a year away from the GAA. The commitment levels were beginning to annoy me, disrupting my going-out time – I was 18 – when I wanted the full college experience, but it was also my first season on the Dublin panel. There was always a game, so I resented not being able to drink on big nights out. I loved Granada, but I missed football so much. Mam was delighted. She knew well I'd feel that way. I've really appreciated wearing the Dublin jersey. It's a huge part of my life, it's an escape hatch, a creative outlet.

'But it makes socialising like other 20-somethings impossible. These winter months are time enough for messing about and cramming in time with people I care about. Also, doing nothing is hugely important. I'm an introverted extrovert! After being in people's company I crave alone time.

'Time management is crucial when playing for Dublin. Eating the correct food, sleeping enough to have the energy to focus on both career and training while also getting to the gym can become very stressful. My current approach to a work-life balance is to leave work in work, as much as possible, to ensure there are as few blurred lines as possible.'

Nicole also spoke about the friendships that have been forged within the Dublin panel, and her appreciation for her team-mates and management, who look out for her.

'There were times,' she explains, 'where you'd be at work all day, and you'd get through the day, and when you're going to training that's when everything would get in on you and you're a bit run-down.

'A few of them would know at this point if I'm a little upset and they'd drag me off for a chat to get away from the noise. Sometimes if you're not in a good mood and the dressing-room is kicking off it's the last place you want to be. It would have been loads of little things like even people you wouldn't be as close to would text every so often to check in and little things like that. I suppose when I talk about feeling valued as a person that's massive, because at the end of the day Mick would have always said that he didn't care how well I was playing so long as I was OK.

'At the end of the day, if we're all unhappy, we're not going to play well either. It's just knowing that the whole team has your back. It's a huge thing mentally.'

So, what then is her message to people who feel they are drowning?

'I wouldn't wish my thoughts as a teenager, or as recently as 2017, upon anyone, but maybe, just maybe, what I say will give a young girl or boy the courage to confide in people they love. If you're struggling, seek help. It's out there. Silence is not the answer.'

7

THE WEE COUNTY v.
THE GARDEN COUNTY

Wicklow v. Louth

All GAA rivalries are contextual. We hold on to them like a discomfort blanket. Fans of Gaelic games only get really engaged when their own team is involved. To that extent great GAA rivalries are in the eye of the beholder. To a fan in Kerry, Louth's rivalry with Meath may not register, but in Louth in many ways it is the only one that matters. When Cavan play Monaghan in hurling, *The Sunday Game* cameras will never be in attendance, but to that most special of GAA species 'the fierce hurling men' (and thankfully increasingly 'the fierce hurling women') in both counties it is *the* big one.

A new GAA rivalry is an Aladdin's cave, a whole new world, with new horizons and vistas of possibility to pursue. In 2007 a new rivalry emerged between Louth and Wicklow during the three games they played in the Leinster championship. Louth eventually emerged on top.

It would have meant so much to Wicklow football to have put one over on their rivals. At the time Sky Sport was asking

58

people leaving the England match after their 1–1 draw to Brazil in Wembley if they were disappointed.

Fan: 'Not at all, I'm Irish. I'm from Bray.'

Reporter: 'But would you not support England when Ireland are not in action?'

Fan: 'No way.'

Reporter: 'Why not?'

Fan: 'Eight hundred years of oppression.'

Reporter: 'Is there ever any time you would support England?'

Fan: 'If they were playing Louth.'

For their part, Louth fans had a conversation of their own.

Father: 'Son, what'll I buy you for your birthday?'

Son: 'A bicycle.'

Father: 'What'll I buy you for your first communion?'

Son: 'A PlayStation.'

Father: 'What'll I buy you for Christmas?'

Son: 'A Mickey Mouse outfit.'

Father, with a twinkle in his eye: 'No problem, son. I'll just buy you the Wicklow football team!'

8

THE SOUL OF THE GAA

Antrim v. Offaly

Some games leave you scratching your head.

One of the biggest shocks in the history of the GAA came when Antrim defeated Offaly in the 1989 All-Ireland hurling semi-final. It also saw one of the greatest displays of sportsmanship when the Offaly team gave the Saffrons players a guard of honour as they left the pitch.

Ciaran Barr went bravely where no one had gone before as Antrim's first All-Star hurler in 1988. Later in his career the former Irish international water-polo player would transfer to Dublin and give outstanding service in the blue jersey. The high point of his career came when he captained Antrim to a memorable All-Ireland semi-final win over Offaly. It was the first time that Antrim had qualified for the All-Ireland final since 1943, as Barr recalls:

'It was a strange situation. We were confident we could beat Offaly, as we had beaten them twice that year. Although it was an All-Ireland semi-final, we didn't think of it like that, we just thought we were playing Offaly. Although Offaly were the form team in Leinster in the '80s we would have been a lot more scared if we had been playing Kilkenny. It was only after we had beaten them that we thought – gosh, we're in the All-Ireland final now.

'Although we started off slow enough, it was a day everything went right for us. Things we had planned in training just came off for us unbelievably well. We were lucky in the sense that we had five or six players who could turn things around for us when the going got tough.'

The Donnelly clan, from beautiful Ballycastle, are the most famous dynasty in Antrim hurling and were at the heart of that Antrim victory. Over a hundred years ago Edward Donnelly co-founded the Ballycastle McQuillans Club in 1907 and was its first chairman. In 1989 his great-great grandson Dessie Donnelly won an All-Star at left full-back for his commanding performances, which carried Antrim to the All-Ireland final that year. Dessie's teammates included his brother Brian and cousin Terry, son of the legendary 'Bear' Donnelly, who hurled with distinction for club and county in the 1950s and 1960s.

Donnelly was presented with his sole opportunity to play on the highest stage within the game in 1989. Everyone was expecting the day of the All-Ireland hurling semi-finals to produce high drama – mainly because the second semi-final was between old rivals Galway and Tipperary. Eleven days previously Galway had hammered the Glensmen in a challenge match, suggesting to neutrals that the Northerners would be like lambs to the slaughter against Offaly.

It was Offaly who made the better start and their half-time lead was 1-10 to 1-6.

It was a different story in the second half, as Dessie Donnelly marshalled the Antrim defence superbly and Antrim ran out 4-15 to 1-15 winners. Ciaran Barr assumed the playmaker role, like a maestro playing the violin to provide ample scoring opportunities for Olcan 'Cloot' McFetridge (who with Donnelly won an All-Star in 1989), Aidan 'Beaver' McCarry and Donal Armstrong.

It was fitting that Armstrong should be part of Antrim's finest hour, as his late father, dual star Kevin and Antrim GAA's most famous son – left half-forward on the team of the century of greatest players never to have won an All-Ireland medal – had starred in the last Antrim team to reach the All-Ireland final back in 1943. After beating Galway by 7-0 to 6-2 in the quarter-final they had shocked Kilkenny in the semi-final, only to lose to Cork in the final.

TROUBLED TIMES

July 2019 brought a reminder of the historical political problems on the island when Tyrone manager Mickey Harte apologised for some members of his squad singing what was perceived as a Republican song on the team bus. Dessie Donnelly believes that the Offaly win was more special because it came during the height of the Troubles. Donnelly came to regard the abnormality of that situation as normal.

'Thankfully the Troubles never had a major impact on me. The only time it was an issue for me was when we were travelling for some of the Antrim matches. Of course, you have to be particularly careful when times are especially tense, like the marching season. There are quite a few places in Antrim that you wouldn't walk down the road on your own, or even in company, with a hurley stick in your hand – especially around the 12th of July.

'Back in the 1970s our changing rooms were bombed. The damage was superficial. I'd say that was more a matter of luck than careful management on the part of the bombers. There were a lot of theories floating around about who did it, as you can imagine, but I can't tell you who was responsible. Definitely, though, when we qualified for the All-Ireland in 1989 it took people's minds away from the violence.'

Donnelly believes the 1989 All-Ireland semi-final with Offaly is a parable for what GAA rivalry should be.

'Both teams and our fans went into Croke Park as rivals. On the field both teams were trying their utmost to win, but when the final whistle went the Offaly team gave us a guard of honour as we walked off the pitch. It was a genuine rivalry, but one which showcased real sportsmanship and all that is wonderful and positive in the GAA.'

9

FROM BITTER ENEMIES TO FRIENDS

Cork v. Meath

GAA rivalries, like most things in life, mutate with events. At its peak, though, this rivalry was a powder keg ready to explode.

Between 1987 and 1990 Cork and Meath dominated the football landscape, winning all four All-Irelands and three leagues between them – but when they played each other the referee was busier than an ice-cream seller in a heatwave. In a repeat of the 1967 final Meath won their fourth All-Ireland in 1987 when they beat Cork by 1-14 to 0-11. In the 1988 All-Ireland both sides drew in an entertaining game played with fierce intensity. Meath were very lucky to get a replay. It was the first draw in an All-Ireland final since 1972 and it took a controversial free in the dying seconds for Brian Stafford to equalise.

In the replay Meath's battling qualities were to the forefront. After six minutes Gerry McEntee was sent off. Yet they went on to win 0-13 to 0-12. It was a tough, uncompromising match which witnessed some hefty changes and it threatened to boil over a few times. Leitrim great Packy McGarty was one of the many people who were unhappy with the spectacle on the day.

'I remember Colm O'Rourke writing an article explaining how Meath beat Cork in the All-Ireland replay in 1988 when Gerry McEntee was sent off early in the game. Their tactic was to foul an opponent out the field and then they were no longer a man down because a Cork player had to take the free. It was very effective, but it was no way to win because it's much too negative and ruins the game as a spectacle.'

A major controversy would ensue about comments made by John Dowling, the then president of the GAA, which were critical of Meath's 'robust style' – one of the few times the Meath manager Seán Boylan was publicly incensed. As a result, some Meath players refused to walk up to receive their medals from Dowling at the presentation ceremony.

In 1990 the sides met for the third All-Ireland final in four years but this time it was the Leesiders that emerged on top. Meath full-back Mick Lyons went to his manager Seán Boylan after losing that game to Cork with a badly bruised face.

'I'm awful sorry, Seán,' he said.

'Why?' Boylan enquired.

'When X gave me that blow into the face, I should have started an almighty row and that would have galvanised us.'

It was a revealing comment and it said so much about the rivalry between the two counties during those years.

THE BOSS

For more than 20 years Seán Boylan drank from a glass that continuously refilled itself, the last long, cool swallow as necessary as the first, his thirst unquenchable.

Boylan's methods reaped a dividend almost immediately as his star corner-forward, Bernard Flynn, recalls.

'We won the Centenary Cup in 1984, which was a big deal and meant a huge amount to us, and for two years things were going great. We lost the Leinster final by two points to Dublin that same year and we were delighted by how far we had come in the pecking order and that we were at the stage where we could compete.'

Flynn's Meath team were quickly to get a bruising awakening about their status in the hierarchy of Gaelic football.

'The biggest lesson that Meath team got came in 1985 when Laois beat us by ten points in the Leinster championship in Tullamore. We were disgusted and to say it was a "back to the drawing board" moment is an understatement. We went to a quiet bar on the outskirts of Tullamore afterwards and we weren't able to eat. We didn't even sit on seats, we sat on the floor.'

It was time for a new approach, which was not going to be for the faint-hearted.

'It was then that Seán and the senior players recognised that we were nowhere near the level we needed to be. From the autumn of 1985 we saw a huge change in terms of physical training and everyone upped the levels. The raw ambition in that team was relentless. Our rivalry with Cork was brilliant because it pushed us to continually raise our standards as any good rivalry in the GAA should.'

The old warriors found talented and willing recruits to take their place in the unique torture chamber that constituted Meath training sessions.

'Boylan learned as he went. We were lucky to have Noel Keating and Kepak by his side. We went from being 15 years behind the times in 1985 to ten years ahead of the times by the late '80s. I would have heard about Kieran McGeeney and how driven he was with his Armagh team, but I guarantee you they could not match what happened in our training sessions. We were nearly stupid and silly and it's only when you retire that you realise the belting that went on. It was unreal. I wouldn't go to training sessions in fear but I wouldn't know if I would come out safe at times. It was that vicious.

'My own experience was that the only time you missed training was on your deathbed. Boylan had instilled that culture into the squad. They were so true to each other, so honest with each other, and so committed to each other. They were committed to the cause to a fault because I believe some of the stuff that went on in training, while it made us, if we had managed it a bit more and released more of the creative spirit within us, we could have won even more. It was madness beyond comprehension, the hitting, the thumping, and the belting that went on, but it was needed at the time.'

There were times, though, when it got very personal.

'The day before one of the Leinster finals there was a doubt if David Beggy was fit. I'm not sure what issue some of the lads had with him but they beat him up and down the field for about 50 minutes. I remember thinking that man shouldn't be able to play for a week, but they were expecting him to play well in the Leinster final the next day. Nobody asked or said anything because we were afraid to, but it was crazy the torture they put him through.'

A LEADER FOR ALL SEASONS

Séan could keep both the long- and short-term view and persevere with single-minded focus, as Flynn recalls.

'The holidays we went on were brilliant. Our girlfriends were treated like royalty. The steaks and the food were incredible. My parents would go to league matches in the mid-'80s and [Boylan] would insist that they came in for the team meal. When I was a manager, I would be pretty strict myself, but what I learned from my days with Meath is that it is important that you have a bit of craic. We would have a few drinks together when

67

the time was right, but once the drinking started Seán would be gone because things might be said when tongues were loosened that mightn't be easily forgotten or forgiven.'

HUMILIATION

Flynn was to discover in a brutal way that there were severe consequences if you broke the code that drove the squad with the fervour of medieval monks.

'The training in Bettystown and the hill of Tara was savage. I hated the running up the hill of Tara sessions. I would always be at the back while fellas like [Joe] Cassells, Terry Ferguson and [Gerry] McEntee would be up at the front. Even when I was vomiting down my top I kept going because you dared not stop.

'The biggest single lesson I got about Boylan's psyche came one night when he brought us over the sand dunes in Bettystown early in my career. It was minus four or five degrees and we were made to go into the water because he loved the healing and therapeutic powers of water and the whole spirituality of that, but we were worried about getting hypothermia. Seán was way ahead of his times because he had a back-up team with him from early on. One of his first nights in Bettystown he had his crew and they had jeeps with their lights on and they were providing the light in the sand dunes.

'It got so bad I was scared I was dying. I actually felt death was coming over me. I have never felt so bad before or since. I was at the back and I fell down and I got sick and I hid in the bush where it was pitch dark. When the lads came running around again, I jumped into the middle and I thought I had got away with it. Seán had been watching me, though, and he saw what I was at and he stopped everybody. He knew I was a young lad and needed a bit of a reality check of what was expected and demanded of me. I was still wiping away the vomit from my top, but he gave me such a lecture and a lesson that I never stopped again in my entire life.

'The lads were looking me in the eyes and some were shaking their heads and I knew they thought less of me because of that incident. It took me a lot of hard work to rebuild some of their trust after that. I felt I had let myself down, and I had let them down, but the one thing I learned was that you never give up. It wasn't a case of Seán putting his arm around my shoulder. He devoured me and tore strips off me and had me nearly crying. I got no sympathy from anybody else and that was the kind of thing that was needed. He has the image of being a lovely man but underneath he is a silent assassin in a way!'

THE SCHOOL OF HARD KNOCKS

In case Flynn was to forget that lesson, there was another painful reminder of the etiquette that was required in the Meath camp, which put a premium on a widely shared sense of purpose and values.

'At one stage the All-Stars were going to play in the Skydrome in Toronto. Robbie O'Malley, myself and a few players from other counties were asked to go over in advance to promote the games and generate the maximum level of interest. We ran it by Seán Boylan and somehow he said yes because we were going to be playing Dublin in the quarter-final of the National League, which was big for us at the time. When we arrived in Toronto we were met by a limousine; we were on the equivalent of *The Late, Late Show* in Canada. There were three live television shows and three or four of the top radio shows. We were treated like royalty and had never known anything like this. We got a few bob for it at a time we had nothing.

'We had a great break and we were asked to extend the trip for an extra two days for more promotion. We managed to get the word back to Seán. We came back on a wet night and the quarter-final was the following Sunday and we went straight to training.

'As soon as we walked into the dressing-room the hatred we felt from the rest of the players – because we had overstepped the mark in their eyes (or they were just plain jealous they didn't get to go) and done something that was unacceptable for Meath players to do – was unreal. I have no doubt, but if it was [Liam] Harnan or [Mick] Lyons who had been asked to go to Toronto they would have said: "Go f**k off and get somebody else."

'We didn't think there was anything wrong in what we had done. What was done to me that night in training meant I physically couldn't walk at the end and stumbled into a car to get me home. I got thumped and belted all over the field. It was not the first time I'd got thumped, but what was different that night was that nobody said anything to me. We were ignored because we had missed one training session and that was sacrosanct.'

A MISUNDERSTOOD MAN

Part of the problem for Flynn was that his colleagues made assumptions about him that did not reflect him in the best possible light. On one occasion Flynn added fuel to that fire in Seán Boylan's eyes. Yet, like all great leaders, Boylan had the capacity for the counter-intuitive response and could understand the voice of resistance. He could change the rules of the game when he felt it was needed and find new possibilities and stay calm and engaged when there was a threat to his authority. Flynn also experienced this side of his manager at first hand.

'I know there was always a culture within the Dublin squad, for example of going for a few drinks on the Monday night after a big match. I got into my head that one Monday night I would go out for a few drinks. Back then Bad Bobs was the place to go and I thought as I was away from Meath nobody would know. I had a great night and made it into work the next morning on time, as I always did. That night I went to training, having had literally no sleep the night before and having had what might be nicely termed as "a rough night". It was one of the few times when I simply couldn't run, and a bit like that night in Bettystown I was really scared that I was going to die because my head was spinning. Seán was running us up and down the hills and up the steps of the stand in Navan and he could see the way I was struggling badly. Normally he would pull up a fella in front of the whole squad, but he knew I was a younger guy and there was a danger that he might push me over the edge. Although I had the height of respect for him, I was fiery and I would take him on the odd time and that was well known within the squad; he probably felt that if he started eating the face off me that night there could be a reaction, and who knew where it would end? There was a bit of a rebel in me – some of the lads would say more than a bit.

'It was only afterwards that I realised how brilliantly Seán handled the situation that night. He pulled me up and he said to the lads: "Bernard is not feeling well. I chatted with him beforehand and I'm pulling him out." I knew that was not the case and I didn't know what was going on. He got me into a corner on my own and never discussed the incident with any other players. I know because I've asked several of them about it subsequently. He said: "If you f**king ever do again what you did since Sunday evening you're finished." He then proceeded to go through all my movements from Monday evening to Tuesday morning: every pub and club I had been to and what time I came and left. He then said: "You are getting one chance, now go home and rest."

'His psychology was brilliant. He weighed me up and felt that this was the best way to handle me because there could have been a major row. And there were a few of them. I respected him and had a little fear of him and there was no way I was going to try anything like that again. I didn't think he would be able to track my movements, but he was letting me know he could. That was his genius. He knew the right card to play in nearly every situation. Without those extreme measures we would never have beaten Cork in those two All-Irelands. It was a huge compliment to our rivalry with Cork that he demanded such high standards from us.'

CAPTAIN FANTASTIC

Billy Morgan led the county to four consecutive All-Ireland finals – initially losing to Meath in '87 and '88 before beating Mayo in '89 and old rivals Meath in 1990. Morgan had captained Cork to an All-Ireland in 1973.

'It was hugely important for Cork to win that year. It was 26 years since we had last won a senior football All-Ireland and the longer it was going on the harder it was becoming. We beat Mayo in the end, but what I most recall was the homecoming. When we got into Cork there were crowds in the station and all the way up MacCurtain Street. The biggest thing was when we turned Barry's Corner. Looking down on Patrick Street it was just a sea of people. I never saw anything like it before. You couldn't see the streets; it was just people all the way down to the Savoy.

'In 1988 I had thought we might be getting such a home-coming when we played Meath. They had deservedly beaten us the year before, but we had a year's experience behind us in '88. We drew the game, even though we should have won it. In the drawn game Dinny Allen had caught Mick Lyons with his elbow and Barry Coffey had tackled Colm O'Rourke and caught him with his shoulder behind the ear. People said Niall Cahalane had "caught" Brian Stafford. All the talk between the drawn game and the replay was that Meath were going to sort us out. My own instructions were, if that was the case, if there was any trouble, stand together and be united.

'It didn't come as a huge surprise when Gerry McEntee hit Niall Cahalane. All our lads got involved in the flare-up. When it was over and McEntee was sent off, I said to our fellas: "OK now, that's it, we'll play football from here on in, no retaliation." I repeated the same message at half-time. It was the biggest mistake I ever made as a manager. What I should have said was "Meet fire with fire, and if necessary we'll finish this game ten-a-side." Fair play to Meath; they beat us with 14 men. I suppose it was sweet, then, to beat them in the final in 1990.'

TEDDY BOY

Cork midfielder during the 1990 double triumph, Teddy McCarthy chooses his words carefully when asked about that years victory over Meath. Did it bring particular satisfaction to the Cork side to put one over on Meath after the allegations that there was a history of 'bad blood' between the sides following their ill-tempered clashes in the '80s?

'Winning an All-Ireland final at any time is great, no matter who you beat. I'm not sure that there was as much bad blood, to use that term, as people thought. There were tensions certainly – much more so with some players in both camps than others. I would say, though, most of us had a lot of respect for the Meath guys … having said all that it would be fair to say that we were glad that after 1990 we had put the Meath thing to rest.'

PERSPECTIVE

Time heals all wounds and can dissipate some deep hostilities. Bernard Flynn saw this at work in the rivalry with Cork when a vein of grief changed the landscape forever and melted away the animosity like tears in the rain.

'One January we were both staying in the same hotel complex in Gran Canaria, and we had as much welcome for each other as a nun would find in a brothel. There was the odd exception. Liam Hayes and Larry Tompkins had a chat one afternoon on a beach in Puerto Rico. One night my wife Madeline and I broke away from the pack to have a few scoops with Shea Fahy, Steven O'Brien and their partners. I was telling none of my team mates that I met up with the Cork lads. They'd walk by each other. The late Mick Holden of Dublin did say to us: "Jaysus, lads, ye'll all be dead and there won't be a football in sight."

'I was in the Canaries when Colman Corrigan phoned to tell me John Kerins had passed. Everything changed after that. Most of the Meath lads went to his funeral. In October 2009, Robbie O'Malley got married. One of the guests that day amidst all his Meath colleagues was Anne Kerins, John's widow.'

Personal adversity, a place where GAA rivalries were forgotten and time went unnoticed, gave Flynn a different perspective when grief cut through him, as surely as any knife.

'In November 2009 I was having a hip replacement. I couldn't sleep. The pain shot through every fibre of my body. I had to grit my teeth. I grabbed the monkey pole above my bed in Mount Carmel Hospital, but I told myself that I was one of the lucky ones. I thought of Jim Stynes, who was fighting cancer and a brain tumour at only 43. He would have loved it if all he needed was a hip operation followed by a knee replacement. I thought of Michael Duignan, who lost his lovely wife Edel to cancer. Then there was Eamonn Coleman, who famously guided Derry to their only All-Ireland. I got to know him when he worked on the buildings in Mullingar. We had many a cup of tea together. Our great rivals Cork in the late '80s also lost Mike McCarthy.

'In 1988 in particular we had a lot of animosity with Cork, but life and death brought everything into perspective. We became friendly with those Cork lads and we both have massive respect for each other now.'

PART II
Classic Hits

On 17 January 2019 the acclaimed American poet Mary Oliver died. She wrote some of my favourite lines in her poem 'When Death Comes' when she spoke of being 'married to amazement'.

Filled with intermittent regrets about the past, occasional forebodings about the future, often barely aware of the present, GAA fans are 'married to amazement'. The rivalry between fans adds another layer to that amazement.

Some GAA rivalries like Dublin v. Kerry, or Cork v. Kilkenny, have long histories. Some intense rivalries have a much shorter shelf-life, like that between Tyrone and Kerry in the noughties, and more recently Jim Gavin's Dublin and Mayo.

Sky Sports described the clash between Kerry and Dublin in the 2019 All-Ireland final as *El Classico*. The game lived up to the hype with a thrilling draw that achieved the unthinkable . . . it left Pat Spillane speechless.

This section celebrates some of the classic rivalries that have lit up the GAA down the ages, as supporters sought to rise above themselves and grasp the world of Gaelic games.

10

KERRY'S DUB-LE TROUBLE

Dublin v. Kerry

The salvation of football.

That is how one pundit summed up Kerry's thrilling win over Dublin in the 2019 National League in front of 12,000 people under lights in Tralee on a cold February night. It was the game that offered confirmation of Ciarán Whelan's thesis that 'Gaelic football is coming out of recession'.

It was just another gripping instalment in Gaelic football's most famous rivalry. The media attention after the match was about the Rachel and Ross from *Friends*-style 'will they/won't they get back together' between Jim Gavin and Diarmuid Connolly, following reports which Gavin quickly rejected that Connolly was having one-to-one training sessions with Bryan Cullen.

LONG-RUNNING RIVALRY

Although Limerick won the first All-Ireland in 1887, Gaelic football really came of age in 1903, when Kerry won their first All-Ireland. They beat Kildare in a three-game saga which grabbed the public imagination. Kerry won the first encounter, but the match was replayed because Kerry had been awarded a controversial goal. So intense was the second game, which finished in a draw, that the referee collapsed at the end. On the third occasion Kerry were comprehensive winners by 0-8 to 0-2.

The following year saw the first taster of what would become one of the great rivalries in the GAA, when Kerry beat Dublin to claim their second All-Ireland. By now the first true star of Gaelic football, Dick Fitzgerald, had emerged. He won five All-Ireland medals, captaining the team to All-Irelands in 1913 and 1914. Like many men of the time Fitzgerald was active in the IRA, as the movement for Irish independence gathered momentum. After the 1916 Rising he found himself interned with Michael Collins in Wales.

THE GLAMOUR TIE

Kevin Heffernan and Páidí Ó Sé are having the time of their afterlives watching the continuing evolution of the Kerry–Dublin rivalry as they lean over the bannisters in heaven. The rivalry between the two superpowers of Gaelic football in the 1970s and 1980s would elevate the game to dizzy new heights on the national consciousness. It is an overused word, but Heffo had *charisma*. It was like electricity, just talking to him and watching his brain computing all the possibilities in an instant.

Pat Spillane became a household name in 1975 when, as a raw 19-year-old, he collected the Sam Maguire Cup when Kerry beat Dublin and team captain Mickey O'Sullivan was en route to hospital.

'It was a dream, only that it was reality. I was very immature and it was something I took for granted. After that, for all of us, there was only one way to go and that was down, which we did.

We were a bunch of youngsters, mainly bachelors, fun-loving lads. We had a great time. We cruised through '75 and thought we were great guys altogether. Success went to our heads and Dublin cut us down to size in '76 when they beat us easily in the All-Ireland final. We got exactly what we deserved – a kick in the pants.'

Oh the Dubs are back. The Dubs are back.

REVERSAL OF FORTUNE

Life is a battle between two thieves: regret over the past and fear of the future. As Dublin's corner-back in 1976 Gay O'Driscoll acknowledges beating Kerry became their all-consuming passion that year.

'Credit is due to Kevin Heffernan because of his ability to adapt to changing circumstances. Tactics did not come into it in '74. The only instruction the backs were given was to win the ball and get it quickly to the forwards. Their instruction was to win the ball. After losing to Kerry in '75 tactics came in the following year and a more professional approach, like watching videos of our opponents. Heffo watched a video of Kerry beating Cork in the Munster final and picked up one of Kerry's key tactics. The Kingdom tried to pull out the opposing full-back line and pump the ball over their heads and get their forwards to turn around and run in. Heffo countered that by keeping either Robbie Kelleher or myself back to act as a kind of sweeper.' *Cause Hill 16 has never seen the likes of Heffo's army.*

Kerry and Dublin renewed their rivalry in 1977 in a classic All-Ireland football semi-final. Kerry's corner-back Jimmy Deenihan was more concerned about the result than its entertainment value.

'It was a very fast game, played at a very high tempo with

quick movement of the ball. The physical competition was intense and there was a great atmosphere because we were craving revenge after losing to Dublin the previous year. We had a large following from the North of Ireland at that stage. But from our point of view it was no good going down in history for having played in the greatest match of all time when we didn't win it.

'Our preparations for that match were hampered by injuries. I had a bad shoulder injury, it was dislocated. Seán Walsh had a serious ligament injury. He played well and got a goal. We were out on a mission to prove that the '76 result was not real. We trained very hard in '77 and went in with reasonable confidence. We felt we had the edge after beating them in the league final earlier that year.

'We had the initiative from the start and were playing comfortably. The only fly in the ointment was that Anton O'Toole ['the Blue Panther', who sadly died in May 2019] had the edge on Ger Power that day and scored a couple of points before half-time. Early in the second half a high ball came in from Tommy Drumm and landed between John McCarthy and myself, but there was hesitancy on everybody's part, including our goalie Paud O'Mahony, and the ball ended up in the Kerry net. Late in the game a soft ball came in towards the Kerry goal. John O'Keeffe had been going well on the day and tried to deflect the ball away from Jimmy Keaveney, but he made a boob and knocked it straight to Tony Hanahoe, who passed it to David Hickey, who scored a goal. Then Seán Doherty made the catch of his life to thwart us as we attacked.'

Does he agree that selection blunders cost Kerry the match, particularly a failure to redress obvious midfield problems?

'The selectors were caught with an embarrassment of riches in terms of players. Páidí Ó Sé was chosen at midfield. He was a great footballer, but he was never a midfielder. We had three natural midfielders in the squad at the time: Pat McCarthy, John Long and Mikey Connor, who were all playing well at the time. Selecting Paídí at midfield caused an imbalance in the team. Pat was brought on when the game was lost. Ger Power was getting a roasting from Anton O'Toole. Both problems were obvious from an early stage but no corrective action was taken. Losing that game, though, was the inspiration for our win the following year. It was a terrible blow for us, worse almost than losing the five-in-a-row in '82. We got a worse reception than we got in '82 when we came home. There was sympathy for us that year, but there was none in '77.

'For the league games, I was rested, as well as Pat Spillane, Ger Power and Paud O'Mahony. I had gone through a run of injuries – I think that they may have felt I was imagining some of them. I think they felt Spillane was too individualistic and not enough of a team player at the time, Ger had not been playing well for a while and I think the selectors blamed Paud for Dublin's first goal. Kerry had a very poor league campaign and only the width of the post prevented them from being relegated in the final match.

'There had been a lot of criticism of management. A challenge had been made openly on Ger MacKenna's position as county chairman. Some of the selectors were replaced. Mick O'Dwyer was booed at a league match in Killarney, I think it was against Galway. That hurt him a lot. We were all irked at the media adulation of the Dubs and the way Kerry were presented as not being in the same league.

'I played rugby all winter for Tralee and was coached by former Irish international Barry McGann, which kept me fit, and I made my comeback to help Munster win the Railway Cup in '78. A big plus for Kerry came in May of that year when we beat Dublin in a game at Gaelic Park, New York. It was a very red-blooded match in every sense! I got my nose broken. Tommy Doyle, Eoin Liston and Pat O'Neill were sent off. We took it very seriously but they took it less so. It was a milestone for us – psychologically, we proved to ourselves that we could beat them.

'There was a lot of pressure on us to beat Cork in the Munster final, particularly as Cork had a strong side at the time, but we did and cruised past Roscommon in the semi-final. The final was a big confrontation for us. We were superbly fit for the game. Most of us lived like hermits. None of the lads went near Tralee races or to the craic in Ballybunion; there were no late nights or alcohol. People who later became heavy drinkers were not drinking at that stage.

'We were very careful with the media that year. O'Dwyer pleaded with us to be very cagey with journalists. We had a press night when all the journalists came down, but O'Dwyer changed the training routine just for that night! In both '76 and '77 Kerry were affected by the media. There was a lot of hype and we believed it. We were a mature outfit, hungry for victory in '78. There were a lot of damaged egos in the side both among the players and among the management. O'Dwyer acknowledged that he had been badly hurt by the booing incident in Killarney.

'We went into the final with a very changed-about team from the previous year, with a lot of positional switches and a much better balance. Eoin Liston, Mick Spillane and Charlie Nelligan came into the side, adding youth and freshness. We were really stretched in the first 15 minutes. I thought it was going to be an avalanche. We were just about hanging on. I remember Robbie Kelleher [the Dublin corner-back] had a shot for a point at one stage, which summed up how bad things were for us. I think they were deluded by the media attention and adulation so much that they left John Egan unmarked. John was not the type of player to be bothered what his marker was doing up the field. He stayed in his position and his goal turned the tide. Then came Mike Sheehy's goal and we were on our way.'

For Deenihan there was a personal disappointment about the final. 'We went in at half-time having absorbed total pressure in front. We just destroyed them in the second half. Everything went our way and we finally produced the type of football we had thought we were capable of for the previous three years. We exploited gaps in the Dublin defence. Their backs were not great second phase markers. A scuffle broke out in front of the goal and John McCarthy and Charlie Nelligan were sent off. I was the loose man and went in goal briefly but the selectors sent on Paud O'Mahony and I was the one taken off. It would have been nice to have finished out the game.

'After that game I remember going back to Killarney, where we got a tumultuous reception, having defeated "the unbeatable Heffo machine". I remember saying, "We're now a mature team. We're savouring the victory but not going to get carried away like we did in 1975." I knew then we could win more All-Irelands.'

The heart becomes a different place when a few All-Ireland medals are stored on the mantelpiece. It would take exceptional powers to keep that Kerry team motivated. In conversation with this scribe, the late Tim Kennelly credited Mick O'Dwyer as the main catalyst for Kerry's success.

'Dwyer was a bit of a rogue, and a really cute rogue at that, but he knew how to get the best out of us. We took everybody by surprise in '75. Going into the '76 All-Ireland we thought we were world beaters. All the backslapping got to us. We were as good as Dublin, but we just weren't mentally ready for that final. The semi-final in '77 against the Dubs was one of the great games. The match was there for the taking. Most of the Kerry players were in tears after the game in the sanctuary of the dressing-room. We had put in a huge amount of training that year but still we had lost to the Dubs again. That certainly dented our confidence. Some of us were thinking, "Will we ever beat the Dubs again?" The next year we got the Bomber on board and I think he was the final piece of the jigsaw.'

Pat Spillane puts the emphasis on the collective.

'What also would have made those Kerry players stand out in any era is that they were an exceptionally intelligent bunch. Their speed of thought was most evident in the way Mike Sheehy cleverly chipped Paddy Cullen with a quick free, which turned the 1978 All-Ireland final in our favour.

'After Seamus Darby's sensational last-minute winner for Offaly against Kerry in 1982, that Mike Sheehy goal is the most famous ever scored in an All-Ireland final. Paddy Cullen's frantic effort to keep the ball out was memorably described afterwards by the legendary Con Houlihan, who wrote it was like "a woman who smells a cake burning".

'I was just watching the tape of the goal recently and I heard Micheál O'Hehir describe it as "the greatest freak of all time". You would have to take him to task for that comment. It was a moment of pure genius in the speed of thought and the execution of a very difficult skill. Absolutely magnificent. Of course it wasn't a free. But that's beside the point.'

THE HEART OF THE MATTER

Another thrilling chapter in the rivalry came when Pat Gilroy's Dublin dramatically snatched victory from the jaws of defeat to Kerry, with Stephen Cluxon famously kicking the winning point in the 2011 All-Ireland final.

Pat Spillane is not convinced that the Dublin–Kerry rivalry was a completely positive thing for the GAA.

'Everyone thought Kerry and Dublin won in the 1970s and 1980s because of frightening physical regimes. This was actually incorrect, but it was a good rumour to throw out at the time. Everyone aped us. What is even worse is that fellas with no knowledge of football earned a great living by training teams at intercounty level, and even more alarmingly at club level, driving players into the ground, running. When people heard about these tough regimes they said knowingly, "Isn't he a mighty man?"

'Two things happened as a consequence. The standard of football dropped because we were producing athletes and runners rather than footballers. The second thing is that these men are responsible for the huge number of crocked ex-players who are the result of that intensive training from these years.

'Too many teams are like sheep. They follow the crowd. If one team does 100 laps a night, the next one has to do 120 laps. If one crowd trained up a 100-metre hill the next found a 200-metre hill, and then the next had to climb a mountain. When one crowd goes for a swim, the next has to swim in a lake and the next go swimming in the sea.'

Spillane, though, also sees a huge plus side to the rivalry.

'The GAA owes the two teams a lot. Gaelic football was not fashionable before the intense Dubs–Kerry rivalry came on the scene, but they did a massive PR job for the game, as was seen in the number of Dublin jerseys being worn at the time, which later spread to jerseys in the other counties, generally when they had a taste of success. Dublin's rivalry with Kerry made Gaelic football sexy because of the hype they generated.'

11

THEM AND US

Meath v. Dublin

VIis mutare aliquid magis excitando tuum?

Do you wish to change to something more exciting? This could have been the question posed to a hurler who was unexpectedly asked to manage the Meath football team – when to the outside world he lacked all the essential qualifications for it.

Seán Boylan became team manager in 1982, at a time when no one else wanted the job. Meath football was in the doldrums and the great powers in Leinster were Offaly and Dublin. He brought organisation into the camp and got players to make sacrifices so that there was no longer any excuse to miss training. Up to then some players would have opted for club football rather than playing for the county team, but Boylan changed all that. He also brought superb interpersonal skills to the job, and above all he knew how to treat people with respect. He allowed players to express themselves in team talks more so than trying to tell players all the time what he wanted. In that way he pulled everybody together.

Boylan's reign did not begin with titles. In 1983, the Royal

County lost to the Dubs in the early rounds of the Leinster championship.

HIGH STAKES

Bernard Flynn saw at first hand the intensity Boylan brought to the Meath job.

'Seán wanted us to be able to hack it with the Dubs, who were up on a pedestal at the time. We had been not just second best to them, but a *distant* second best to them and he was determined to change that. This was going to take a lot of pain and sacrifice. Whatever extreme measures had to be taken, he was willing to do it and that is a real backhanded compliment to Dublin.

'Gerry McEntee's brother Andy was on the Meath panel and, like me, he was very fiery. He was Meath minor manager and brought them to the All-Ireland final some years before, and of course he became the senior manager. But, with the greatest respect to him, he could be a bit of a nuisance in training. He was by no means alone in that respect in the squad.

'One of the reasons I became a good player was that I generally marked Robbie O'Malley in training and those clashes with him brought me on so much. He was so good that I had to push myself to the very limits to match him. One night Robbie wasn't able to train and I found myself marking Andy instead. He was anxious to get on the Meath team and wanted to make his mark and he hit me a dirty belt in the ribs. We had words. Then he hit me a second time. I said to him, "Andy, if you do that again I'll f**king bust you." So he hit me again and I did strike back.

'Seán Boylan was furious, not because we were hitting each other but because we were doing it in a way that was disrupting what he wanted to get out of that session. He said, "That's it. Ye're going to do laps for the rest of the night." I'd say there were about 800 to a thousand people watching us because we often had big crowds at our training sessions and this was going on in full view of everyone. Andy and I started running but we had only got to the corner when we started beating the heads off each other.

'Seán was so annoyed that he abandoned the training and ran over to us. What nobody realised was that he was ferociously strong and fit. Instead of stopping the fisticuffs he hit me in the stomach with a belt and said, "Ye think ye're so f**king hard, I'll take both of ye on." Andy and I looked at each other. Seán was up on his toes and he was skipping like a real hard man. He was beckoning us forward with his fingers and he said, "Come on, ye think ye're hard. Come on and take me on. I'll f**king take both of ye on." We could do nothing because we were in such a shock. If we threw a punch he was going to hit back and he had ferocious power in his arms. He cut the aggro stone dead. We didn't do it again. It was a master class in man-management.'

REGIME CHANGE

Meath seemed to have turned a corner in 1984 when they won the Centenary Cup, marking the GAA's 100th anniversary, by beating a strong Monaghan side in the final. Later that year they reached the Leinster final and ran Dublin to four points. It was back to the bad old days in 1985, when they suffered a humiliating defeat at the hands of Laois in the Leinster championship by 2-11 to 0-7 in Tullamore. Questions were asked about Boylan's stewardship and he had to survive a vote at a county board meeting to remain in office.

Although it was without doubt a low point for the Meath team it proved to be a blessing in disguise. Boylan found six new players who would play key roles in the coming years: Terry Ferguson, Kevin Foley, Liam Harnan, David Beggy, P.J. Gillic and Brian Stafford.

The tide finally turned when Meath beat Dublin in the 1986 Leinster final. Meath went on to win back-to-back All-Irelands in 1987 and '88. They also won five out of six Leinster titles from 1986 to 1991 in the greatest run in the county's history, losing All-Ireland finals in 1990 and 1991 to Cork and Down respectively.

Dublin reigned supreme in Leinster from 1992 to 1995. Boylan faced another apparent crisis in '95, when Meath lost the Leinster final to their great Dublin rivals by ten points. Boylan had to face another election. Again, he reacted to major defeat by rebuilding the Meath team and was rewarded with another All-Ireland title in 1996.

AN EPIC SAGA

After Italia 1990 it seemed as if the Irish nation fell in love with soccer. To some it was as if the GAA's premier status in Irish society was under threat. But in 1991 an epic four-game saga between Meath and Dublin reignited the public love for Gaelic games once more. There was one incident that highlighted for Bernard Flynn the worst and the best of Meath's rivalry with Dublin.

'Dublin's Davy Sinnott and I worked together. The week before the 1988 Leinster final Davy and I were in the papers every day because we were going to be marking each other in the game. The hype was incredible. Tennent's milked it for all it was worth and arranged a reception for 60 publicans after the match.

'On the match day, my wife was in the stand with Davy's wife, Marie. Davy was a clean player; he had burst on to the scene the previous few years and was a breath of fresh air.

'I got the first few balls and then he hit me. Then I got a score and he did it again. I said, "Davy, cop yourself f**king on. You

hit me twice and if you do it again I will bust you." The ball
came out towards the middle of the field and I caught him with
my elbow as far as I could and burst his nose. The referee didn't
see my elbow but did see Davy turning around and giving me
a box. The game stopped. The crowd were going crazy. Davy
was sent off. As he walked off, he started to pump blood and
the referee couldn't understand why. I remember him pleading
with the referee that I hit him first.

'I was lying on the ground and thinking of my job – the first
decent job I had in my life, my new Opel Ascona that made me
feel that I was Don Johnson. I thought of my boss, who was
watching me playing, and I was worried that I would lose my
job and my car. I thought of the publicans who were going to
be at our reception. I thought of Marie and Madeline together
in the stand. All of these thoughts went through my head in
seconds.

'There was a huge euphoria after we beat Dublin in the Leister
final but then I met Madeline, and Marie was with her, and she
was inconsolable. She had a bit of a go at me. Then Davy didn't
show up at the gig. Although it was one of Seán's big things
that the team went together after the match, I got the word back
to him that I had to find Davy before I went back to the gig.
Hours went by and still no Davy, and Marie was very worried.
My boss decided to have a party in his house in Swords and
Davy arrived. After an hour of drinking and thrashing it out,
we made up.

'I crashed my lovely car late that night. I had to do a promotion in Gibneys in Malahide the next day. I was in a state. Who
was the guy who put his arm around me and got me through
it? Davy Sinnott. What did he do? The next day was a bank
holiday Monday. Great man that he was, Davy drove me to the
promotion and got all the stuff I needed and helped me with

my promotion in the pub. That's what the GAA is all about it. I'll never forget him for that.'

There remains a strong sense in Flynn that his Meath team, for all their success, did not achieve their potential, even though their rivalry with Dublin drove up their standards.

'When we meet up, I always contend that we underachieved. There is still strong debate about that amongst us. I believe what made us held us back. If we had managed ourselves a bit better, we would have won at least one more All-Ireland. The last time we had the debate I told the lads, "If we had a little less f**king brawn and more f**king brain we would have won much more."'

12

D'UNBELIEVABLES

Tipperary v. Kilkenny

In no other rivalry has the incredible shaken hands with the inexplicable so consistently. Nobody knows this with as much intimacy as Babs Keating. He was one of the great masters of the ancient game. Playing Kilkenny brought out the best in Babs Keating.

'Coming from where I was in rural Tipperary, we all had the dream of wearing the jersey, of walking behind the Artane Boys Band and playing in Croke Park. The one thing we had was the confidence that if we got to an All-Ireland we would win it because of the power of the Tipp jersey.

'Football was in my blood. My granduncle Tommy Ryan won two All-Irelands with Tipperary. He was playing in Croke Park on Bloody Sunday and helped remove Michael Hogan from the pitch after he had been shot by the Black and Tans. I played football for ten consecutive years with Munster. The fact that I came from a football area meant it came easier to me. I could play football just by togging out because I was brought up with a football, whereas with hurling I had to work a bit harder.'

Babs did not taste immediate success. 'I had huge disappointment at under-age, losing four All-Ireland finals at minor and intermediate level. Then, having won an Intermediate All-Ireland in 1963, three of us arrived on the Tipp senior team for the first league game against Galway and played most of the games in the league but of the three new boys I was the most vulnerable because the Tipp forwards were so strong.

'A highlight for me was playing in my first All-Ireland against Kilkenny in '64. Seamus Cleere was the hurler of the year in '63 and he was an outstanding wing-back. The one thing about that Tipp team was that they had the forwards thinking like backs and the backs like forwards. Seamus Cleere had scored a couple of points from the half-back line in the final the previous year. When you have a half-back scoring like this, he's a seventh forward. My role was to stop Seamus. Lucky enough, the first ball that ran on between us I got it and scored a tricky point. I made a goal for Donie Nealon as well as doing my own job, so I ended up as Sportstar of the Week and on a high. The hype at home then was as big as it is now. The only thing was that the media coverage wasn't anything like as intense as it is today. I was back at work on the Tuesday morning. There was no such thing as banquets here, there and everywhere. Having said that, there was a better atmosphere in Croke Park then, because you were closer to the ground.'

For Babs, the '71 All-Ireland final against Kilkenny has special significance.

'Long before players were handed out gear for free, we were very conscious of the importance of equipment. I had the very best pair of football boots, but the night before the final my bag was stolen with the boots in them. I got a spare pair, but they didn't suit the conditions, so I took them off. Micheál O'Hehir famously described me in his commentary as "Barefoot in the

Park". I was marking Fan Larkin, and guys like Fan and Ted
Carroll were not the sort of fellas to be walking around without
some sort of protection. Fan never stood on my feet. He tried it
a few times, but I was gone before he could make contact!'

THE BLACK AND AMBER

Ernest Hemmingway defined heroism as 'grace under pressure'. By that criterion Eddie Keher is one of the GAA's greatest
heroes. When you have won six All-Ireland medals, ten Leinster medals, ten Railway Cup medals, five All-Star awards and
a Texaco award it is more than a little difficult to isolate one
great sporting moment, but Eddie Keher only hesitated briefly
in making his selection.

'Beating Tipperary in the '67 final was very important because
we hadn't beaten them at that level for 40 years, I think. There was
an attitude then that you'll never beat Tipperary in a hard game.
Although we always play a certain type of game in Kilkenny, I
think we toughened up a bit for that game and it made for a very
satisfying victory, particularly as we proved our critics wrong.'

Stoical as ever, Keher has mixed feelings about his greatest
game. 'From a personal point of view, 1971 was very satisfying.
Things went well for me on the day in the All-Ireland final and
I scored a then record score in an All-Ireland final of 2-11 – a
record which was broken by Nicholas English in 1989. I rang
him up a few days later to congratulate him. Coincidentally it
was Tipp who beat us in the final in '71 and we can have no
complaints with that because they had so many great players,
like Babs Keating, who was hurler of the year that year.'

ENGLISH LESSONS

In the late 1990s Nicky English would take on the job of
managing the Premier County. At the time the omens did not

seem favourable. 'When I was approached to take on the job as manager I got lots of advice not to take it because the belief was that the players in the county at the time were no match for Clare or whoever. To be honest, everybody told me not to take it. But I couldn't stop myself.

'I think we were unlucky in 1999. I feel that the referee made a bad decision to give a penalty to Clare at the end of the match, which Davy Fitzgerald scored. We had a young team and our lads thought it was easy after that game – although Clare were still a great team, we had more than matched them. That Clare team had some of the greatest players in the history of the game, like Seánie McMahon, Brian Lohan and Jamesie O'Connor, and in the replay they really upped their performance and blew us away. I've heard Loughnane and some of the Clare lads saying since that was their best-ever performance.

'I learned from my own mistakes during that game. I had left Declan Ryan on the bench with a view to getting the Tipp crowd going when we brought him on. We sprung him after 20 minutes but the match was lost at that stage. I was talking with Seán Boylan shortly after the game and he said he had made the same mistake once, leaving Gerry McEntee on the bench. That day taught me that you play your best players from the start. We made it to the Munster final the next year, but a lot of our lads got distracted by sideshows, like getting tickets for the game and the crowd, and we lost to Cork.

'I knew that in 2001 we had a great chance of winning the All-Ireland if we could get over Clare in the Munster champion-ship. By then we were a battle-hardened team and were ready to make the big breakthrough, especially with Eoin Kelly arriving on the scene. People talk a lot of nonsense about motivation. I think motivation is a really simple concept. It's about getting a player to give his best but also to do what is best for the team.

Before the final I told the players to go out there and make as many mistakes as they could. I wanted to free them up. The last thing you want is players closing in on themselves. People talk about the importance of having a great leader but the best leaders are not always the best players. We had great leaders on that team, like Tommy Dunne, Eddie Enright, Paul Ormond and Declan Ryan.

'My abiding memory of that All-Ireland was that the referee played four minutes of injury time. That was sheer agony because we were just two points up at that stage and if Galway got a goal we were beaten. I couldn't wait for Pat O'Connor to blow the whistle. It wasn't like winning the All-Ireland as a player. What I felt was sheer relief. There is so much pressure on the manager because you are expected to know on a Saturday what everybody knows on Monday.'

Having reached the summit in 2001, Nicky English would have a less happy time in '02.

'Kilkenny beat us in the All-Ireland semi-final the next year and I saw Henry Shefflin saying recently that was one of their greatest ever performances. That was the end of the road for me. Kilkenny are the benchmark. They beat us that day but they had to be at their very best to do so. Tipperary and Kilkenny is one of the biggest rivalries in hurling – one of the great things of this rivalry is that both teams get the best out of each other because both set of fans demand nothing less.'

THE ADMIRERS

The healthy aspect of the rivalry is the respect the teams have for each other. Babs Keating acknowledges the great players on Brian Cody's team.

'When you talk about the complete player, you have to talk about them in relation to the position they play in. You are talking about Mick Kavanagh, Noel Hickey and Tommy Walsh. J.J. Delaney was the complete left-back. You can't compare Henry Shefflin with DJ Carey because they played in a different position, though you could have played DJ full-forward, depending on who was full-back. DJ went through an All-Ireland final without scoring, but I don't think Shefflin would do that. The scores that DJ got were spectacular. I don't want to make comparisons. Henry Shefflin was perfect.'

For his part, Nicky English is equally generous to Kilkenny.

'It is hard to compare players. DJ was one of the best I've ever seen. He had such skill, great hunger, could get inspirational scores, but above all he had blinding pace and no defender could handle him at his best. In a different way Henry Shefflin was also an outstanding player and one of the greats. For such a big man he had such skill. I was close to him in the stand when he hit the first ball against Waterford from close to the sideline in the 2008 All-Ireland final. I knew from the sound of the ball hitting the hurley that he had caught it sweetly: I didn't even have to look to know it was going over the bar. The only other time I've heard that sound was Tommy Dunne's first ball in the 2001 All-Ireland final. Again, I didn't need to look. It was going to take an exceptional player to come out of DJ's shadow and Henry did that.'

English is also keen to pay tribute to Brian Cody.

'I don't believe in the cult of a manager. The way I see it is a bad manager will stop you from winning an All-Ireland, but a decent manager will win the All-Ireland for you if he has the players, and that's the key. It is players who win the All-Ireland, not managers. The one exception I would make is that I rate Brian Cody very highly. He has achieved so much over such a long period, but above all he has changed the tradition of Kilkenny hurling. He has brought in a new system and a way of playing which has become part of the hurling culture in Kilkenny.'

Part of this culture is one of Cody's favourite phrases: 'savage intensity'. The journalist Dermot Crowe provided two vivid vignettes of Cody's intensity.

The Kilkenny manager was examining portraits of the Black and Tans and the Kilkenny hurlers of the 1920s at an art exhibition. When someone commented on the similarity of the images, Cody observed, 'Both killing machines.'

When he was asked if he wanted a player who would die for the Kilkenny jersey, Cody replied, 'No, I want a lad who would kill for it.'

THE CATS GET THE CREAM

Of course, the 2009–11 All-Ireland finals brought a new intensity to the rivalry.

In 2009 Kilkenny, courtesy of two late goals – one a result of a contentious penalty decision – wore down the Tipperary challenge on a 2-22 to 0-23 scoreline. Tipp would get their revenge a year later, with Lar Corbett famously scoring three goals, and Kilkenny would restore their superiority when the counties met again in the 2011 final.

Tommy Walsh claims that Jackie Tyrell's motto is 'Go hard or go home.' The entire Kilkenny team turned up with that attitude in 2011.

Then came the never-to-be-forgotten All-Ireland semi-final in 2012, when Lar Corbett strangely spent the game following Tommy Walsh and Kilkenny won by 18 points – their biggest winning margin since 1897. Both sides have produced thrilling league finals, with Kilkenny winning 5-14 to 5-13 in 2003, and in the 2009 final in Thurles a stupendous long-range point from Eddie Brennan securing a Kilkenny victory in a match that went to extra-time and yielded 49 scores in a 2-26 to 4-17 result.

A TALE OF TWO THRILLERS

In 1973 and 1974 Limerick and Kilkenny had a brief rivalry when they contested consecutive All-Irelands. Limerick emerged on top in '73 and Kilkenny exacted revenge the following year. In 2018 and 2019, the rivalry surfaced again. In 2018 Limerick had two points to spare over Kilkenny in a thriller in Thurles in the All-Ireland quarter-final. In 2019 Kilkenny got revenge when they ended Limerick's reign as All-Ireland champions in another thriller in the All-Ireland semi-final. The Cats won by a whisker, just a single point proving further evidence of a great hurling truth: Kilkenny are Kilkenny.

As with all great rivalries there was controversy when Limerick were denied what appeared to be a clear 65, and the opportunity to equalise, with the last play of the game. With true grace afterwards the Limerick manager John Kiely did not use it as an excuse or engage in a whinge-fest.

There was also a wave of sentiment. Thirty-seven years after his father Brendan won an All-Ireland football medal with Offaly, Shane Lowry was presented to the crowd a week after he won the Open. The rapturous reception he received was confirmation that he is one of Ireland's favourite sons and of the unique love GAA fans have for the Lowry family. Shane follows the Johnny Pilkington school of knowing how to enjoy yourself after the prize is won, which endears him to fans.

Wexford and Tipperary have had brief rivalries down the years, like in 1997, when Tipp ended Wexford's reign as All-Ireland champions. In 2019 the rivalry was rekindled when the teams clashed again in the All-Ireland semi-final. To add fuel to the fire, Wexford were managed by Davy Fitzgerald. In his last game playing for Clare against Tipperary, Davy showcased his great love for their old rivals in his exhortation to the team beforehand: 'Let's f**king go for them, boys.' In the 2019 instalment, in yet another thriller with a number of controversial decisions, 14-man Tipperary came from behind to win 1-28 to 3-20. There was a competition among the fans as to who would first get to proclaim the old hurling adage: Tipp are Tipp.

So, the hurling gods decreed that Kilkenny would renew their rivalry again in the 2019 All-Ireland final, their sixth clash in the final in 11 years. Another instalment of Liam Sheedy v. Brian Cody.

The conventional wisdom is that you should never go back, but Liam Sheedy in his first year of his second term as Tipp boss claimed his second All-Ireland in 2019. He sprinkled his magic dust and Tipperary won by 14 points. There was controversy afterwards about whether it was the correct decision to send Kilkenny's Richie Hogan off.

In the words of the team captain Séamie Callanan, who scored his eighth goal in eight consecutive championship games in the match, immediately after the final whistle: 'It's f**king everything we dreamed off.' In this unique rivalry the extraordinary has become the new normal.

13

UP DOWN

Down v. Kerry

The hardest arithmetic to master for fans of Gaelic games is that which enables us to count our blessings.

In 1991 Down won their fourth All-Ireland, their first in 23 years, when they beat Meath. On their way to the title they beat old rivals Kerry in the semi-final by 2-9 to 0-8. It was the fourth championship meeting between the two teams and the Mournemen maintained their 100 per cent record against the Kingdom.

Pat Spillane got Kerry's only score in the second half that day. He concedes that Kerry's rivalry with Down was a bit special.

'Tradition is a big thing in sport and in life. We are very modest in Kerry – we know we are the best! Although our best-known rivalry is with Dublin, we never feared the Dubs. That Down game was a little bit different because our older fans had never known anything other than losing to Down in big games and they were nervous about getting beaten by them once again – and sure enough, they beat us.

'While I was playing, when we were not at our best we won

games we shouldn't have because other teams feared us and didn't believe deep down they would win – that Down team, though, had no such fear. When they took the field, their history told them, in a way no other county had, that they had the upper hand over us.'

Spillane concedes that Down were the best team on the day.

'When I want to think very positively of Ulster football, I do so by recalling the great Down team managed by Pete McGrath that won All-Irelands in 1991 and 1994 at a time when Ulster football ruled the roost.

'Gaelic football at its best is the beautiful game – played with strength and speed, with courage and skill, with honesty and humour. It has the capacity to stop your heart and leave the indelible memory of a magic moment. Think back to that Down team of Pete's in the early 1990s, a forward line of footballing artists like James MacCartan, Ross Carr, Mickey Linden and Greg Blaney. This is why I wanted to play the beautiful game. Pete won two All-Irelands in 1991 and 1994 playing football the way it should be played and I take my hat off to him.'

Spillane, though, is annoyed about one aspect of that 1991 All-Ireland semi-final.

'I am still not convinced by all these new methods teams are going in for today. To take one example, it is now accepted orthodoxy in the GAA world that the night before big games a team use a "buddy system" in the hotel, in other words a senior player rooms with one of the more junior players on the panel. The idea is that the senior player helps the younger man to settle and handle his nerves better. I do not go along with that at all. I think you should room with the player you want to room with, rather than finding yourself rooming with someone you have nothing in common with. In 1991, the night before the All-Ireland semi-final I found myself rooming with a young sub on the Kerry team. I always liked to relax the night before a match by staying up late and watching television. My room-mate wanted to go to bed early and I felt obliged to do so for his sake. The problem was that because I was deviating from my normal routine I could not sleep at all and therefore it was very hard to be at my best playing a huge match the next day. Well, that's my excuse anyway!'

Down's ace forward Ross Carr saw their rivalry with Kerry in positive terms.

'We grew up watching the great Kerry team of the 1970s and the 1980s and they inspired us. So when we played them in '91 we really wanted to beat them, not so much to continue the great Down tradition as to show them that we were better than them. The rivalry got the best out of us.'

THE PIONEERS

In 1960 the All-Ireland final between Down and Kerry generated great interest in Ireland and in the diaspora. The biggest crowd ever of 87,768 witnessed history as the Sam Maguire trophy crossed the border for the first time. Down's 2-10 to 0-8 victory was the biggest defeat Kerry ever suffered in an All-Ireland final. The following year in front of over 71,000, a record for a semi-final, Down beat the Kingdom by 1-12 to 0-9.

Jimmy Magee saw that Down team as pioneers.

'Like the great Kerry team of the 1970s and '80s that Down team were full of stars and had some of the greatest players ever. They were one of the great innovators of Gaelic football. They were one of the first intercounty teams to wear tracksuits, which aroused great curiosity at the time. One young boy captured the bewilderment of the fans when he turned to his father and asked, "Why did they not take off their pyjamas?"'

In the 1968 All-Ireland final, Down beat Kerry by 2-12 to 1-13 with a virtuoso performance. The northerners had the advantage of a lightning start, taking a 2-3 to 0-1 lead after just eight minutes. The star of the team was Seán O'Neill.

In conversation, Seán said, 'The rivalry between Down and Kerry has been good for the game. Our tradition has been of two great teams going at it hammer and tongs, but the key thing is that we did so playing positive football and doing everything in our power to win. I really think we need to recapture the spirit of that rivalry because today so many teams have as their priority not to lose and to stop the other team from playing football. This is a total distortion of what our games are really about.'

14

THE GREEN AND RED v.
THE GREEN AND GOLD

Mayo v. Kerry

In recent years Kerry and Mayo have served up some thrilling games, notably Kerry's epic 3-16 to 3-13 victory in the 2014 All-Ireland semi-final replay after extra time in the Gaelic Grounds in Limerick. At the end of normal time Mayo goalie Rob Hennelly had a chance to win it for the Westerners, but his last gasp free fell short. In 2017, Mayo got revenge with a 2-16 to 0-17 victory in the All-Ireland semi-final replay. The rivalry between the counties has a long history.

MASTERS OF THE PIGSKIN

The first Connacht team to win an All-Ireland was Galway in 1934. Two years later Mayo won their first All-Ireland. The star of the Mayo team was Henry Kenny, as his son, the former Taoiseach, Enda, recalled for me.

'My father was particularly famous for his fielding of the ball. He grew up on the same street with Patsy Flannelly, another of the stars of the '36 team. They had no football as kids, so they went to the butcher's shop and got pig's bladders to use instead of footballs. Dad always said, "If you could catch those, you could catch anything."

'The other thing he was noted for was his ability after he caught the ball in the air to turn before his feet touched the ground. When my brothers and I started playing, his advice to us was always "be moving before the ball comes". He found a big change in the way the game was played, especially when they started wearing lighter boots like the soccer players. When he saw a pair of them, he said, "These boots are like slippers." He didn't have much time for the solo runs and that's why he called it "the tippy toe". He said he would "beat the solo runner with his cap".

'In 1936 Seamus O'Malley captained the Mayo team to the All-Ireland. He travelled to Dublin by train the evening before the match. On the day of the match he announced that he could not stay for the celebrations and got a lift back to Mayo after the match. The Sam Maguire Cup was put in the boot of the car. He had to go to work as a teacher the next morning. He left for work by bicycle with the Sam Maguire Cup strapped on his back! The times have changed.'

Tom McNicholas was the last survivor of the 1936 Mayo team and was best equipped to give an objective assessment of Henry Kenny.

'There wasn't the same cult of personality back then, but there was no question that the star of our team was Henry. He was wonderful at catching balls in the air. He had great duels with the mighty Kerry midfielder Paddy Kennedy and was probably one of the very few players, if not the only footballer, who could hold his own with Kennedy. This was particularly the case in the 1936 All-Ireland semi-final in Roscommon when we beat Kerry 1-5 to 0-6, when Kennedy was the new star in the game.

'Henry was known as "the man with the magic hands". He had big hands and he could hold the ball in one hand. Now our game has become more like basketball, there is so much hand-passing. Back then, though, it was a game of catch and kick, and nobody did it better than Henry. I don't think any of our team would believe the way the game has changed, especially the emphasis on stopping teams from playing, and above all the number of times people pass the ball backwards. We believed in positive football and playing your own game rather than the opposition's. Down the years Kerry broke our hearts many times but in the early days of the rivalry we came out on top.'

In the 1940s the rivalry between both counties stepped up again.

YES, MINISTER

Before the Department of Health became known as 'Angola', Seán Flanagan served as Minister for Health for three years (1966–69) and then Minister for Lands for four years (1969–73). He was elected to the European Parliament in 1979, having first been elected to the Dáil in 1951. However, his fame in Mayo resides chiefly in his achievements on the football field, which saw him captaining the county to All-Ireland titles in both 1950 and '51. He was selected at left corner-back on both the Team of the Century and the Team of the Millennium.

Even as a teenager in St Jarlaths College, Flanagan was showing his true colours on and off the field. In one anecdote, having captained the school to its first junior championship, he discovered that there was no cup to be presented, so he impro-vised and borrowed a golf cup from one of the priests in the college. When he played for Connacht Colleges in 1939, he was involved in an early example of player power. The team suffered a bad beating and the manager, a priest, thought they had disgraced the province and refused to give them their jerseys. The players staged an immediate revolt on the basis that they had tried their best; they held a sit-in in the team hotel until they got their way. When the priest said 'I give you my word of honour as a priest', one of the players, showing an untypical lack of reverence for the clergy for the times, replied 'We need your word of honour as a man.' Victory went to the players, at least in the argument.

Things were also tense when Flanagan began to play for Mayo. Relations with the county board were less than harmonious. Such was Flanagan's frustration with the incompetence of the county board that he resigned from the team in 1947. The county secretary, Finn Mongey, wrote back to say he had placed his letter before the board, who asked him to reconsider and make himself available for the '48 season. The league was beginning in Tralee, but Flanagan said he would not travel. Following intense moral pressure from his friend and teammate Eamonn 'George' Mongey, he was eventually persuaded to go.

When the team reached Tralee, Flanagan was addressed by a man who asked him what position he played in. When Flanagan told him he was a corner-back, the man said in a strong Kerry brogue, 'Aren't you a bit small to play full-back? Kerry always have great backs, big strong men.'

Flanagan's blood was boiling and he retorted, 'Mayo came here in 1939 and we beat the lard out of you. We propose to do the same to you tomorrow.'

The incident did not so much light a flame under Flanagan as a powder keg. All his hesitancy was vanquished. The Kerry game had become a 'do or die' issue for him. Although Mayo had only a squad of 15 players, they drew with the Kerry men, who had contested the historic All-Ireland final the previous year in the Polo Grounds in New York. So desperate were Mayo that the only subs they could tog out were the county secretary and the rather rotund team driver. The situation could not be left unchallenged. Flanagan and the established players on the team drafted a letter which left no room for ambiguity.

'Year after year we have seen the county board bring to nought the hours of training which we have put in, but yet, believing it was outside our sphere as players, we have desisted from drawing your attention to the matter. Events in Tralee last Sunday have banished our indecision, however, and we feel the time has come when something must be done before football disappears completely in Mayo – unwept, unhonoured and unsung.'

Two Connacht titles were secured, but Mayo failed to win the All-Ireland. A view emerged within the more progressive elements of the county board that Sam would not return to Mayo until Flanagan was made captain. The problem was that Flanagan 'only' played for a junior team. This required a change of rule at the Convention giving the captaincy of the senior team to the nominee of the county champions. Flanagan duly repaid the county board for their benevolence by immediately banning them from any contact with the team until after they had won the All-Ireland! He did make an exception for the chairman of the county board and the county secretary Finn Mongey. One other member, a man of the cloth, thought he should be an exception and paid a visit to the team during their collective training. Flanagan was over to him immediately and coolly informed him, 'Get out and I'll see you when I have the Sam Maguire.' While this did nothing for his popularity, winning the next two All-Irelands did surmount any residual problems in that area.

A WAKE-UP CALL
In 1982, having just established himself on the Mayo team, Dermot Flanagan found himself training with Dublin's Kerry-

based players. In the best GAA tradition this was an accidental by-product of a controversy. Mícheál Ó Muircheartaigh was training players like Mick Spillane and Jack O'Shea in UCD, but a newspaper made a big issue of the fact that none of the players involved were attending UCD. A Gaelic football solution to a Gaelic football problem had to be found. As secretary of the UCD club, Flanagan wrote and invited the Dublin-based Kerry lads to join the UCD players involved in summer training.

'Micheál was very welcoming. The first night he pointed to me and said to the Kerry lads, "You'll see that man winning an All-Ireland." I deeply appreciated his comments. His training methods were very modern and sophisticated. When I went back to train with Mayo, I was noticeably sharper because the training was so crisp. The big thing for me was that in March they were training for September, whereas counties like Mayo were only training in four-week bursts until the next match. Psychologically I found that the Kerry way made you believe you were an All-Ireland contender rather than hoping you might possibly be one.'

THE MAURICE FINAL

The rivalry between the two counties heated up again in the mid-1990s, as Dermot Flanagan remembers.

'We played some super football in 1996 and were tremendous when we beat Kerry in the All-Ireland semi-final.'

A fine lobbed goal from James Horan was the highlight of their 2-13 to 1-10 win. Flanagan has a more personal regret about the loss to Kerry in the All-Ireland final in 1997.

'I had got a nick in my hamstring ten days before the final, as had Maurice Sheridan. Both of us thought we were good enough to do a job, but neither of us lasted the match. The ironic thing was that psychologically I never felt better in my head for the game. I had taken a month off work and was really psyched. There was no point me going in for just five minutes, if that's all I thought I could last – which is all I did. It is a huge regret of mine that I never got to contribute more to the team that day.'

Since his retirement Flanagan has had ample time to appraise his career.

'Eugene McGee once asked me, "Why don't you play gobshite football?" I didn't understand what he meant then, but I do now. We were not cynical enough.'

ON THE SIDELINE

In 1996 when Mayo lost the All-Ireland it was the referee who was in the firing line; in 1997 when Mayo lost the All-Ireland it was Mayo manager John Maughan himself who was in the firing line.

'I took a lot of flak after the game for the way we didn't replace Dermot Flanagan directly but made a series of switches, but above all for leaving Pat Holmes on Maurice Fitzgerald. The best man to have marked Maurice would have been Kenneth Mortimer, but we needed him up in the forwards. With the benefit of hindsight, we maybe should have put someone else on Maurice with ten or fifteen minutes to go, but we felt then it was best to stick to our guns.'

Pat Spillane views Maughan's performance that day with nothing less than incredulity.

'His tactical expertise was sadly lacking and brutally exposed in the way he left Pat Holmes on Maurice Fitzgerald for the 70 minutes. It was unbelievable. Anybody could have seen Holmes was getting an almighty roasting. When Dermot Flanagan was passed fit to play in an All-Ireland, when everyone knew he was injured, that was another disaster. He had to be taken off after only a few minutes. It took about six switches to cover his position, which caused a lot of disruption in the Mayo defence.'

Although the despair lingers like a stubborn cobweb, Mayo selector that day Peter Ford still believes they acted correctly.

'I stand over what we did. We played an army team about ten days before the game and Dermot Flanagan got injured. Looking back, we shouldn't have played that game. Dermot was the sort of player who liked to keep fresh, so we didn't push him into lots of fitness tests. We had a plan if he didn't work out and had prepared for that eventuality and decided on the switches we would make. If we'd had someone on the subs of the same quality, we would have brought him on straight away, but we hadn't, so it ended up as multiple switches rather than one.

'Maurice Fitzgerald scored three points from play that day. Pat Holmes did what any good defender is told to do in these situations. He forced him out to the sideline. Normally there would be no danger, but Maurice could kick points from there. It's very hard to find anybody to mark any player that good in that sort of form. It was almost freakish.'

15

THE ARISTOCRATS AND THE REBELS

Cork v. Kilkenny

Donal Óg Cusack described the Kilkenny team of the noughties as 'Stepford Wives' because of what he saw as their 'robotic' style. Kilkenny great Jackie Tyrell said of that Cork team, 'We didn't just want to beat them, we wanted to trample on them like dirt.' Simply put the Cork team of the era really didn't like the Cats and the feeling was mutual. Seán Óg Ó'Halpín went so far as to liken the hostility between the two teams at the time to that between America and Russia during the Cold War. It was not always thus.

FROM A JACK TO A KING

As we grow old the world becomes stranger.

When you ask someone who held the unique distinction of winning six senior All-Ireland medals in consecutive years (1941–46) what his favourite personal sporting memory is, the last thing you expect to be told about is an All-Ireland final he lost! Yet such was the case for Jack Lynch.

'It may be paradoxical but the games of which I have the

most vivid memories are the ones we lost. Of these I remember best the first All-Ireland hurling final in which I played. It was Cork versus Kilkenny on 3 September 1939. I was captain of the team and hopeful of leading Cork out of a comparatively long barren spell. Cork had not won a final since 1931, when they beat Kilkenny in the second replay of the final.

'The match I refer to has since been known as the "Thunder and Lightning" final. We had all kinds of weather, including sunshine and hailstones. It was played on the day that the Second World War commenced. I missed at least two scorable chances – of a goal and a point. I was marking one of the greatest half-backs of all time, Paddy Phelan, and we were beaten by a point scored literally with the last puck of the game. I can remember more facets of that game than almost any other in which I played.

'Although I was lucky enough to play in many All-Ireland finals, all the wins over Kilkenny were special. It was always about more than sport. It was a social occasion where men drank in manly moderation, but probably more than any other moment in the calendar it defined our identity. Looking back, there was a lot of hardship in those days, with rationing and so on. To take one example, both Tipperary and Kilkenny were excluded from the 1941 hurling championship because of an outbreak of foot-and-mouth disease. Yet no matter how bad things were, like Christmas, beating Kilkenny was always guaranteed to put a smile on people's faces in Cork.'

SLEEPING BEAUTIES

Joe Dunphy has a rare distinction in Kilkenny hurling, captaining his native county to two consecutive All-Ireland minor titles in 1961 and '62. Although Dunphy won a National League medal, the game's highest honour eluded him. Despite the colour and excitement outside, the dressing-room of a team that has just lost an All-Ireland final is like Hell's Kitchen without the charm. Dunphy has experienced that sinking feeling.

'In 1966 Kilkenny lost the All-Ireland to Cork, although we were red hot favourites. Cork won by 3-9 to 1-10. I scored a point, but it wasn't a happy memory for me because I had missed a goal a couple of minutes earlier! The papers the next day were full of talk about "the year of the sleeping pill". It was the first year players had taken them before an All-Ireland final. There was a lot of smart comments afterwards that we took them too late because we hadn't fully woken up until after the match!'

THE SECOND COMING

In 1999, after a young Cork side defeated the hot favourites Kilkenny in the All-Ireland hurling final, Jimmy Barry-Murphy stated that Brian Corcoran was the greatest Cork hurler of his generation. Barry-Murphy is not a man given to wild statements or hyperbole, so it was not a remark to be taken lightly. The hurling pundits nodded sagely in agreement.

Corcoran exploded on to the Gaelic games scene in 1992. A series of masterful performances in the Cork colours saw him crowned as hurler of that year. In 1999 he reclaimed that honour. Not long after that the cumulative wear and tear of unending training sessions and games took their toll. Corcoran retired prematurely from inter-county football and hurling.

The arrival of a young family also played a major factor in his decision to quit at the top of his game.

'To be honest, hurling had become a chore. I'd be on my way home from work and all I wanted to do was play with the baby, and instead I was being dragged away to do something that I didn't want to do. By the time I came home from training she was asleep. It got to the stage where I was getting up in the morning and saying, "Oh no, I've got training tonight."'

Initially he did not miss the game. For a time it seemed as if Cork could get on without him too, and as if the Cork hurlers were more interested in off-the-pitch activities than on-the-pitch stuff when they famously went on strike to get better facilities and conditions from the county board.

In 2003, in the course of Cork's triumphant march to the All-Ireland final, a new sporting icon was launched on Leeside. Setanta Ó hAilpín thrilled the Cork public in the same way Jimmy Barry-Murphy had inspired Cork to All-Ireland final glory at 19 years of age in 1973. Cork fans were bitterly disappointed at losing the final to Kilkenny, and their sense of misery was compounded when they heard that Setanta had gone Down Under to carve out a new career for himself as an Aussie Rules player. After his departure, only a true legend could fill the void. The time was right for Corcoran's second coming, not least because the expectation of a success-craving county, awaiting retrieval of its oldest sporting prize, demanded another All-Ireland.

'It was a big gamble to come out of retirement. I could have fallen flat on my face and Cork could have struggled. Some people told me that I had twice been hurler of the year and I had nothing to prove. But you make decisions and you live by them. To be honest, I was half-afraid of going back. I wasn't sure if the lads would be welcoming me back, with me being out so long. They did. I went back to win an All-Ireland. The fact that we did it over our great rivals Kilkenny made it all the more special. The rivalry we had with them was great for the game and raised standards in hurling, as a good rivalry should.'

REBELS AND CATS WITH A CAUSE

The rivalry between the two counties was put aside in March 2019 when the Marble County received an uncharacteristically generous welcome on Leeside when they played Cork as a fund-raiser for Kieran O'Connor. The former Cork star was fighting his third bout of cancer. John Myler, the then Cork manager, captured the respect between the counties when he said afterwards, 'It emphasises the whole family aspect of the GAA, the way it all comes together when someone is in need, or needs urgent help. Kilkenny are great ambassadors for hurling and there is great credit due to them, their team and county board, for facilitating the match. It's a fantastic gesture from them.'

16

COME ON, THE ROSSIES!

Roscommon v. Kerry

The summer was hot and something was coming to the boil. The 1940s saw the most glorious era in the history of Roscommon football, with the county's only All-Ireland successes in 1943 and 1944, both under the captaincy of Jimmy Murray. It marked the beginning of a rivalry with Kerry that would flare up over the years, as Jimmy told me.

'The first time I lined-out in an All-Ireland final in 1943 and an hour before we got to Dublin I was nearly standing up just to get my first glimpse of Croke Park. That was my dream come true.

'One of my most vivid memories of my playing career is my brother Phelim telling me that the prince of midfielders, Paddy Kennedy, came over to him in the 1946 All-Ireland final and said, "Phelim, I think it's your All-Ireland." Phelim replied, "You never know, anything can happen, there's still over five minutes to go." Phelim's words were prophetic because Kerry got two goals in the dying minutes to draw the game and they went on to win the replay.'

Brendan Lynch was right half-back on that Roscommon team.

'I made the most impact on their great midfielder Paddy Kennedy when I had a head collision with him and he had to be stretchered off. He asked me, "Jaysus, what did you do to me?"'

Lynch's Roscommon were to come within a whisker of taking another All-Ireland in 1946.

'It was a Mickey Mouse ruling in the GAA that cost us the title. We played Mayo in the Connacht final in Ballinasloe. They had a goal disallowed and then we got a goal that was going to be disallowed. Jimmy Murray grabbed the green flag and waved it and we were awarded the goal. After the game Mayo lodged an objection. What should have happened was for the referee to have produced his report saying Roscommon won the match and that would have been that. Instead we had to go into a replay, and on top of the heavy collective training we were doing we didn't need another match. We lost Frank Kinlough with a leaky valve in his heart and Doc Callaghan, our full-back, was injured. By the time we faced Kerry in the All-Ireland final replay they were getting stronger and we were getting weaker. I was never as happy as when the final whistle sounded in that game because the whole year had been absolutely exhausting, with the two replays and all the collective training. It finished us as a team.'

PRIMROSE AND BLUE

Gerry O'Malley was the star of the Roscommon team that caused a sensation in 1952 when they beat the great Mayo team led by Seán Flanagan, which famously won All-Irelands in 1950 and '51. Because of a national newspaper strike, many people around the country only heard the result on the Tuesday after the game, and when they did most thought it was a mistake.

Given his stature in the game, all neutrals wanted the 1962

All-Ireland final to be 'Gerry O'Malley's All-Ireland', only for Roscommon's star player to be injured in the game and Kerry to beat the men in Primrose and Blue by 1-6 to 1-12. The passage of time allowed O'Malley to see the black humour in the occasion.

'I had to be taken to hospital after the All-Ireland and I was in a bed beside a man I had never met before. My "neighbour" knew who I was and we got to talking the way you do. The next day a fella came in with the newspapers who didn't recognise me from Adam and my new friend asked him, "How did the papers say O'Malley played?"

'"Brutal," came the instant reply, and it certainly left me feeling even more brutal!'

EARLEY DAYS

In 1980 Roscommon would face Kerry in the All-Ireland final again. It was a real thrill for Dermot Earley to be there.

'It was just incredible to reach the All-Ireland final in 1980. Our manager Tom Heneghan had us really well prepared. He arranged for us to get two weeks off work and for those two weeks we trained twice a day, at noon and in the early evening. By night time you couldn't wait to get to bed. We had Kerry reeling early on, but I feel we lost because we weren't attacking enough. We had great attacking half-backs, and on the day they did a good defensive job, but we didn't use them to attack Kerry. Offaly beat Kerry in 1982 by attacking them. We had the class to do the same, but we didn't.

'We were gutted afterwards, especially for the supporters. They gave us a massive reception when we got home. What stays with me is that there was no real celebration from the Kerry players or the fans. That's what hurt me the most. Winning had become so routine it didn't seem to matter to them. When they won in 1997 you could see it did matter to the Kerry lads because they hadn't won an All-Ireland for 11 years at that stage.'

That evening a convoy of cars and buses made their way home. The normal buzz of chat and banter was noticeably absent. One of the songs that came on the radio was the big smash from Abba at the time, 'The Winner Takes it All'. Those five words said it all for Dermot Earley.

'It was not a great All-Ireland final. Both sets of defenders were well on top and scoring chances were at a premium. Marking was extremely close and this resulted in too many frees from each team, but it was not a dirty game. However, many of the decisions left the players bewildered, not to mention the crowd. Roscommon suffered more than Kerry in this area. We became frustrated and our game suffered as a result. Kerry deserved to win because they took their chances well. We had the winning of the game from placed balls alone, but the concentration slipped and so did the opportunity for victory.

'I was disappointed that Eoin Liston did not play, as it was a shame for any footballer to miss the All-Ireland final for any reason but particularly for ill-health. We felt all along we could have beaten Kerry with him because in Pat Lindsay we had a full-back who could have held him.

'The start was magic – a goal from John O'Connor followed by sustained pressure from Roscommon and a further point from Seamus Hayden. Then Kerry took over and threw the ball around, but our defence was good. Gerry Connellan and Mike Sheehy appear to be booked by the referee and then Tommy Doyle and I got our names taken. This happened as Kerry came forward. I turned hard to the left to follow the attack and bumped hard into the back of a Kerry player. He turned and let me have one in the face. The ref called us together as I got off the ground. The Kerry man was my former army colleague, Tommy Doyle.

'The referee booked me. I asked him, "Why are you booking me, ref?"

'He said nothing. He booked Doyle, then moved away.

'Tommy and I looked at one another. We shook hands. There were no hard feelings, but I was disappointed to be booked in my first All-Ireland final.

'Micheál O'Hehir in his commentary said, "Tommy was a lucky man, he wasn't sent to the side-line." But then the referee decided to hop the ball and O'Hehir wondered who hit who. Now I got frustrated, as I felt doubly punished, booked and lost a free to a hop ball.

'We had the wind and we didn't want to waste time. Tom Heneghan was told to stay in the dug-out. Mick O'Dwyer was up on the line for much of the first half and nothing was said to him. Time was being wasted and selective justice was administered – more frustration.'

The pattern of growing annoyance intensified for Earley.

'Gerry Fitzmaurice and Pat Spillane were involved in an incident off the ball. It was also off-screen. Pat was on the ground and took an age to get up. Time went by and many efforts were made to assist his recovery, to no avail. Eventually he staggered up. Both players appeared to be booked and play resumed with a hop ball. Micheál O'Hehir wondered, "Is Pat Spillane really hurt or is he in line for an Oscar?" Much time had been wasted again. Thirty-seven minutes after the ball was thrown in at the start of the game the first half ended. Two minutes of extra time were played. Spillane must have been down for about four minutes, not to mention the other stoppages. It was 1-3 all and now we had to face the wind.

'The final score was 1-9 to 1-6. Kerry won, and deservedly

so, before a crowd of 63,854. As I pondered the result it stood out that the difference between the teams was Mike Sheehy's accurate free taking. He scored six frees and a goal from play. Although Roscommon scored 1-4 from play to Kerry's 1-3, we missed frees we should have scored. After a marvellous start, Roscommon seemed to change their style of play, as the openings which were there in the first few minutes were quickly closed off by the Kerry defensive unit. I have explained this change of play many times as a self-conscious feeling that Kerry would whittle down our early lead. What happened was that the fear of losing overcame the will to win.

'My feeling of emptiness was almost overwhelming. I can remember turning around and shaking hands with Seánie Walsh. I recall Ger Power being close by and there was a clap on the back and a smile. I turned around immediately because I was absolutely shattered and completely disappointed and I then walked to the dressing-room. Seán Kilbride, who was a sub on the team that day, caught me by the arm. I looked around and realised that the disappointment was there, but you had to get on with your life and had to do things correctly.'

THY KINGDOM GO

Twenty-six years later Earley got the postscript he wanted.

'Every year Roscommon plays in the Connacht championship there's an expectation that we can do something significant. The Roscommon supporters really rally behind the team, as was shown in Ennis in 2006 when Roscommon beat Kerry in the replay of the All-Ireland minor final. The atmosphere was incredible and, judging by the massive traffic jam on the way home from the game, every man, woman and child in the county was at the game. That Roscommon team played football the way I think it should be played: with great support play, no fouling and enormous commitment. Of course, it really added to the occasion that we beat the mighty Kerry.'

THE EYE OF THE TIGER

As he leaned over the banisters of heaven in 2019 to watch Tiger Roll win the Grand National for the second consecutive year, Dermot would have smiled at how a horse owned in Westmeath but trained in Meath could have temporarily halted the rivalry between the two neighbouring counties.

His characteristic big smile would have been even broader than normal that same day as a new chapter in the Roscommon–Kerry rivalry was written in the All-Ireland Colleges Senior Football B final, with CBS Roscommon's last-minute victory over Kerry's Scoil Phobail Sliabh Luachra. With his keen eye, Dermot would have spotted a connection between both epic events: one of the horses running in the Grand National had a name that summed up the Rossies' rivalry with the Kingdom.

Us and Them.

17

SKIRTING AROUND THE RIVALRY ISSUE

Kilkenny v. Cork

They take their rivalries seriously in camogie. The strangest story must be about a camogie club match in Westmeath in the 1970s when Cullion were so determined to put one over on their bitterest rivals they had a man on their team. What was stranger was that nobody noticed the difference until after the match. The headline in the local paper read: 'When is a girl not a girl?'

Camogie's most famous star is Kilkenny's Angela Downey. As a girl, Downey always had a hurley in her hand and her theatre of dreams was her backyard. As a teenager, there was not much to do other than camogie: no discos, no cinemas locally, although she did cross-country running for Kilkenny City Harriers. She practised by hitting stones on the roof of the slaughterhouse in her father's butcher's shop. Her heroes included Liz Neary and Helen O'Neill.

Not surprisingly she has been immortalised in folklore and is to camogie what Christy Ring is to hurling. Hurling was in her genes. Her father was the legendary Shem Downey, who starred for the black and amber in the 1940s and 1950s, and won an All-Ireland medal in 1947 in Kilkenny's classic triumph over old rivals Cork. Shem brought the passion he exhibited in the county colours onto the sidelines when he watched his daughters on the camogie field.

THE FINAL FRONTIER

Angela played in her first senior All-Ireland final with Kilkenny in 1972 against Cork when she was just 15. It was to be a rare reversal for the young player, but all present that day remember their first acquaintance with Angela and knew intuitively that something special had arrived on the sporting scene. In the coming years, they were destined to see her glide through bedraggled defenders, making a feast from a famine of poor possession. It might be unfair to say that a Kilkenny forward line without Angela was like *Hamlet* without the Prince, but if that is the case it is a marginal call.

Although she would be defeated in '72, she went on to win seven consecutive All-Irelands for Kilkenny from 1985 to 1991 in a team trained by Tom Ryan. In total she would win 12 All-Irelands; the first would come after a replay against Cork in 1974. She captained the county to All-Ireland successes in 1977, 1988 and 1991. In 1986 Angela became only the third camogie player to receive a Texaco Award.

To add to Angela's joy, all her All-Ireland medals were won with her twin sister, Ann. In 2010 both were jointly presented with the Lifetime Achievement Award in the *Irish Times* sportswoman of the year awards.

Angela epitomises the power of rivalries in camogie in her determination to do what is needed to beat Kilkenny's great rivals, Cork. During an All-Ireland final against Cork she was goal-bound when her opponent, Liz O'Neill, made a despairing lunge at her, which caused Angela's skirt to end up on the ground. Undeterred, Angela kept on running and even when Cork goalie Marian McCarthy whisked the hurley from her hands she palmed the ball into the net and then calmly returned to collect her skirt. Even more telling was her subsequent comment: 'Even if she had pulled off all my clothes I was going to score a goal first!'

The following morning the picture of her in a state of undress appeared on the front page of the *Irish Times*.

LATE, LATE SHOWS

In recent years the Cork and Kilkenny rivalry has resurfaced. It began in 2016, when rank outsiders Kilkenny, managed by Ann Downey, prevented a Cork three-in-a-row with a seven-point victory that gave the county a first title in 22 years. The following year it looked as though Kilkenny were about to confirm their status as the new queens of camogie. But in dramatic fashion two magnificent injury-time points from Gemma O'Connor and Julia White saw Cork through by 0-10 to 0-9. In 2018, in another thrilling crescendo, a late free from 60 metres out on the left wing from Orla Cotter gave Cork a one-point victory over their great rivals and Kilkenny hearts were broken again. Cork won a fourth title in five years with survivors from the team that played in eight successive finals in the noughties. Gemma O'Connor won her ninth All-Ireland medal to cement her place in the GAA immortals.

NEW SHOOTS

2019 saw the emergence of a new rivalry between Kilkenny and Galway, which culminated in an exciting All-Ireland final between both counties that breathed new vitality into camogie.

18

THE FLYING '50s

Wexford v. Cork

In the long conversation about hurling it is often difficult to trace how or when the subject comes to a shift. From time to time, though, it is easy. Hurling was to get a welcome new lease of life in the 1950s with the emergence of a new power, as Micheál Ó Muircheartaigh recalls.

'The first hurling team to make a lasting impression on me was the great Wexford team of the 1950s. I had seen John Doyle's great Tipperary three-in-a-row side of '49 to '51, but because of Tipperary's tradition you somehow didn't wonder at that. It was different with Wexford because they came from nowhere. Remember, this was a county that had only won an All-Ireland in 1910, and by the 1950s they had only added a solitary Lenister title, which they won back in 1918. They showed they had promise when they reached the National League final in 1951 only to lose to Galway. They took another step forward by reaching the All-Ireland that year, even though they lost heavily to Tipperary. By the next year they were able to run Tipp to a point in the league final and then they swept all before them in 1955 and '56, winning two All-Irelands and coming from 15 points down against Tipperary at half-time to win by four points in a pulsating league final. The '56 All-Ireland final against Cork was an epic, with a late surge ensuring perhaps their greatest ever triumph.

'In the 1990s there was a famous racehorse called Danoli, a Cheltenham winner, who was known as "the People's Champion". It may not have been fully on the scale of the reaction to Clare's triumph in 1995, but when Wexford won in '55 they became the People's Champions.

'The star of that side was Nicky Rackard, but sometimes the invaluable contribution of his brother Bobby is neglected. Bobby was probably the best right full-back I have ever seen. He started off as an elegant centre half-back, but because of an injury to their great full-back Nick O'Donnell he had to move to plug the back there. When Nick recovered, Bobby was slotted into the corner and he produced a string of astounding performances there. He had a marvellous ability to catch the sliotar – high or low – and send it far out field in sweeping clearances. He was key to Wexford's supremacy over Cork at that time.'

The Slaneysiders' All-Ireland-winning manager Liam Griffin sees the 1950s as a golden era for hurling and the rivalry that existed between Cork and Wexford was critical to this. Griffin believes that there are historic reasons for the breakthrough. He feels 'Wexicans' carry the spirit of the 1798 Rising in their DNA. 'We were the only ones who stood up when Ireland needed someone to take on the Empire.' Eamon Sweeney claims, 'Other supporters go to a match, Wexford fans go on a crusade.'

Liam Griffin believes that one man was critical to transforming Wexford's fortunes.

'Nicky Rackard was one of the most colourful characters I ever met. He changed the whole sporting and social structure of Wexford. He went to St Kieran's College in Kilkenny and developed a love for hurling which he brought home to his brothers and to his club, Rathnure. Wexford had traditionally been a football power going back to their famous four-in-a-row side. But Nicky Rackard turned Wexford almost overnight into a recognised hurling bastion. He was crucial to Wexford's two All-Irelands in 1955 and 1956. It was a tragedy that he died so young. As people know, he had his problems with the drink, but I spoke to his brother Bobby at his funeral, who told me it was a great shame he died because he had been doing great work for AA at the time.'

Griffin has no doubt about the high point of his county's rivalry with Cork. 'Everyone has their favourite memory of Micheál O'Hehir. If he could only be remembered for one broadcast, I would like to suggest the 1956 final between Cork and Wexford, one of the greatest hurling finals of them all, which will be remembered above all for Art Foley's save from Christy Ring. Anyone who ever saw either Christy Ring or Art Foley play would have a very clear mental picture of the handshake that passed between them after the save, listening to O'Hehir.

'It was a match which captured the imagination like few others. Tradition favoured Cork. Going into the game, they had won 22 titles against Wexford's two. Such was the interest in Wexford that two funerals scheduled for the day of the final had to be postponed until the following day because the hearses were needed to transport people to the match! More than 83,000 people attended. The match had to be delayed until 23 September because of a polio scare in Cork. The authorities did not want a huge crowd assembling in any one place.

'The crucial contest was that between Christy Ring, playing at left corner-forward, and Bobby Rackard. Ring went into the match in search of a record nine All-Ireland senior medals, having won his first in 1941. Outside Munster, Cork's greatest rivals were Wexford at the time. It was the Wexford man who would win out in every sense.

'Wexford had the advantage of a whirlwind start, with a goal from Padge Keogh after only three minutes. Two minutes later Ring registered Cork's first score, with a point from a 21-yards free. Wexford went on to win by 2-14 to 2-8.'

Wexford had a special place in Ring's affections.

'We in Cork treated Tipperary as our greatest rivals, but I always loved our clashes with Wexford in Croke Park. It was a different climate in Croke Park because you didn't have the pressure of the Munster championship on your back. It was the same for Wexford; they didn't have the pressure of beating Kilkenny on them. Both of us could relax a bit.'

Liam Griffin sees the rivalry between the two counties as a parable of all that is good in the GAA. 'After the 1956 All-Ireland final, which was the great Christy Ring's last match for Cork, the Wexford players carried him off the pitch. It was a stunning act of sportsmanship. While the match was going on, both teams would have done everything to win, as true rivals should, but when the match was over the rivalry was put on hold to honour probably the greatest player to have played that game. If you ever wanted to know what makes the GAA so special that incident tells you all you need to know.'

19

THE WEST'S AWAKE

Galway v. Mayo

Although Galway crushed Mayo in the 1982 Connacht final, the game did produce some moments of theatre, as a by-election was taking place in Galway at the time. The Fianna Fáil government did not have an overall majority, hence the importance of the outcome. Martin Carney still recalls the showbiz.

'Charlie Haughey and half the cabinet were there. There were helicopters landing in the stadium, which was unheard of at the time in a GAA match. It was more like the Epsom Derby than a Connacht final.'

THE MASTER

When I asked Jimmy Magee who was the greatest Gaelic footballer he had ever seen, he replied, 'The first man I would have on a team of all-time greats would be Galway's Seán Purcell.'

My only meeting with Seán Purcell is a memory that will stay with me forever. He transmitted vitality and enthusiasm like electricity. In his early days in the maroon of the Tribesmen he was in the right place at the wrong time.

'I came on the intercounty scene in the late '40s. Mayo had a wonderful team and overshadowed us for years. I will never forget one day they beat us very badly in Tuam. I happened to be in Galway that night and I met a great old friend of mine, Mayo's greatest ever forward Tom Langan. Tom was a very quiet man who didn't have much to say. But he'd had a few pints that night and he came over to me and he said, "Don't let that worry you. I played in six Connacht finals before I won one." I think that gave me heart. Before we played Mayo in the Connacht championship in '54 we decided we had to give it everything, that we had a chance. We beat them against all the odds and after that then we took off. From there on, things fell into position easily enough.'

THE GREEN AND RED OF MAYO
The depth of Mayo's rivalry with Galway was evident when I asked John Maughan what his proudest moment in football was.

'My greatest day was when we beat Galway, who were All-Ireland champions at the time, in Tuam in the Connacht final in 1999. Tuam had always been a bogey ground for us. Every year is sweeter in Mayo when we beat Galway because the tradition of rivalry with our old enemy is so embedded into the Mayo psyche.'

BOTH SIDES NOW
Having played for Mayo and managed Galway, Peter Ford is ideally equipped to comment on the rivalry between both counties. 'I think immediately of 1990. Mayo had great expectations, having reached the All-Ireland the year before. Not for the first time our hopes were dashed.

'In 1990 we played sh*t and were arrogant. We had a trial

game before we played Galway in the Connacht champion-ship and the B team beat us badly. Galway, too, hammered the daylights out of us. I marked a guy I didn't rate, which was part of the malaise, and he gave me a hard time. With that level of complacency, our chance of progressing from '89 was gone.'

Having taught in Sligo, gained a reputation as a coach in Summerhill at schools level and having had success in Mayo at club level, Ford found himself managing Sligo in 2001.

'I was half-hoping that I might get the Mayo job, but I had three brilliant years with Sligo. We lost by a point to Mayo in the Connacht championship, having missed a penalty in Castlebar in 2001, but I suppose the first highlight came some weeks later against Kildare. They had been in an All-Ireland final three years before and had won another Leinster title after that, and under Mick O'Dwyer they were one of the glamour teams. On 7 July we were the first Sligo team to win in Croke Park. Even though we lost, playing Dublin then in Croke Park was a wonderful occasion. I suppose one of the real high points came when we beat Tyrone the following year, as they were the team of stars and had so many household names. We then went on to draw with Armagh and were unlucky to lose the replay. We could have got a penalty in the last minute.

'We were punching above our weight. We were performing well, getting great support and there was such goodwill towards us in the county. We also had great players. Everyone knows about Eamonn O'Hara, but Dessie Sloyan was a fantastic forward who would consistently score for you, and we had other great fellas like Kieran Quinn and John McPartland. The team brought a lot of enjoyment and it was a happy county in 2002. There was no bitterness when we lost.

'In 2003, things started to go wrong and, within the local media in Sligo, there was a section that turned on us. That didn't help and it does affect the players. We had three or four injuries to key players, and no matter how much talent you have you can't win without your big players. The desire wasn't as strong and we had become complacent.'

Having raised Sligo up to new heights, Ford found himself filling the large shoes of John O'Mahony as Galway manager.

'My father was from Galway and I had gone to college there, but I also took the job because I thought I had the chance to win an All-Ireland. We won a Connacht title and an under-21 All-Ireland in 2005. We lost the first three league matches in 2006 and that put a strain on us. An element within the local media turned on us. Players started to have doubts. Although we qualified for the league final, things did not go to plan in the championship. The nadir was losing to Westmeath in the qualifiers. I was absolutely disgusted. A part of me wanted to walk away after that, but I felt that would be the cowardly thing to do. I wanted to try and put things right.

'In 2007 we were really right for the match against Mayo. The older lads were psyched to put one over on John O'Mahony, who was back managing Mayo. We did, but we were never able to get up for it again that summer in the same way and losing to Sligo in the Connacht final is not acceptable in Galway. Losing to Meath in the qualifiers was a real downer. I accepted the blame for the defeats, but my three years were up and it was time to move on.'

Having served under both John O'Mahony and John Maughan, Ford is ideally equipped to assess the respective merits of both.

'They are similar in the sense that they are both strong characters who bring a big work ethic, great self-belief and very good organisation to the job. They are very dissimilar, though, in the way they operate. John Maughan is more in people's faces, John

O'Mahony less so. Both styles will suit some players better than others. Maughan is an extrovert who enjoys the hype and likes to blow things up. O'Mahony likes to keep a low profile and stay out of the limelight. O'Mahony is more into psychology, Maughan is more into tactics.'

Ford's reply is immediate when asked about the frustrations of being a manager.

'When you are building up to a big game and have your plans based around a player or players, it is incredibly frustrating when they get injured. It's a killer on morale. Another problem is that some players play the way they want to anyway, no matter what you say, often to the detriment of the team. The dilemma is whether you are better off without them.'

A subtext in Ford's review of his career is the role of the media. When I raised the issue, he shot me a look that could have cut through steel.

'If a main GAA figure in the local media is constantly critical of the team or individual players it has a very negative effect. Players have wives, girlfriends, fathers and mothers. They find constant negative articles upsetting, which in turn affects the players in question. These are guys who make huge sacrifices to train and they find it frustrating to read a constant level of abuse.'

Was Ford himself badly affected by media criticism?

'What killed me was losing. After losing some of the big games in Galway I wouldn't want to show my face in the county for days, sometimes weeks. I put on a brave face in interviews after the games, but I took the defeats very badly. I was very depressed for weeks after some of our bad losses.'

So how does Ford see the rivalry between the two counties?

'It is one of the great traditional rivalries. There is seldom much between the teams when they play in the championship.

If there is a downside to the rivalry, it is that both sides put so much into beating each other in the Connacht championship in the past that they peaked too soon and were unable to sustain the momentum in the business end of the championship when they got to Croke Park. I found this out up close and personal in 2007.'

20

OLD RIVALRIES

Leinster v. Munster, 1790

No, the date is not a misprint! The clash between Munster and Leinster in the Phoenix Park in 1790 was faithfully recorded by the English authors, the Halls. The hurling match was 'got up' by the Lord Lieutenant and 'other sporting noblemen' and was attended by all the nobility and gentry belonging to the Vice-Regal Court, and the beauty and fashion of the Irish capital and its vicinity.

The Halls' match report tells us, 'The victory was contended for, a long time, with varied success; and at last it was decided in favour of the Munster men, by one of that party, Matt Healy, running with the ball on the point of his hurley, and striking it through the open windows of the Vice-Regal carriage and by that manoeuvre baffling the vigilance of the Leinster goals-men, and driving it in triumph through the goal.'

As apprehension mingled with the ache of deprivation, the Clare shout was starting to spill over the line between the urgent and the frantic. It was an occasion of red faces, virile voices and nerves stretched to brittleness. The sense of what might have been lost reached achingly into everyone who had ever admired the Munster team. But it must have felt like a disembowelling knife to Leinster fans, for whom the imminent defeat was the latest in a series of disasters visited upon them by their Munster rivals. Denial was their crutch. The match report is of interest because it shows that even a hundred years before the GAA was founded partisan rivalries were at the heart of Gaelic games.

ME AND JIMMY MAGEE

Jimmy Magee lived up to his nickname 'the Memory Man' as he trawled through the history of the GAA in the corridors of his mind.

'Wicklow have always produced great footballers, though never enough at the one time, like the county's first All-Star in 1990, Kevin O'Brien in the 1980s and 1990s. In the 1950s Andy Merrigan was very strong and a real slogger. It was like hitting a brick wall clashing with him. He was an iron man. They talk about Paddy McCormack, who was very tough also. Wicklow's finest, but one of Ireland's greatest, was Gerry O'Reilly in the 1950s. He was right half-back on the team of the century for players who never won All-Ireland medals, and he was one of the nominees for the team of the millennium. He was a sensational wing-back, but the only time you'd see him play was on St Patrick's Day in Croke Park, for Leinster. That evening people would be saying what a marvellous player Gerry O'Reilly was and how they'd have to wait for another year to see him perform again.

'At that time, Railway Cup football and hurling were prestigious events, and to be selected to play was the highest accolade of recognition for a player of exceptional talent. From the 1940s through to the 1960s, the rivalry between the provinces was as strong as it is between counties today. Once the Railway Cup finals were shown on television in the early '60s they became huge national events and the interprovincial rivalries took a hold on the nation.'

21

KEEPING UP WITH THE JONESES

St Patrick's College Armagh v. St Jarlath's College Tuam

It is the stuff of dreams.

Schools like St Mel's Lonford, St Patrick's Maghera, St Patrick's Navan in football and St Kieran's Kilkenny and St Flannans Ennis in hurling, among many others, have generated great rivalries which have adorned the GAA for decades. Games between these sides are often the best theatre in town and they generally come without any admission fee. The first great colleges' rivalry was between St Patrick's College Armagh and St Jarlath's College Tuam.

The great Italian racehorse breeder Federico Tesio once said, 'A horse gallops with his lungs, perseveres with his heart, and wins with his character.' If he had applied those criteria to Gaelic football, he would have used them to describe Tyrone legend Iggy Jones. He first came to prominence on the national stage in 1946 in the inaugural All-Ireland colleges' final when his three goals helped St Patrick's College Armagh, make a great fightback to snatch the title from St Jarlath's College Tuam. The Northerners, who also had Eddie and Jim Delvin in the team, trailed at half-time by 2-3 to 0-6, with Jones having scored four of those points. In the second half Jones scored three goals – the highlight of which came from a solo run when he spreadeagled the entire defence, having collected the ball deep in his own half before unleashing a rocket of a shot to the Tuam net. The Galway side were powered by the great Seán Purcell. Previously, colleges' football had been played only at interprovincial level. Indeed, by 1946 Iggy had played for Ulster colleges for four years and for the Tyrone senior team for two years.

The following year in the colleges' final the results were reversed, with Seán Purcell dominating. By that stage Iggy had left school. He was overage to play on the Tyrone minor team that won the Ulster minor championship in 1946. It was the start of a great period in underage football in the county, as they won the minor All-Irelands in both 1947 and 1948. Barney Eastwood, later to find fame as the manager of Barry McGuigan, was corner-forward and free-taker on the '48 team.

PART III
A Town Called Malice

Where would Ireland be without the GAA? In rural Ireland in particular it dominates all aspects of life. Every Sunday and Monday morning, throughout the summer especially, the topic of conversation is Gaelic games in an oddly pleasurable routine. It pervades Irish life and drives anguish and astonishment. Ireland owes the GAA a great debt of gratitude. What really turns Gaelic games into a national soap opera is when there are major controversies that create a form of existential pain that becomes unbearable – like a short-lived youthful passion. In its long history, the GAA has produced its fair share.

Anxiety is a great diluter of attention. Nothing fuels GAA rivalries like controversial incidents. Impulsive decisions become settled arguments. This section considers some of them where the heroes are avenging angels and agents of retribution for past humiliations, and opposing fans look across at each other through the desert of hostile incomprehension.

22

NO ORDINARY JOE

Galway v. Tipperary

The failure belonged to everybody. There was no place for scapegoats.

Having suffered a number of defeats to Tipperary, 2017 was the year when Galway put Tipp to the sword in the All-Ireland semi-final. Fittingly the game was won with a sensational point from distance and close to the sideline by Joe Canning. Joe sees the score as a means to an end.

'Winning the 2017 All-Ireland was a big thing for the Galway team. You're always going to feel pressure when you're going into an All-Ireland but the big thing for this group of players was that a lot of the guys were on the team in 2012 and 2015. We didn't want to lose three on the bounce. We didn't want to be on another losing team. It had been 29 years since Galway last won it – in our own minds, enough was enough.

'It was also a big deal for my family. My brother Ollie played for Galway almost 15 years and never won it, he was unlucky not to win it. It was a sense for him that we have it in the family now. I could've got taken off ten times in that game and my dad wouldn't have minded. He was more overjoyed than anything.

'It's great for the next generation, for the kids. For 29 years they've never witnessed the All-Ireland hurling championship in Galway. If we can inspire the next generation of Galway hurlers, then that's the main thing.

'For us to win just our fifth All-Ireland was pretty special. We have to embrace and celebrate it as well, and they don't come round very often. It was brilliant because Galway isn't a traditional county for winning All-Irelands; it was only our fifth ever All-Ireland compared to the likes of Tipperary.'

HOT AND HEAVY

In the 1980s the rivalry between Galway and Tipperary was explosive.

For star forward Noel Lane, his abiding memory of these games is not of Tipperary.

'In '88 I was back starting on the team, but after scoring 1-5 in the All-Ireland semi-final to my amazement and disgust I was dropped for the final on the Tuesday night before the game. I hadn't seen it coming. I let Cyril Farrell [the team manager] know my feelings on the subject in no uncertain terms and in choice language. I left Ballinasloe in a hurry and went home feeling sorry for myself and believing an injustice had been done to me. I proceeded to Loughrea and drank 12 pints of beer. On the Thursday night, realising that I was lucky to be there at all, I went up to Cyril and said, "You heard what I did in Loughrea and you heard what I said to you on Tuesday night, but if you want me Sunday I'll be there."

'I came on after half-time. It was one of the great All-Irelands. There was a great rivalry and a number of great duels. One of the decisive factors was that our full-back, Conor Hayes, had

Nicky English in his grip. If they had moved English, we would have been in trouble. I think the captaincy played on Nicky. I got in around the square and scored a goal that was instrumental in us getting the result.'

For Lane, their coach Cyril Farrell was critical.

'The week before the All-Ireland final the team was training in Ballinasloe on the night the team was due to be announced. There was a terrible storm that evening, with thunder, lightning and incredible rain. [Brendan] Lynskey and [Tony] Keady did not travel down from Dublin. Farrell felt like shooting the two miscreants but knew he could not win the final without them. Things were tense for a while, especially as he never picked a team until the squad were there to hear it first. He arranged a training session for the next evening and this time the two stars were back and victory was secured.

'Cyril always preached we were better than everybody else. He had great passion and would get us to see the opposition in terms of what they didn't have, more than what they did have. He inherited Babs Keating's team in '79 but really showed his skills with his "second team" from 1985 to 1990. He would have worked with most of that team at minor and under-21. He knew everything about them: what they ate and drank, who they slept with, and their strengths and weaknesses.'

REGRETS: I'VE HAD A FEW

In both 1987 and '88 Galway deprived Tipperary of All-Ireland titles. Babs Keating looks back wistfully at the aftermath of the 1987 Munster final replay.

'The one regret I have is that we didn't have the courage to take the team away the next weekend for a break. We had drawn the Munster semi-final and had needed extra-time in the replay to win the Munster final. The team were dead and the three of us couldn't lift them for the semi-final. That's not to take away from the fact that Galway were a great side and deserved their two All-Irelands.'

Nicky English echoes those sentiments.

'Galway had learned a lot from losing in '85 and '86 and were ahead of us in their development. They deserved to win in '87 and '88. The rivalry between us was very strong because I think we were so far ahead of all the other counties in those years. Things came to a head in the '89 semi-final. Galway were really hyped up by "the Keady affair" [when Galway's Tony Keady was suspended for playing illegally in New York]. They felt that a major injustice had been done to them. They were going for a three-in-a-row and until 2008 with Kilkenny we saw how hard it was to do this. We knew we would be seen as failures if we returned home defeated three years in a row. Given the tradition in Tipperary that was not acceptable. People often say you have to lose one before you win one, but losing can make it more difficult to come back too. Jimmy Barry-Murphy said it's as easy to win your first All-Ireland as the last. By losing in '87 and '88 we maybe made it harder for ourselves in '89, but it was going to be a defining game for us.

'Both semi-finals were played on the same day. Before the match we got the news that Antrim had defeated Offaly in their semi-final. Both teams knew that our match was really the All-Ireland final, and that upped the ante. It was a thundery day and there was a black cloud over Croke Park, so there was kind of an eerie atmosphere in the crowd. It was an ill-tempered game and, although we won, the fact that Galway had Sylvie and Hopper McGrath sent off took a bit of the gloss off it.'

Nicky English talks easily and eloquently about the complexities of the financial markets and all matters hurling. There is only one subject he is not forthcoming on. When asked directly for his opinion on Sylvie Linnane, he replies, 'I have no comment on that topic.'

Babs Keating also regrets the atmosphere on that day.

'In many ways 1989 was unusual. We beat Waterford in a horrible Munster final. The build-up to the semi-final against Galway was dominated by the Keady affair. What really hurt me about that was that Galway people blamed Tipperary for setting Keady up. Tommy Barrett, the county secretary, was the Tipperary delegate and he spoke in favour of Tony Keady being allowed to play. He never remembers anyone thanking him for it. I thought it was a very noble thing and I don't think we could have done any more. We never got involved in the politics of it. At the end of the day Galway had delegates from their own province who didn't support them.

'Everybody knew the rules. Tony Keady knew the rules. The Galway people in New York knew the rules. Tony Keady was such a fine player, but the Galway people who played him in New York let Galway hurling down by playing him.

'The atmosphere was very bad before the game. There was a lot of aggression. It was a pity. Galway had beat us in the league final that year and it was a superb game.'

With typical reserve Nicky English makes no mention of an incident in the 1991 All-Ireland semi-final against Galway when he was struck a blow above the left eye, which might have caused him permanent eye injury but instead required nine stitches. The flow of blood came with the intensity of the Niagara Falls. Despite repeated nudges, no comment on the incident is supplied.

By then injuries were starting to catch up with English. Given these injuries, Babs Keating once said to him, 'Nicky, if I had legs like yours, I'd be wearing nylons.'

23

THE IRISH ARE WIMPS

Ireland v. Australia

Joe Brolly is one of the few players who turned down the opportunity to get involved in the International Rules series. On a day when autumn was speedily bleeding into winter, he told me, 'I was asked about it a few times and I couldn't run away from it fast enough. I'm too much of a coward!'

International Rules football, sometimes called 'Compromise Rules', is a hybrid code of football which was developed to facilitate international representative matches between Australian Rules footballers and Gaelic footballers.

The first games played were test matches between Australia and a touring Meath Gaelic football team which took place in late 1967 after Meath had won that year's All-Ireland senior football championship. Following intermittent international tests between Australia and an All-Ireland team, which began in the centenary year of the GAA in 1984, the International Rules series gained a unique place in the GAA landscape.

The series really entered the popular consciousness in 1986, following a major controversy. One of the Irish players on that tour was Pat Spillane. What are his memories of that tour?

'There was controversy before we went to Australia when the Dublin coach Kevin Heffernan was appointed as tour manager ahead of Mick O'Dwyer. Micko is the most successful Gaelic football coach of all time and he has never managed the International Rules team, which is extraordinary.

'However, what really made the tour come alive was when the manager of the Australian team, John Todd, described the touring side as "wimps" following complaints about the "excessively robust play" of the Australian players. His remarks provoked a storm of outrage not just among the Irish team but also back at home in Ireland. It was a huge story throughout the country. It wasn't quite as big as Roy Keane and Mick McCarthy during Saipan, but it was pretty close. Todd's comments were taken as a slur on the Irish character and, as a result, people who had no interest in the game back home in Ireland became fascinated by the series. It became a matter of national pride for us to beat the Aussies. Thankfully, the fighting Irish provided the most effective rebuttal possible to Todd's comments when we won the series.

'Although people constantly bemoan violence on the pitch, a lot of people love watching the games because of the physical contact. The controversies and the violence generated brought the games to everyone's attention, and I guarantee you that when there is massive interest in the series it is because people are wondering if there will be more violence.

'From my point of view, it was a tremendous honour to be invited to play for my country and I was delighted with the chance to be part of the experiment to give an international outlet to Gaelic football. Of course, it did come as a shock when you were on the ball that an Aussie player could come up and knock you to the ground by any means necessary – and keep you pinned down. I do think we could learn from them. Everything was much better organised and facilities are so much better over there. There is a very high emphasis on the basic skills because they believe you shouldn't make elementary mistakes in a match. If you were to introduce "back to basics" training sessions with senior teams in Ireland, you would be laughed at, but as Kerry showed with Kieran Donaghy in their defeat of Armagh in 2004 there is still a major place for "catch and kick" in Gaelic football.

'It is great for players from so-called "weaker counties" in particular to get the chance to play alongside the cream of the GAA talent and to showcase their talents to the nation. Take a player like Westmeath's Spike Fagan, who could really show the country how good a player he was on live television when he played for Ireland.

'I wonder, though, is it possible to play a compromise game between the two codes? For example, I think asking the Australians to play a game without a tackle is like asking the Irish soccer team to play a game without heading. I sometimes wonder if it would be better if we went out there to take them on at their own game and they came to play us at ours. Having said that, the rivalry between the two countries when the series was at its peak really energised fans of Gaelic games.'

24

EVERYBODY NEEDS GOOD RIVALS

Clare v. Galway

Change is inevitable, except from a vending machine.

In his second autobiography, Davy Fitzgerald departs significantly from his first by having harsh words for two of his former teammates, Brian Lohan and Jamesie O'Connor. However, he goes perhaps surprisingly gently on Ger Loughnane, given some of the critical comments written about him in Loughnane's newspaper column. Fitzgerald does have a cut at Loughnane, though, for fuelling the rivalry between Clare and Galway to the detriment of the Banner in 2016.

After Kilkenny beat Galway in the Leinster final Loughnane, with characteristic understatement, described the Westerners as 'made of absolutely nothing' and as having 'no guts whatsoever'. With the peerless Joe Canning calling the shots, Galway were determined to crush Clare when the sides met in the All-Ireland quarter-final after Loughnane's incendiary comments. And they did. As Clare manager at the time, Davy described himself as 'hugely let down' by Loughnane's 'diatribe'. Although Fitzgerald dismisses his critics as 'empty vessels making noise' he nonetheless expresses his frustration about 'one Clareman setting up another for a fall'.

ONE FINE SUMMER

Fitzgerald and Loughnane were on the same page against Galway in the '95 All-Ireland semi-final, as Loughnane explains.

'I was aware of a dramatic escalation of the rivalry between Clare and Galway before the semi-final. When I visited a town like Gort, which is so close to the Clare border, the Galway fans were always keen to let me know who had the best team!

'In the All-Ireland semi-final against Galway in 1995 Brian Lohan damaged his hamstring. He was on Joe Cooney, and Cooney had got a couple of points off him. I went down to the sideline and looked at him. I did more than look at him, I needn't tell you! He started to hurl out of his skin. Lohan said afterwards, "I saw Loughnane coming down the sideline and decided it was time to start hurling!"'

Anthony Daly identifies one moment when Loughnane's contribution was particularly significant at the time.

'No one will ever forget the night the training was bad and Stephen McNamara had complained of a stomach bug. Loughnane brought us all back into the dressing-room because we were so lethargic in training. He gave a tyranny of a speech and began with me. "It starts with the captain ..." He lambasted me and then everybody else, and eventually he came around to Stephen McNamara, who had skipped training because of illness, and he hit him a kind of belt in the stomach. "Sick Mac! Sick is coming out of Croke Park beaten."

'I think that was a turning point because we weren't going to settle for winning Munster – we were going to go all the way. When we took on Galway in '95 the rivalry was very keen between the fans because we are neighbouring counties and it was such a novel pairing for an All-Ireland semi-final, but, to be fair to him, Loughnane had us in the right frame of mind.'

INTO THE WEST

In 2006 Galway fans temporarily put aside their rivalry when Loughnane began an unsuccessful two years as Galway manager. A significant section of the Galway hurling community attributed the reason for the failure largely to the man from Clare.

Ever the diplomat, Loughnane had a jaundiced view both of some of the county's hurling officials and the training facilities.

'I was on the Hurling Development Committee, which tried to persuade Galway to come into the Leinster championship. When we met them, one official fell asleep at the end of the table. That's a fact. Another official's only concern was that the kitchen was closing at 9 p.m., so the meeting had to be over then, so that he'd get his meal. They weren't the slightest bit interested.

'Ballinalsoe is like a sheep field. Loughrea is an absolute disgrace – a tiny cabbage garden of a field. Athenry is the worst of all. I asked myself what were these people doing in the 1980s when they had all this success? It was Pearse Stadium they concentrated on – the stand, not the pitch. Because the pitch is like something left over from famine times, there are so many ridges in it.'

25

FAMINE DAYS AND DONKEY DERBYS

Tipperary v. Cork

The worst surprises are those we think we see coming.

Talking down your rivals is a dangerous business. In February 2019, before Kilkenny played Limerick in the National League, former Kilkenny great Jackie Tyrell said that Limerick were not even in the top three teams in the country despite the fact that they were the All-Ireland champions and had won their previous two league games very easily. Limerick went into Kilkenny's fortress, Nowlan Park, and won by nine points.

DONKEYS DON'T WIN DERBYS

Nicky English retains vivid memories of Tipperary's rivalry with Cork.

'We won the All-Ireland again in '91 and it was important to us that we beat Kilkenny in the final because there were those who devalued our win in '89 because it was Antrim we beat and not one of the powers of hurling. Of course, that's very unfair on Antrim, but we had to show to the hurling world that we were worthy of a place at hurling's top table. My hamstring went in that year, and I came back too soon for the semi-final against Galway and it went again. It went a third time because I didn't make it through the final. I think although we won the All-Ireland the injuries were starting to catch up, and although we won the Munster title in '93 and a league in '94, we never could scale those heights again. I was glad we won that second All-Ireland for Babs's sake.'

Nicky is keen to defend Babs from one long-running criticism: Keating's comments that 'you can't win derbys with donkeys' before Tipperary played Cork in the 1990 Munster final were seen as a spectacular own-goal when the Cork donkeys won.

'We did make mistakes in terms of selection for that match. I think after we won the All-Ireland in '89, our first in 18 years, we coasted a bit and never had the same application as the previous year. We went to Toronto for a week in March to play the All-Stars and that was another distraction. When Cork beat us, Babs was blamed for his remarks. People said that because it suited them. It might have been used as a motivational tool in Cork, but it was not the reason we lost. Cork were hungrier than us and that was the crucial difference.'

Babs addresses his controversial comments head on.

'It was a stupid remark and no more that. It was used against us that year. We were decimated with injuries. It was a bluff game with us. We had no sub for the backline with injuries. We took a chance with Declan Ryan at full-forward, even though he was lifting bales with his father the day before and he just wasn't fit to hurl. Mark Foley got three goals that day and he never played liked that, before or since.

'The next year both Mark Foley and the Cork full-back Richard Browne didn't perform well. Both of them are dentists. The boys in one of the pubs in Clonmel put up a sign: "Wanted for Cork: a centre-forward and full-back. Dentists need not apply."

'I knew we needed to win a second All-Ireland to be seen as a great team. We had one thing mitigating against us. I brought 11 subs with us on our trip to Florida and the Bahamas, but none of them really contributed to the team afterwards. We needed to find one or two new players to cover for injuries and we didn't. The underage teams weren't going as well as I would have liked. Nicky basically didn't play in '91 because of injuries.'

SUPERMAC

In September 1990 Teddy McCarthy wrote himself into the annals of the GAA. He starred in Cork's historic double: defeating Galway in the All-Ireland hurling final, and a few weeks later would add the second leg to a remarkable double when he helped the Leesiders beat old rivals Meath in the All-Ireland football final.

With the Keady affair if not exactly behind them then at least in the background, Galway had a seven-point lead over Cork in the 1990 All-Ireland final and appeared to be cruising to another All-Ireland title, particularly as Joe Cooney was giving a torrid time to Jim Cashman and calling the shots. However, two goals from Cork's John 'Schillaci' Fitzgibbon turned the match decisively in Cork's favour and they ran out comfortable winners. While obviously winning such a unique double meant a lot to him, neither All-Irelands were necessarily his fondest memory of the year, as McCarthy explained to me.

'Nobody outside the county expected us to beat Tipperary in the Munster final in Thurles. They looked as if they were going to be winning All-Irelands back-to-back, particularly having got their Galway bogey out of the way. It was a sweet victory for us, particularly in Thurles, and bearing in mind that Tipp were going for their first four-in-a-row in Munster.'

THE MIGHTY QUINN

When he scored three goals for Tipperary in the 1954 National League final against Kilkenny, the late Billy Quinn, father of former soccer star Niall, was propelled into national prominence. He had a unique insight into Tipperary's rivalry with Cork.

'The big thrill was to be changing around with the senior team. The Munster final in Killarney was a classic match, though I'd an awful experience when a Cork man dropped dead beside me with the excitement of the game. The crowd invaded the pitch a few times and Christy Ring had to escort the referee off the pitch.

'This was not a new thing. A decade earlier also, such was the intensity of one Cork–Tipperary match that a man had to be anointed on the ground. The entire crowd knelt down as a mark of respect.'

Quinn's intercounty career coincided with a barren spell in Tipperary's fortunes in the championship.

'We played Cork in 1956 and Seamus Bannon got the best goal I ever saw, when he ran down the wing and lashed the ball into the net. But one of our lads threw his hurley 20 yards in celebration – the referee disallowed the goal and Cork beat us. It was the greatest injustice I ever saw in hurling. We got dog's abuse listening in to the All-Ireland in Thurles because everyone was saying, "Ye should be there if ye were any good."

'I think the 1950s were a golden era for hurling because you had a lot of great teams like Cork, Tipperary and Wexford. Not only had you great players on all those teams, but go back and you'll find that each of those counties had five or six great players competing for each position. Christy Ring was the greatest player of the time, but Jimmy Doyle would run him a close second. He would get scores from left or right.'

THE FAMINE IS OVER

Babs Keating glows as if he is transmitting electricity while he recalls the 1987 Munster final replay when his Tipperary team defeated Cork in one of the most memorable matches between the two old rivals. 'It was one of the days of our lives. You could cut the atmosphere with a knife.'

Nothing captures the unique magic and tribalism of the GAA more vividly than that Munster final. Michael Lowry has been one of the most controversial figures in recent Irish political life, but he was to play a significant role in the revival of Tipperary's hurling fortunes in 1986. His meeting with Babs Keating would change hurling history.

'When Michael became county chairman, he asked to meet me. We met in a private house, the late Seamus Maher's home, because I wanted to meet in secret, knowing the stories that would go around. To be fair to him, he gave me the power to pick my own selectors. I'll always remember he said, "You have the job, but we have no money." The county board was broke after hosting the centenary All-Ireland in '84 and the economic situation was very bleak. I got the idea to start the supporters' club. Then I decided we would raffle a racehorse, and Christy Roche bought an ideal horse for us. I got everyone I ever knew to buy a ticket, like Charlie Haughey and Jack Lynch. I remember being at home one morning and getting a call from Niall Quinn when he was at Arsenal. He told me he had sold seven tickets for me and listed off a who's who of Arsenal greats who had bought one.

'My back-up team was Donie Nealon and Theo English. They had played for the county for about 12 years and I don't think Cork ever beat them. They couldn't understand why there was such fear of Cork and they transferred that attitude. Our captain, Richie Stakelum, would always say that Tipperary had such fear of Cork at that stage.

'People talk about the great team Tipperary had in the '84 Munster final but that team brought Tipp into Division Two. We played our first league game away against Antrim and won it fairly impressively. The great thing that happened to us was that in our second league match we played Laois and they beat us by ten points in Thurles. We got rid of six or seven players and went in a different direction. If that defeat had come later in the campaign, it would have been much harder to regroup. As with everything in life, you need a bit of luck. We got it with that game in Laois.

'One thing I did every January was to take out the two selectors and their wives for a meal and told them to pick the team they would play in the All-Ireland that year. The three of us had 13 identical choices that night in '87, so we only had to find two players.

'We had huge confidence going into the Munster final, even though Cork were 3-1 on. We had come from nowhere in Division Two and had 12 new personnel. We had money behind us. When we travelled away for big matches, we stayed in five-star hotels. I will never forget the first game we played against Cork. Both of us got to the ground at the same time. Our bus was in the Tipperary colours. The Cork players were in their jeans and jumpers. Our lads looked like film stars in their blazers. Richie Stakelum said it was worth five points to us.'

Nicky English won six All-Stars in seven years and was hurler of the year in 1989. He is ideally placed to give an insider's guide to the game.

'When I came on the scene, Tipperary changed managers almost every year because we weren't winning Munster championships. It is a bit like what was happening in Galway for a decade. In a county where you have a lot of hurlers there is a massive turnover of players with each new manager, and that means there is little or no continuity. A lot of good players are thrown out in the wash before they have the chance to develop. We came close in a high-scoring Munster final that we should have won in 1984 when Seánie O'Leary scored a late goal to win for Cork.

'Things changed when Babs came on board. He did things differently. He raised a lot of money and arranged things in what was a radically different way back then, though county players take it for granted today. He got us blazers and we stayed in hotels before matches. Things were tight economically in the 1980s. There was no money around. The Tipperary county board were putting all their money into upgrading Semple Stadium. All their financial focus was on infrastructure, not on looking after players. Up to then we would drive through the traffic and invariably get stuck in it. Anything we needed in terms of gear or hurleys was got for us. Before that you got your own hurleys and handed in receipts, and often there was a long delay before you got your money back. Sometimes you wouldn't get your money back at all. It is hard to quantify how much it all helped us on the field of play, but it did make an impact. Babs blazed the trail, and every football and hurling team followed to a greater or lesser extent. He brought a whole new attitude and confidence. Babs believed and we believed because of him.

'Winning the 1987 Munster final was my greatest day in hurling. The fact that we beat Cork after extra time in a replay added to it. Tipperary hadn't won a Munster final since 1971, so that's why Richie Stakelum's comment that the "famine days are over" struck such a chord. The emotion our victory unleashed was unreal. Nothing has ever matched that feeling.'

Nicky English is responsible for one of the most iconic scores in hurling when he kicked the ball past Ger Cunnigham into the net in the '87 Munster final at Semple Stadium, with a bend on the sliotar that George Best would have killed for.

'I was lucky to have scored goals in big games. I was giving out to myself that day because the one good ball I got in the whole game I had no hurl. I was tackled by Cork's full-back Richard Browne and lost my hurley. As a youngster I played a lot of tennis and often afterwards we played soccer with a tennis ball. I had no option that day but to kick the ball and many times after that I tried to bend the sliotar the way I did that day but never could. So I was really lucky it came off for me that day.

'The 1987 Munster final replay was the day of days as an event and from an emotional point of view. The thing is, though, when I look back at the game I am embarrassed. The standard is very poor. That's why I despair when I hear people saying hurling used to be much better in "the old days". Hurling is way better now and will be even better in a few years' time.'

26

JIMMY'S WINNING MATCHES

Donegal v. Mayo

In the foggy no-man's-land between dreaming and waking there are special moments for Donegal fans.

In 2012, in the first Ulster–Connacht All-Ireland final since 1948 (when Cavan, captained by 'the Gallant John Joe' O'Reilly, defeated Mayo), Donegal beat Mayo 2-11 to 0-13 to win their second All-Ireland. It was the best possible start for Donegal, who led by 2-1 to no score after 11 minutes, with goals from Michael Murphy and Colm McFadden.

The following year Mayo exacted revenge when they routed Donegal in the 2013 All-Ireland quarter-final. Alex Ferguson-style mind games are now in vogue in the GAA. Former Donegal selector Rory Gallagher aired his conspiracy theory before the game: 'We suspect there was a bit of collusion between Mona-ghan and Mayo. [James] Horan [the Mayo manager] works to a premediated script and I think Kieran Shannon [then team psychologist and columnist with *The Examiner*] is behind a good bit of it.'

Colm Parkinson immediately described it as 'Mind James'.

For many fans the real rivalry between the counties came in 1992.

THE YEAR OF LIVING DANGEROUSLY

The promise of reaching the All-Ireland final in 1989 for Mayo was not built on, and Dermot Flanagan looks back on the experience as a lost opportunity.

'The winter of '89 saw a form of euphoria because we had reached a final after such a long time and had played well, which really took away from our focus. What should have happened is that we should have cleared off for a week and realised we had lost. People thought we were on the crest of winning an All-Ireland, which created a lot of distractions and left us vulnerable in '90.'

To this day, Flanagan finds it difficult to assess the way events unfolded after Mayo's defeat in the Connacht final replay to Roscommon in 1991.

'John O'Mahony departed in controversial circumstances. John has never spoken in public about all the details and I suppose we should let him have his say on that. It is probably fair to say that part of the reason was that he was not allowed to choose his own selectors. Looking back, the circumstances of Mayo football were not right then.

'Brian McDonald came in as his replacement and a year later would find himself in a huge controversy. Were there any winners? Everybody was a loser to a greater or lesser extent. Brian had been a selector with Liam O'Neill in 1985. To be fair to Brian, he had a lot of good ideas about the game, but whether he was the man to get the best out of players was another question. The first thing he asked me when he took over as manager was if I was committed to Mayo football. I was totally committed. I was the first guy to do stretching before training and after training. Long before it was fashionable, I was doing acupuncture, watching my diet, reading sports injury books and doing power weightlifting – anything that would give me an edge or improve me as a player – so it came as a shock to be asked that.

'The issue that got into the media was about the players pushing cars as part of a training session. That was not the underlying problem. You needed to have a very strong skin to be able to handle Brian's comments in a training session. That was OK for the senior players, but repeated exposure to this for the younger players could have undermined their confidence. We had a lot of younger players in the squad at the time.

'Again, in fairness to Brian, we did win a Connacht final in 1992 and could have beaten Donegal in the All-Ireland semi-final. We were not in the right frame of mind for an All-Ireland semi-final. There were a lot of problems with organisation. I was a man marker, and I was on Tony Boyle for a short time in the game and did well on him, but I wasn't left on him and he played havoc with us.

'Afterwards, the controversy broke in the media. The team was going nowhere. There were no winners in that situation. The tumultuous saga reflected very badly on the whole scene in Mayo. The county board had been deaf to any complaints. John O'Mahony had left under a cloud. These situations don't come from nowhere. A lot of mistakes were made.'

The sins of the father were revisited on Flanagan.

'My dad wouldn't have been hugely popular with the county board in his playing days. One day he turned around and asked the county chairman if he wouldn't mind leaving the dressing-room. For that reason, some people believed that I was the most likely instigator of the "revolt" against Brian, but I had nothing to do with it. I never had to push cars because I was training in Dublin and was too busy in my legal career to be "master-minding a coup".'

THE MAN WHO PLAYED FOR TWO COUNTIES

Although he won an All-Star that year, T.J. Kilgallon's memories of the All-Ireland semi-final in 1992 are not very happy. Heartache pounded through his soul.

'There was kind of a bad vibe all year, and even though we won the Connacht final there was a sense in the camp that things were not going well. Probably the most memorable incident happened when Enon Gavin broke the crossbar in Castlebar and the match had to be delayed. The management had brought back Padraig Brogan earlier that year – I'm not saying it was a popular move with the players. When we played Donegal in the All-Ireland semi-final, it was probably the worst game ever seen in Croke Park. Padraig had played for Donegal the previous year, and when the Donegal lads saw him warming up you could see that it gave them new energy.'

In 1985 Brogan wrote his name on the consciousness of the GAA world with a stunning goal against Dublin in the All-Ireland semi-final – it won the prestigious 'goal of the season'. In conversation with this writer, Brogan recalled his eventful career.

'I had a lot of personal problems. I really lost control of my life for a few years when I let myself be taken over by drink. I can't describe how bad things became. I lost everything, maybe what I lost most was my self-respect. I reached rock bottom and I really mean that. It was as if I brought myself to hell on earth. Thank God I got myself sober.'

Brogan's inter-county rehabilitation surprisingly came in the Donegal colours but after one and a half years with Donegal he abruptly returned to Mayo for the 1992 championship, only to find himself coming on as sub when Mayo played Donegal in the All-Ireland semi-final.

'I had great times with Donegal, but I'm a Mayo man and blood is thicker than water, so I was glad to come back and play for Mayo. I didn't take it personally when some of the Donegal fans booed me. I still have great friends there and I was obviously very close with the lads on the Donegal side.

'I think it was a very silly thing for the management of the team to bring me on in that game. It was a factor in Donegal's win because it lifted their team. The management should have played me from the start or not at all.

'I was very disappointed afterwards. Although I was delighted Donegal won the All-Ireland, I had mixed emotions, thinking if I had stayed on I would have an All-Ireland medal now.'

DONE IN DUNNES

T.J. Kilgallon recalls the controversy after the loss to Donegal.

'Things got ugly after that. It was more personal than it should have been. It was probably an early example of player power. We said that if there wasn't a change of management a lot of us would walk away. I was asked recently if we really did spend a training session pushing cars. We did! It was at the Dunnes Stores car park in Castlebar and the cars were really big. There was not a great humour in the camp and the manager had to walk the plank. John O'Mahony had stepped down in 1991 because he was not let to choose his own selectors and maybe that's when we should have acted.'

A significant insight into Peter Ford's character is provided by the fact that a narrow loss in the All-Ireland semi-final to Donegal in 1992 is not one of the big regrets of his career, but the immediate aftermath.

'A lot of controversy was generated by the stories that surfaced about the training methods of our manager, Brian McDonald. Brian's family got a lot of abuse afterwards. That should not have happened. I was captain that year, and whatever grievances we might have had with Brian's training methods there's no way they should all have got into the media in that fashion, nor should Brian have got such a pillorying. I didn't realise till later how much Brian's family had suffered, through terrible phone calls because of the controversy, and I still feel terrible that they had to go through it. It is one of the big regrets of my career.'

Of the semi-final itself, he also has a couple of regrets.

'I had a shoulder injury before the game and had to take a painkilling injection. I was marking Tony Boyle and he did terrible damage that day. As captain, the management had promised me that, no matter what happened, Padraig Brogan would not be brought on as a sub, even if the game was in balance, because he had played for Donegal the year before and the sight of him would gee on the Donegal side. However, he was brought on, with exactly the result that I had anticipated.'

Pat Spillane has a different take on the car-pushing controversy.

'I often think of what would have happened if Mayo went on to win the All-Ireland in 1992. They came within a whisker of beating the eventual All-Ireland champions, Donegal, in the All-Ireland semi-final. In a highly publicised saga afterwards, the Mayo players signed a petition which called for the removal of Brian McDonald and in the process released a list of training methods which they had used during the year which seemed to border on the farcical. Only one side of the story was told in public. Player power saw McDonald bowing out, and Jack O'Shea taking his place, only for Mayo to be absolutely massacred by Cork the following year in the All-Ireland semi-final.

With a bit of luck, though, Mayo could easily have beaten Donegal in 1992, and who knows what would have happened against Dublin in the All-Ireland final? McDonald, being very cute, got the squad to push cars around the car park when there was no pitch available. If Mayo had won that All-Ireland, everyone would have said McDonald was a genius and car-pushing would have become part of training.'

SHUT THE F**K UP

Tensions between Mayo and Donegal flared up again in February 2019 after Corofin beat Gaoth Dobhair in the All-Ireland club semi-final. Former Mayo star David Brady took to social media to raise questions about the Donegal side's commitment.

'They will, when the dust settles and time passes, in a quiet moment ask, did they pass up on the opportunity of a lifetime … posting multiple pi**-ups won't win you an All-Ireland and that's not what winning is about.'

After winning the Ulster title, former Donegal All-Star Kevin Cassidy had posted several videos showing the exuberant celebrations in Gaoth Dobhair. His response to Brady was:

'Shut the f**k up. I'm not even a midfielder and I would still take you to the cleaners, you muppet.'

27

FROM THE CLARE SHOUT TO JIMMY COONEY

Offaly v. Clare

It has become the conventional wisdom that the 1990s in hurling were 'the revolution years' because between 1994 and 1998 the three traditional hurling superpowers – Kilkenny, Cork and Tipperary – were deprived of an All-Ireland, with the honours shared in those years between Offaly, Clare and Wexford. But, if so, it was a very short-lived revolution. From 1999 through to 2012, the three superpowers restored the 'natural order' and jealously kept the Liam McCarthy Cup between themselves.

What the 1990s did, however, was to make hurling 'sexy'. No team did more to make this happen than Clare, and no man was more to the forefront than Ger Loughnane. At the start of 1995 not even Biddy Early herself could have foreseen that the rivalry between Clare and Offaly was destined to become the new national soap opera.

MR MOTIVATOR

Jamesie O'Connor feels that Clare's victory was due in large part to Ger Loughnane's unorthodox motivation style.

'He was looking for a particular type of player – a player who wouldn't roll over. If a guy was going to roll over here in Shannon, he wouldn't survive in Croke Park. Much of the training was psychological. They were testing you and looking for a certain reaction. They were looking for a type of guy who would bite his lip and grit his teeth and say, "I'll prove you wrong." Ger would have said tough things to me. The guy who used to mark me in training was Christy Rusty Chaplain and I would have awful battles with him. I remember one wet evening he was cleaning me out and Loughnane would let out this roar: "Good man, Christy, you have him cleaned." I'm saying under my breath, "You bollox," but at the same time gritting my teeth to win the next ball. That's what he was doing. If you sunk down in your boots, you were going to be no good to him in Croke Park. That was part of his psychological approach.

'I used to live in Galway and ten days before the All-Ireland final I went down to a summer camp in Woodford. One of the men running it was Paddy Kirwan from Offaly. Paddy is a fierce hurling man, but I just got a sense from him that he didn't rate us. Ger said to us a week before the game that if we made a battle out of it nobody was going to beat us and I remember thinking: he's dead right.'

Hurling can lift the shadows from the heart, but buried deep in the collective subconscious in Clare was a nagging doubt. Loughnane was always looking for an opportunity to stress that this team were not for turning or rolling over.

'The night before the '95 All-Ireland we met them in Cusack Park just to tell them the arrangements for the following day. You wouldn't believe how relaxed they were. They were confident.

'I always believed that the last serious training session set the scene for what was coming up. I remember the last training session before the All-Ireland final in '95 came the Saturday week before the match. I blew the whistle up early, but they wanted to go on for another five or ten minutes. I said I wouldn't let it go on. When they want more, you know you're ready. We could always judge how ready they were. They always knew when things were exactly right, when to push and when to pull back.

'The morning of the All-Ireland in '95 we were driving out to the airport from the Oakwood Hotel in Shannon. We had met there as usual at 8 a.m. Instead of turning in the yard, the bus driver decided to drive right around the hotel and come out via the back exit. When we arrived there, we found the gate was locked. The bus driver said he would turn around. I told him no. Tony, Mike Mac and one of the players got off the bus with me and we lifted the gate off its hinges. A clear message was being sent out to the team. Unlike Clare sides in the past, we were never going to turn back and no obstacle was going to stand in our way. That was the message.'

RAISING THE BANNER

Although it was only one step in a long climb that the team had to make if there was any chance of surviving among the best in the country, Clare's Munster final victory was more feverishly acclaimed than any other in recent decades. Even when the small hairs stood on the back of his neck and the war-whoops of victory echoed all round him, Anthony Daly never imagined the attendant fanfare that might accompany it from a generation of Clare fans who had learned stoicism about Munster final defeats almost in the cradle from their fathers. It quickly became evident, though, that they had to forget about that game if they were to capture the All-Ireland title from the holders, Offaly.

'We were different people and there was a swagger in our

steps going into work and thus we were nearly like new men. The Sparrow [Ger O'Loughlin] and myself went for a swim the day before the final and I asked him what did he think and he said he thought we were going to win. I said I felt the same. I had bought in to the theory that it was our year.'

The match got off to a fiery start. One of Offaly's stars on the day, Daithí Regan, has spoken out about the Offaly manager Eamonn Cregan's sense of the occasion.

'He warned us to be prepared for the roar once the Clare team ran onto the pitch because they had not been in a final for so long. He was right. Croke Park seemed to shake with the roar. As I walked around in the parade and looked into the stands and saw the place teeming with Clare people, I thought to myself: Is there anybody from Offaly here at all?

'I had played poorly the previous year, even though we won. I was determined to redeem myself against Clare and I was going to be ruthless to do it. I "did" Ollie Baker at the start of the match and scored a point after 16 seconds and I was flying.'

Anthony Daly, though, took it all in his stride.

'There was a bit of magic in the air in Croke Park that day. It just seemed the way things fell into place. I just felt that on the day Offaly got two fortunate goals but we never dropped our heads. We came out and hurled away and got the break with the goal two minutes from the end. Offaly got the goal just before half-time and everyone says that's a great time to get a goal but it is probably a better time to get one with two minutes to go.

'When the All-Ireland started, everything was going grand. Seánie McMahon scored two great points to set us off. We were doing everything we planned. It was a war of attrition. We were blocking them and hooking them.

'Then just before half-time disaster struck. Michael Duignan came along under the Cusack Stand and he seemed to try and lob the ball over the bar but it fell short. Fitzy [Clare's goalie Davy Fitzgerald] tried to control the ball with his hurley, which was unusual for him, but the sliotar skidded off into the net. It looked like the classic sucker punch that could destroy us. If there was any fragile area in our make-up that would undo us.'

Ger Loughnane was relaxed throughout.

'There was no discernible air of tension. We had been through the semi-final against Galway, which in a way is a more difficult occasion to cope with. There were very few words spoken. We just told them that Clare people were there in their thousands and that people had come from all over the globe to be here, so a massive effort was needed. Above all we stressed that all the plans we had for Offaly were to be implemented and stressed the importance of work-rate, discipline and taking any opportunities that came our way because they would be scarce. We also emphasised that if they suffered any disappointment or setback, they were to put it behind them. When they left the room, they nearly took the doors off the hinges they were so charged-up.

'Then just before half-time Michael Duignan scored a fluky goal. Then the Sparrow scored a brilliant point from the side-line, and instead of going in on a downer everyone was in a different frame of mind. In fact, Fitzy's mistake turned out to be a good thing because at half-time everyone was on to him, saying, "Not to worry. We're still going to win." We held up the jersey in front of them and asked them to give every last ounce of energy for Clare.'

A PROPHECY

In '95 the outcome of the All-Ireland final seemed clear-cut. As the historic contest entered its decisive final minutes Offaly were travelling so smoothly that it seemed they should win as easily as a nun gets to heaven. Twelve months earlier Limerick had outplayed Offaly throughout the All-Ireland final, and held an apparently unassailable five-points lead with just minutes remaining, but they were caught by the Dooleys. Back-to-back titles seemed inevitable for the Midlanders, but the Clare team had a morale so tough that railway sleepers could be broken across it.

Managers are selected for winning matches, certainly not for the quality of their post-match interviews. They have no obligation to produce either profundity or entertainment for the microphones and notebooks that cluster round them in the half-time interval. Yet at half-time Loughnane had boldly told the television audience, hungry for direct evidence, that Clare were going to win: 'We're going to do it.' Cockiness is no crime, especially in a world where undue reticence is a recipe for being left behind, but Gaelic games is one of the areas where the penalties of overdosing on self-approval are especially severe. With five minutes to go the manager's confidence had apparently been exposed as the creation of a romantic and deluded imagination.

Loughnane explains. 'The second half was tense. We were going well and then Johnny Pilkington scored a second Offaly goal. The ball should have been cleared. We had always said, "For certain we'll make mistakes. For certain we'll have a lot of wides but don't panic, stick to the plan and work, work, work until the last second."'

THE STRIFE OF BRIAN

One player gets special praise from Loughnane.

'With about 20 minutes to go, Brian Lohan pulled a hamstring and he gave a signal. We had built up such an understanding that at any time, whether it was in a dressing-room or out on the field, a look was all it took. There was no need for words most of the time. It was the look, and especially how you sent the look, that sent the message, especially with players like Daly, Seánie, Lohan and Doyler [Liam Doyle]. It showed the terrific understanding there was between everybody and that applied with the selectors as well. Colm Flynn said to me, "Jesus, his hamstring is gone." I replied, "Tell him he's not f**king coming off." I turned my back and walked in the other direction after Lohan called me. Colm went in and broke the news to Brian. No reaction whatsoever. He just got on with it and pretended nothing was wrong with him. When you talk about mental toughness, what Lohan did in the All-Ireland – it was out of this world. It would never happen in soccer. If a player pulls his hamstring in soccer, the stretcher is brought in and there's a big exit.

'In the last 20 minutes he used his head, stayed goalside of John Troy and whoever else came on, and played away with a torn hamstring. He wasn't able to train for three months after-wards. For those last 20 minutes he held out by sheer guts. For a Clare player to do that in an All-Ireland final was incredible and said everything about the difference between the team I played on and the team I managed. There's no way I'd have done that when I was playing.

'He got through it by cutting down the angles. It was a measure of his courage and his intelligence. He used his head to survive with a torn hamstring. He was willing to go through the pain barrier because the team needed him to do so.'

In this zone everything else melts away. Loughnane was determined to get his message across.

'The '95 All-Ireland was a case in point. I had noticed that Offaly players were brilliant at finding a loose man whenever they were tackled. If I ever saw two players on the one man in training, I'd shout, "Get the f**k on the loose man!" There was a stunning photo taken during the All-Ireland of Brian Lohan and John Troy going for the ball. Instead of looking at the two of them, Anthony Daly was in shot looking for the loose man. It was driven home again and again: *it's not the man in possession you watch but the loose man.* That was how we kept Offaly down to 2-8 in that match. With all the talent Offaly had, that must have been a record low score of points for them.'

IT'S A LONG WAY FROM CLARE TO HERE

Loughnane's towering gifts as a manager – the priceless 'feel' for players and commanding urgency of his voice, the cold nerve and iron determination, the judgement that springs a sub at precisely the right moment to suit their capacities – have never been better exemplified than in his icily patient delivery of the D'Artagnan of the big square, Eamon Taaffe, in that final. The melodrama belonged in the last reel of one of the classic Western films in which John Wayne battled against the odds to snatch victory from the jaws of defeat. The Banner's gifted team were suddenly buzzing and Clare were on their way to victory, as Jamesie O'Connor recalled.

'The second half was tense. We were going well and then Johnny Pilkington scored a second Offaly goal. With the clock ticking Anthony Daly and Eamon Taaffe combined to get us the goal we needed. Offaly came down the field again. They hit the post, but the ever-reliable Frank Lohan was there to relieve the danger. The ball was cleared and we got a 21-yard free, which I pointed. Then the crowds descended on us. Every inch of Croke Park was covered with Clare people.'

Ger Loughane watched on agog.

'With the clock ticking, Anthony Daly, a master at the height of his powers, lobbed the sliotar into the square. Taaffe connected and the umpire was reaching for the green flag. It

MY BALL: Galway's Gearoid McInerney evades the Limerick resistance in the 2018 All-Ireland final.

THE CLASH OF THE ASH: Cork's Julia White and Kilkenny's Collette Dormer battle for possession in the 2018 All-Ireland final.

© INPHO / Tommy Dickson

THE REBELETTES v. THE BLUES SISTERS: Cork's Aine O'Sullivan challenges Dublin's Lauren Magee in the 2018 All-Ireland final.

SPOT ON: Tyrone's Peter Harte beats Dublin's Stephen Cluxon from the penalty spot in the 2018 All-Ireland final.

© INPHO / Ryan Byrne

© INPHO / James Crombie

OLD RIVALS: Wexford's Harry Kehoe clears the ball despite the best efforts of Kilkenny's Kieran Joyce in 2017.

CLEAR AND PRESENT DANGER: Limerick's Tom Murphy goes bravely for the ball with Tipperary's Padraic Maher lurking ominously in the 2019 Munster final.

© INPHO / James Crombie

© INPHO / James Meehan

KEEPERS OF THE FLAME:
Cork's Fergal McCormack breaks through the Tipperary defence during another instalment of one of hurling's most famous rivalries.

LEAP OF THE DAY: Cork's Shea Fahy and Kerry's Ambrose O'Donovan soar like eagles to claim the ball in 1991.

THE BRADY BUNCH: Mayo's David Brady contests with Galway's Joe Bergin in the 2001 League final.

© INPHO

© INPHO / Patrick Bolger

FREE WILLIE:
Kildare great Willie McCreery goes head to head with Meath's Hank Traynor in the 1998 Leinster final.

SHOULDER TO SHOULDER:
Tyrone's Peter Harte and Armagh's Tony Kernan renew an old rivalry in 2015.

FAT LARRY LOOMS: Donegal's Martin McHugh breaks away from Mayo's Anthony 'Fat Larry' Finnerty in 1992.

GAME OF THRONES: King Henry Shefflin leaves Tipperary's John O'Keeffe in his wake in the 2011 All-Ireland final.

SUPERMAC: Dublin's Philly McMahon gives Meath's Conor McGill his full attention in the 2019 Leinster final.

LAST NIGHT I HAD A PLEASANT DREAM: Leitrim's Ryan O'Rourke breaches the Roscommon defence in the 2019 Connacht Championship.

© INPHO / Ryan Byrne

© INPHO / Evan Logan

THE CLIFF EDGE: Kerry's newest superstar David Clifford takes on Dublin's Jonny Cooper in 2018.

SHANE'S WORLD: Cork's Shane Kingston goes man to man with Waterford's Shane McNulty in the 2019 Munster Championship.

was from this point on that the game slows down in my mind. After Offaly equalised, Ollie Baker forced a 65. Dalo was facing up to it, though Seánie should have been taking it. Daly had made up his mind. There was somebody injured and the game was delayed. I ran into Dalo and said to him, "Give it a right lash." I'd say he never even heard me. He was looking at the posts the same as if it was Cusack Park. I was standing on the sideline and was shouting a point before it had gone halfway.'

Across the nation enthralled radio listeners were tuned into the peerless Micheál Ó Muircheartaigh with breathless enthusiasm saying the magic words: 'We're gone 45 seconds into injury time. It's all over and the men of Clare of '95 are All-Ireland champions.'

Perhaps this match had not been the best showcase of the team's communal talents, but at that moment they were the happiest team in the world, and they deserved to be. As all around him were swept up in the madness, the manager looked out on the hallowed sod, lavishly garlanded on the day with thousands of ecstatic Clare people who spread out like a tree that blocked the sun, in the stunning clarity of autumnal light and quietly plundered its pleasures for himself. For the kind of man who can euphemise fanaticism as common sense, who can disguise obsession as the only sensible way to behave, his restraint was almost treasonable. From the peculiar terrain that champions inhabit he was wearing the smile that only the vindicated know. His faith in his young team was magnificently justified, and it was right that the gods should refuse to throw a shadow across their dreams.

'When the cup was presented, I didn't go up the steps. It was just a thrill to stand there and soak it all in. It was surreal. Those players will be heroes forever and that is more lasting than cups or medals. The best way I can think of summing up the day is to use an idea taken from a Paul Simon song; it was one of "innocence and wonder".'

Clare triumphed over Offaly in 1995, but their rivalry would only really ignite three years later in a saga that had more twists and turns than a bad bog road. In 1982 Charlie Haughey gave a new word to the political vernacular 'GUBU' – an acronym for 'Grotesque, Unbelievable, Bizarre and Unprecedented'. The year 1998 would see hurling's equivalent. Offaly would get the opportunity for revenge in the All-Ireland semi-final.

HURLING'S YEAR OF GUBU

The whole Irish sporting world seemed to be swept up in the myth of Ger Loughnane in 1998. Having travelled the stoniest road to stardom, it seemed that the outrageous vicissitudes of his career came to a climax that summer. As the fallout from the Colin Lynch controversy grew like a monster out of control [Lynch had been suspended for three months after the Munster final], Loughnane's role in helping to lift hurling to unprecedented heights was seldom mentioned. Such was the media frenzy that when Clare faced Offaly in the All-Ireland semi-final the fact that his team were just 70 minutes shy of a third All-Ireland final appearance in four years seemed almost secondary. Hurling's capacity to outreach the wildest imaginings of fiction was shown that year.

Loughnane's primary purpose, to which he returned again and again during his infamous Clare FM interview, was to encourage the Clare fans to lift the team, especially the new players that would have to come on the team the following Sunday. The interview achieved its objective.

'After the Munster final there was so much unfavourable comment in the media that the Clare players were starting to wonder when I was going to reply to it. I wanted to leave it as close as possible to the Offaly match to lance the boil and I got a lot of things off my chest when I went on Clare FM! When I came into training that night, all the players were looking at me. Although they said nothing, I knew they were relieved I had taken on the criticism. In all of the controversy I never spoke to any of them about anything that was going on off the field. I wanted them to concentrate just on the hurling.

'In my experience of Gaelic games, I've never seen a team as united with its supporters as that first day against Offaly. When we came onto the pitch there was just an electric feeling and a great ovation. It was an incredible feeling of oneness with the crowd and, considering that at that stage we had already won two All-Irelands, it was just incredible.'

THE FAITHFUL DEPARTED

After player power had led to Babs Keating's departure as Offaly manager, the Offaly players had a major point to prove, of which Loughnane was keenly aware.

'Offaly were going to be out for revenge for '95 and had such outstanding players and leaders on the pitch, like Brian Whelahan, Martin Hanamy, Hubert Rigney, Johnny Pilkington, the Dooleys and Michael Duignan. Lohan's loss through suspension was incalculable that day. We had a new full-back and he played well, but obviously he didn't have the experience for such a match and was caught out for the Offaly goal.'

For their part, Offaly came into the game after a period of disarray. After they lost the Leinster final in '98 to Kilkenny, Babs Keating controversially described the Offaly players as 'sheep in a heap'. Babs met with the county board and decided to stay, but the next morning he resigned because he was 'shocked' by an interview in a newspaper by Offaly's star midfielder Johnny Pilkington, who had questioned Babs's record with the county, stated that Babs had abandoned Offaly's tradition of ground hurling and questioned the tactics against Kilkenny.

Pilkington is not someone to hide his feelings.

'It really got to me. Babs was manager of Offaly. We had some very bad wides on the day and we had conceded two soft goals in the last 15 minutes. It just seemed he was passing the buck. Maybe it was the players' fault but he was the manager and he could have come down on Tuesday night and said what he had to say in the dressing-room. He always referred to Offaly as "them" – never as "us". It was a case of "they" were poor out there and "they" did things wrong.

'Michael Bond came on the scene after about a week. He just said he liked Offaly hurling and off we went training. Nobody knew who he was. Nobody knew his hurling credentials or anything. We knew he was a teacher. Someone told us he was a principal. He spoke Irish and some of his instructions were in Irish. The training sessions upped significantly. We were a group of lads who were down at the bottom of the barrel. We were after speaking out against the manager. It wasn't anyone else's responsibility to pick it up – only the 30 lads who were there. After Bond came in, there was a great buzz in training and we were thinking we were great lads again. We played Kilkenny in a challenge match, though, and they gave us an even bigger beating than they had in the Leinster final! So where did that leave us?

'Loughnane took his eye off the ball before we played Clare in the All-Ireland semi-final. If they had been playing Kilkenny or Galway, it would have been a different story. He took Offaly for granted.'

Not surprisingly Babs Keating's reading of the events of '98 differs sharply from Pilkington's: 'Johnny Pilkington took great exception to my remark, but one of my biggest battles at the time was to get Pilkington to train.'

FIGHT BACK

In the semi-final Clare led Offaly by four points with ten minutes to go, but it required a late free from Jamesie to tie the match at 1-13 each after Offaly scored 1-2 without reply. In the circumstances Loughnane was delighted: 'I was relieved we had survived and I knew we would play much better in the replay.'

Much of Clare's performance in the replay was a monument to patience, nerve, courage and technical brilliance, the mature masterwork of a great team. As normal, Clare concentrated on setting a dominating, draining pace. This was essential for a team in which goals had to be mined like nuggets for Loughnane.

'What I always felt about our team was that in order for us to be effective we had to play the whole game with the pedal to the floor. It had to be constant, constant going, constant closing in on the opposition. When you faced into draws and replays it just sapped your energy. No matter what you did, you didn't have the same zip as if you had a break between games.

'After the three games with Offaly in '98 everybody felt that the end was nigh. In particular we felt the second Offaly match was like the end of the road. The hurling we produced that day was absolutely out of this world. For the first 40 minutes of that game the Clare hurling was exceptional. The speed of the game, the quality of the scores were excellent and then, like Kilkenny had done against us the previous year, Offaly came back. We let them back in but were still winning by three points with two minutes to go and Barry Murphy was goalbound on the 21-yard line.'

PREMATURE INTERVENTION

Clare's calculated challenge was intensifying towards its thrilling crescendo, but Jimmy Cooney intervened and blew full-time two minutes prematurely. There was a very thin line between laughter and loss for Loughnane.

'When the game was over there was no sense of elation, except a sense of anger. The question in my mind was: why the hell did the ref blow as Barry was going through? I said to Colm [Flynn], "What he's doing?" Colm said, "It's over." He started jumping up and down. I felt no sense of exhilaration. I was preparing to give the team the most ferocious bollicking in the dressing-room for taking the foot off the pedal and allowing Offaly back into the game. Jimmy Cooney didn't deprive us of the All-Ireland that year, but he did deprive us of getting there.'

Unfortunately, Cooney would suffer badly because of the saga.

'After I blew the final whistle, I saw my umpire and he had his hand out with his five fingers up. I thought to myself, "Oh Jesus." All the photographers were nearly pushing themselves out of the way to get a picture of me. The umpires told me afterwards that I didn't tog in for two hours. I don't remember it but I remember my wife eventually coming into the dressing-room and she was crying, of course. We went to the Ashling Hotel and twas news time and I was flashed across the screen. The waitress looked at the screen, then looked at me. Before she said anything, I said, "That's me." I just wanted to get home. We had a young family and I knew there could be phone calls.

'There were lots of calls. If one of the girls answered, they asked if their daddy was a referee. When they said yes, they were told that their daddy was going to be killed and their house was going to be burned down and if they didn't pass on the message they would be killed as well. When I got to the phone and offered to meet the callers face to face, they hung up quickly. It would have lasted till Christmas and after that.'

THE MORNING AFTER OPTIMISM

A new hurling soap opera was about to unfold, with Loughnane cast as the central character.

'After that match, I was sitting down in the Burlington Hotel when someone came in around seven o'clock and said there was a call for me. It was Marty Morrissey telling me that RTÉ had been put on standby for 3 p.m. the following Saturday in Thurles. I had just been talking to Phelim Murphy, who is on the Games Administration Committee [GAC], about the rumours that had been circulating about a replay and he said it was pure rubbish. There was a massive confusion that night, but I said if we were going to have a replay we had to have Colin Lynch back.

'I knew the late Joe McDonagh [then President of the GAA] was supposed to be in the hotel, so I asked John Glen, then manager, who had told me that Joe was staying there, to arrange a meeting with him for me. He told me that McDonagh was gone down to Galway to present medals that night but he would be having breakfast in the Berkley Court in the morning and I might be able to meet him then. I had the very distinct impression that the president of the GAA did not want to meet me then, with the controversy about Colin Lynch at its height.

'So I rang our county secretary, Pat Fitzgerald. He was halfway home at this stage. He rang me back and told me there was a GAC meeting set for ten o'clock the next morning. Then I knew something was definitely up. All the players were in the pub drinking, so I went in and said, "Take it easy, lads. There's going to be a replay on Saturday." Anthony Daly summed up the attitude of the players when he said, "Ah, f**k it. We'll take them on again. If they bate us, what about it. If we're going to lose it, let's lose it on the field."'

For *Hamlet*, the 'play was the thing', but in 1998 the replay was the thing. The spectre of another replay floated into the consciousness. Loughnane summoned all the officers of the Clare county board for a council of war meeting for 8 a.m. in his room in the Burlington the next morning. Meanwhile he had instructed Pat Fitzgerald to arrange a meeting with Liam Mulvhill, the GAA's Ard Stiúrthóir, with a view to getting Colin Lynch back into the fold.

In his notorious interview on Clare FM, Loughnane had raised a few eyebrows by invoking the name of Don Corleone, but there were echoes of a film about the mafia in the way events unfolded later that morning. Galway were playing Derry in the All-Ireland football semi-final that day, but nothing on the pitch could compete with the intrigue off it, as Loughnane recalls.

'I drove Pat Fitz's car into the back of Croke Park. This man in a black suit and dark glasses opened the gate and waved us through. He told Pat to get out and ordered me to drive over to the Hogan Stand side. Pat went into the labyrinth of the Cusack Stand and we waited and waited for him to come back. About five minutes before the GAC meeting was due to start Pat returned and said, "There's going to be a management meeting on Wednesday night. We can't say for definite, but you can take it for granted that Colin Lynch will be back."

'The Offaly delegation, Christy Todd and Brendan Ward, were waiting in the corridors and looked really uptight. I said to them, "What's to worry about? There's definitely going to be a replay."

'They asked, "How do you know?"

'I replied, "Sure what are we here for? There's going to be another game. It's going to be next Saturday in Thurles at 3 p.m."

'Both of them were looking at me. "But there's going to be an investigation."

'"There's going to be no investigation. It's already sorted."

'They lightened up then. We went in first and Pat Fitz presented our case as to why there shouldn't be a replay, just as a formality, knowing it was just a whitewash. There was very little argument on either side. Offaly went in and came out as the next step of the charade was played out. Then we were both brought in together and given the verdict.'

To nobody's surprise in the Clare camp, they were told that there would be a replay in Thurles on the following Saturday. Additional features were that the money generated would be given to the Omagh fund (after the atrocity in the town that killed 31 people) and that there would be a 'big' donation to the holiday fund of both counties. The only shock was the news that Dickie Murphy would be refereeing it, as the practice at the time was that the same referee who officiated at the original game refereed the second game. At this juncture Loughnane intervened to ask why Jimmy Cooney would not be in charge. He was told that the Galway man had asked not to be considered. Loughnane stated, 'I want to make it quite clear that we have no objection to Jimmy Cooney refereeing it.' His comment appeared to fall on deaf ears.

'Then I said, "We have no problem taking on our great friends here from Offaly next Saturday." They were all aghast because they were expecting a massive row over it. My attitude was, once you win anything on the field if there's any question mark over it what good is winning it? I also believe that no matter what else happens the All-Ireland is sacrosanct. We would do nothing that would jeopardise or compromise its status in any way.'

The following Wednesday after the Jimmy Cooney affair Colin Lynch's appeal was heard by the management committee in Croke Park. Lynch travelled up for the meeting with Pat

Fitzgerald but was not asked any question or afforded the opportunity to speak. The Munster council produced a witness, a Mr McDonnell from Tipperary, who claimed to have seen Lynch striking Tony Browne.

At the meeting the chairman and secretary of the Munster council claimed that they received calls from Joe McDonagh, urging them to take action following an incident in the Munster hurling final replay. This was one of their strongest arguments in upholding the suspension. This intervention raised questions in the Clare camp. Did any members of the GAC receive similar calls from Joe McDonagh following the All-Ireland semi-final replay?

Resentment over the episode in Clare was compounded by the failure to take comparable action against an Offaly player. As there were no similar disciplinary measures taken against Michael Duignan, even though his blow had been captured live on television and reproduced in a photograph in the national newspapers, the feeling in Clare was that Joe McDonagh had left himself open to very serious questions of partisan behaviour.

Following his retirement in March 2001, in an interview with Brian Carthy, Michael Duignan admitted that he was very lucky not to have been sent off for what he described as a 'desperate' challenge on David Forde. He generously conceded that Clare fans must have felt a great sense of injustice with the way he got off without any sanctions, whereas Colin Lynch received such a severe punishment.

At the meeting Lynch was told that the GAC could not grant him clemency. As it was the Munster council who had suspended him, only they could shorten his sentence, as Loughnane recalls.

'Lynch wrote to the Munster council and delivered it personally to Donie Nealon's house, but Donie didn't recognise him. He asked him who he was and then took the letter from him.'

The Clare camp were understandably keen to have Lynch's appeal heard before the second replay, only to be confronted by the type of labyrinthine bureaucracy associated with the decaying Ottoman Empire – a mindset so brilliantly satirised in *Little Dorrit* in Charles Dickens' creation of the 'Department of Circumlocution'.

'That night I went to Pat Fitzgerald's house to see if we could get the Munster council to meet before the game to discuss Colin's case. Pat knew that the chairman of the Munster council, Seán Kelly, was on holidays in Wexford, but was told by another prominent official that the only way they could contact him was from a payphone half a mile from where he was staying.

'Months later, after the controversy had died down, Seán Kelly contacted me and asked if he could meet me for dinner. To his credit he wanted to bury the hatchet between the Munster council and us. We had a great chat for six hours. At the end I asked him if the only way the Munster council could have contacted him when he was on holidays in Wexford was from a payphone up the road. He said in this day and age that was nonsense. Enough said!'

WHEN HOPE AND REASON DO NOT RHYME

Loughnane, like all great leaders, was a dealer in hope. Yet it was a real struggle to generate any optimism going into the third Offaly match.

'On our way to Thurles, we stopped at the usual hotel in Cashel. We were walking up the steps when Tony Considine said to me, "I feel awful tired." This really surprised me because Tony is never tired. I replied, "I don't feel a bit tired." There was a total atmosphere of deadness on the bus from Cashel to Thurles.'

Loughnane's problems combating the fatigue factor were

compounded by the ever-increasing toll of injuries. In the dressing-room the players looked exhausted. Now more than ever Loughnane needed one of his famous motivational ploys.

'I had to do something to try and lift them. Just before they went out onto the field, I put up the picture of Michael Duignan striking David Forde and said, "Are we going to let that beat us?" Give them their due, they all woke up and went out fighting.'

The hallmark of the Clare team in the Loughnane era was their ability to build up a momentum which no rival could live with. In '98 they had gone to the well once too often. The laws of attrition reaped their vengeance yet again.

'We were in trouble all over the field. Doyler and Brian Quinn were really struggling. At half-time I was late getting back into the dressing-room. They were all exhausted. We were facing demolition. I had to do something dramatic to get them going again.

'Ollie Baker was lying on the treatment table. Colm Flynn said to me, "He's f**ked. He'll have to come off." I said, "Baker, get off that f**king table. Do you realise what state we're in? There is a war on here. We're going down the swanny. Get out there. I don't care if you are on one leg. Doyler has done it already. Now it is your turn." He jumped off the table and went out and had a brilliant second half. He almost single-handedly brought us back into the game.'

There are lies, damned lies and statistics, but it was significant that Clare's tally of 13 points, in the final twist in this tale of the unexpected, was the lowest recorded by them in the championship since the 1993 Munster semi-final against Cork, when they managed just 2-7. And yet were it not for the brilliance of Stephen Byrne in the Offaly goal …

It has been said that the best part of winning is that it's not losing, but losing was a lens through which Loughnane could see himself and his team more clearly. From time to time a keenly contested defeat made him feel better than a victory in which the team didn't perform to its optimum.

'I went into the dressing-room and sincerely congratulated the Offaly players. It was bedlam inside. All the journalists were there. The previous Saturday evening we had been drinking with the Offaly lads and they were slagging us about giving them a replay. When I walked in after we lost, Joe Dooley said to me, "A week is a long time in hurling, Ger." On the day, Offaly were the better team and deserved to win.

'When I got back into our dressing-room Michael Bond, who is really sound, said a few words. I shut the door after he left and said, "In years to come, you'll look back on this as a brilliant year. There are a lot of lessons that can be learned about life, about trust, and the way people behave. I'm prouder of you today than on the day you won your first All-Ireland."

'As we walked out to the bus the place was thronged with Clare people and they gave us a fantastic reception. It was so emotional that some of the players were in tears. It was the first time I'd ever seen any of them crying.

'When we got to the hotel, I met Kilkenny selector Dick O'Neill. He said, "It's a pity ye didn't win." I replied, "Ye were waiting for us. Now ye're in right trouble." I knew that with this kind of momentum Offaly would be unstoppable. I then met Eddie Keher, one of the nicest, most genuine people you could meet, and he has a great love and knowledge of hurling. Very few ex-players have such a knowledge of the current hurling scene as he has. It was nearly a relief that it was over. I was exhausted.'

UP HIS OWN ASS

Memories from 1998 continue to linger in both counties. The film *Four Weddings and a Funeral* made Hugh Grant a star. It also spawned one of the biggest-selling songs of all time from Wet, Wet, Wet, 'Love Is All Around'. On Valentine's Day in 2014 love was all around again – well, almost. It was the day Ger Lough-hane chose to write in his column in *The Star* that Offaly were the 'only team in the modern era with fat legs, bellies and arses'.

Twitter went into meltdown. Daithí Regan had a response that raised an intriguing biological question: 'Someone give Ger a replica Liam McCarthy Cup, stamp it "1998 winners" and then he might crawl back up his ass.'

PART IV
Everybody Needs Bad Neighbours

All-Ireland finals are often settled by explosions of effectiveness, and nobody explodes more lethally or plunders more consistently than star players. Their mesmeric wanderings totally flummox many a defence and neutralise many a tactical plan drawn up to sabotage their domination. You can teach a player many things, but there is something you cannot transmit: natural talent. It is a mystery which only the player and God can really know about. Their effortlessly exquisite touch, their blazing pace and the fluency of their every movement unfailingly troubles opposing defences. They can consistently promise to fill the minds of fans with glittering memories and deliver on that promise with a series of sublime performances. Everybody loves watching them – except rival fans.

GAA rivalries come in different shapes and sizes. There are many elements that constitute rivalries, from tradition to controversy to all-out violence. One factor, however, that accentuates such rivalries is when two counties are close neighbours. This section celebrates some of them.

28

ONE-IN-A-ROW, JOE

Derry v. Down

Seán Boylan lives by the philosophy that a candle loses nothing of its light by lighting another candle. He takes some of the credit for Joe Brolly's elevation to the highest level as a player.

'In 1993 I got a call from the then Derry manager Eamonn Coleman and he asked me in that strong Derry accent of his, "Can we win the Ulster title?"

'I replied, "Do you want to win the All-Ireland?"

'He came back and said, "That's not the question I asked. Can we win Ulster?"

'I answered, "I know what your question is. Yes, ye can win Ulster. But I am asking if you want to win the All-Ireland?"

'"Of course I would like to win the All-Ireland!"

'"Well, if you want to win the All-Ireland, ye need to get that young fella off the terraces and onto the pitch."

'For a number of years I was involved in picking the Sigerson team of the year. Joe Brolly was a star of the Trinity College team and I knew he would make it. Eamonn picked him and they went on to win the All-Ireland that year. Joe was excellent in both the semi-final and All-Ireland final.'

ON THE DOWNSIDE

For his part, Brolly believes that they would not have won the All-Ireland without the intervention of their great rivals, Down.

'Looking back at the 1970s and the 1980s, the reason why the teams from Leinster and Munster always wanted to play an Ulster team in the All-Ireland semi-final was because Ulster teams were defeated before the match even started because of psychological reasons. Deep down they didn't believe they could win.

'I'm as sure as I can be about anything else that the man who changed the face of Ulster football was James McCartan Jnr. He changed everything. In part it was because his father had played on three All-Ireland-winning teams in the 1960s and James had inherited the winning mentality from his dad. The Down team was moribund until he came along. Ross Carr, Greg Blaney, Mickey Linden were all there before. Then McCartan comes in as an 18-year-old. He had scored three goals in a McCrory Cup final and taken Down to an All-Ireland minor title. He was a force of nature. I had never seen anything like him. I still haven't. Dermot McNicholl was the closest, and like James he had that exciting and swashbuckling quality, but he didn't have the fine skills that James had. McCartan changed that entire team. In a way, I think he shamed them all because of his bravery, his courage, the way he played and his electrifying confidence and self-assurance.

'In 1991 James was in his second year with Down. He was irresistible. He scored five points in the All-Ireland final against Meath. He changed everything. If Down hadn't won that All-Ireland, you could have forgotten about Derry winning an All-

Ireland, you could absolutely forget about Donegal winning an All-Ireland, or there wouldn't be Tyrone or Armagh All-Irelands. All of those titles were grafted on the back of Down's '91 win. Donegal realised they could win an All-Ireland and there was a sense of it being inevitable that Derry would win the All-Ireland in '93 and Down came back to win another final in '94. If you had to isolate one reason for all of that, it would be James.

'The strange thing was that he burnt out so quickly. Perhaps it was his size. He wasn't big, and took a lot of hits. He was a constant target because of the way he played. He was a phenomenal athlete and is the seminal influence in the way he changed Ulster football.'

A GAME CHANGER

When the Oak-leaf county succeeded Donegal as All-Ireland champions in 1993, Brolly was fast becoming a star name in Gaelic football.

'I always wanted to play for Derry because of the great team of the '70s that won back-to-back Ulster titles. It was very clear from an early stage that the team was going somewhere. We had a lot of very strong characters on the team. An important catalyst for our success was Lavey winning the All-Ireland club title in 1991. Our captain was Henry Downey from Lavey and he was driving us on. He would tell us we were not training enough. So when Lavey won the All-Ireland club title, we all bought into the belief that the Downey way was the right way. We were training five nights a week.

'Our manager Eamonn Coleman was also crucial. Then Mickey Moran came in. He is a quiet man who was a terrific coach and a football fanatic. He worked very well with Eamonn. The broadbrush stroke man who had the philosophy behind everything was Eamonn, while Mickey was the nuts and bolts man. I know in hindsight that Eamonn was not a good trainer, but when Mickey came in all of a sudden everything was right.

'The other thing that was important to us was Down winning the All-Ireland in 1991. We had nearly beaten them that year in a titanic game in the Athletic Grounds. We were a point up at the end when they got a free 60 yards out. I was close to the ball at the time and I heard Ross Carr saying to Enda Gormley, "I'm going to drive this over the bar." Enda told him, "Wise up, you f**king eejit." But Ross sent it over the bar and they went through instead of us, but when they won the All-Ireland it inspired us because it made us realise how close we were.

'I've never seen either the 1993 semi-final or All-Ireland final, but anyone who has tells me they never had the slightest worry that we would win either, although it was very close against Dublin in the semi-final, and even though Cork got a whirlwind start scoring 1-2 in the first five minutes in the final we beat them without any problems.'

REVENGE

After the high of 1993 Derry made an early exit in the championship in 1994, as Brolly recalls.

'Our great rivals Down beat us in an epic game in Celtic Park. Eamonn Coleman took them for granted because we had beaten them by 18 or 20 points the year before. Eamonn positively laughed at the notion that Down could beat Derry at Celtic Park. Mickey Linden kept them in it in the first half. Then, in a classic smash and grab, they beat us with a late goal. After one game, we were gone.

'There had been a lot of discomfort in Derry about Eamonn. He was a players' man, not a county board man. He would have literally told them to f**k off and there was a lot of jealousy. All of a sudden he was sacked. In his first year he won a National League. Derry's previous league title had been in 1947. In his second year he won an All-Ireland. He had won a minor All-Ireland himself as a player and had coached Derry to an All-Ireland minor title, with his son Gary as captain. He had coached an All-Ireland under-21 team. When he was sacked, it killed the spirit within the team. It had been a very special group, but Eamonn's sacking spread a poison through the team. It is a fact that three or four members of the county board undid all the good work. It is also a fact that they weren't the slightest bit interested in winning All-Ireland titles or having success cos that put them under the spotlight. They were only interested in running things and getting tickets. That was their mentality. They screwed him. It was impossible to pick up the pieces. Mickey Moran stood in, in controversial circumstances. He never had the team with him. We won the National League the following year on autopilot. The interest was gone.'

29

WHERE TWO COUNTIES MEET

Longford v. Westmeath

In 1967, when he was eight years old, John McEnroe played his first tennis tournament – the Douglaston Club under-12s – after playing tennis for just two weeks. He got to the semi-finals with three other boys, all of them 12, and lost. Two weeks later he competed in his second tournament with the other three boys and this time he won. His first coach, Dan Dwyer, said afterwards, 'I'm predicting we are going to see John at Forest Hills someday.' There is a particular thrill at watching a young prodigy emerge.

One of the games most etched onto the mind of this writer was witnessed while being part of the 12,000 people who attended the All-Ireland colleges football final at 'the Hyde' in Roscommon in 1976 between the now sadly defunct Carmelite College Moate and St Jarlaths Tuam. It was a remarkable attendance for a colleges' game and I have never forgotten the electric atmosphere.

Carmelite College's prominence in the GAA world turned Aidan O'Halloran into a superstar and in my lifetime only Joe Canning had so many plaudits heaped on him at such a young age. Aidan would go on to transfer from his native county,

Westmeath, to the county he worked in, Offaly – an episode which stirred up a hornets' nest in the deep rivalry between the neighbouring counties. He went on to win an All-Ireland medal with Offaly in 1982.

Fans always answer in the affirmative when their team asks, 'Will you still love me tomorrow?' However, for many GAA fans it is their rivalries that root them, guide them and define them.

The Longford–Westmeath rivalry is innovative, infectious and addictive for both set of fans and is one of the most keenly contested in football, as was apparent in the Leinster championship. An old Longford fan was dying, and when it was obvious that he had very little time left the local priest, a Westmeath man, was sent for. After the priest administered the last rites, he asked the old man if he had any last wish. He was astounded when the man asked if he could join the Westmeath supporters' club. The priest duly pulled out a membership card for the man and helped him to sign his name for the last time. When the priest left, the man's seven stunned sons crowded around the bed and asked their father why he had made this extraordinary request. With practically his dying breath he said, 'Isn't it better for one of them to die than one of our lads?'

For their part, the Westmeath fans have an assured composition of their own. 'The Longford forward line couldn't strike a match.' Even more damningly, swelling with emotion and critical reflection, they add, 'Avoid excitement, watch Longford.'

In the summer of 2019, as 'the Ballymahon Bombshell' Maura Higgins exploded into the national consciousness, one Westmeath fan observed, 'Finally Longford are going to make a big breakthrough. Of course, they'll never win the Leinster title but at least they can win *Love Island*.'

These are just the nice things both sets of fans say about the other.

30

DISPATCHES FROM THE SOUTH

Cork v. Kerry

For those of us of a certain age the defining image of the Cork–Kerry rivalry saw Páidí Ó Sé knocking Dinny Allen onto the seat of his pants in the 1975 Munster final after Allen had thrown the first punch. Then came a moment of classic comedy when the referee, running in to admonish the two bold boys, slipped on the wet ground. To add to the sense of incredulity, neither player was sent off.

A more recent example of the nature of the rivalry, Cork under-20 manager Keith Ricken's verdict on the danger posed by Kerry before the 2019 Munster under-20 final: 'That's as obvious as tits on a bull, as the man says.'

MORAL VICTORIES?

Jimmy Magee paid a nice tribute to Teddy McCarthy, which sums up his place in the pantheon of GAA greats: 'He will always be remembered for his high-fielding. He is a man apart, with an achievement apart [winning All-Irelands with both Cork footballers and hurlers in 1990] in the modern games.'

Like other players featured between the covers of this book, Teddy's collection of football medals is much lower than it could have been because his career coincided with the golden era of Kerry football. How difficult was it for him to keep going when they were losing to Kerry almost every year in the Munster final?

'God, there were times when it was hard. It did get demoralising. However, I would have to say we never went into those Munster finals not thinking that we were going to win. We never had any inferiority complex, even though they beat us well a few times. We always enjoyed those matches. Mick O'Dwyer always hyped us up by saying Cork was the most difficult opposition he expected to meet all year. We always got on well with the Kerry lads. I played with most of them for Munster and I always felt that they gave us plenty of respect. So it was a deep rivalry, but a different type to the one we had with Meath. It was competitive but mutually respectful. We didn't beat them often but when we did it was wonderful to go on and win two All-Irelands.'

Pat Spillane feels the intensity of the rivalry has diminished in recent years but still has a power because of its tradition.

'In the late '80s and early '90s Cork were a real power under Billy Morgan, but when he was succeeded by Larry Thompkins things started to go downhill. Larry is a lovely fella and a gentleman. He was probably the first professional Gaelic footballer – not in the sense that he was getting paid but because he trained morning, noon and night, seven days a week. He devoted his entire life to it. The problem was that even though he captained Cork to an All-Ireland in 1990, people in Cork to this day think of him as a "blow-in", which means he was grudgingly accepted.

'After Larry, Billy Morgan was expected to be the second

coming of the Messiah, but it did not work out that way. Cork's fall from grace had been gathering momentum for some time. There are three main reasons for this. Firstly, the standard of club football in Cork has been poor. Secondly, there are far too many GAA officials in Cork who are so focused on the rule book, pre-occupied with outdated ideologies, and so narrow-minded in their outlook that they have lost sight of the bigger picture. Thirdly, hurling is the number one game in the county and football has to settle for being second best.'

In 2019, two further issues would push the state of Cork football down the agenda – the poor state of the pitch in Páirc Uí Chaoimh and the big cost overrun of the new stadium. One Kerry fan helpfully suggested that Cork needed the services of Bob the Builder.

During Spillane's playing days, things were very different.

'When people think of the great Kerry team of the 1970s and '80s they automatically assume that our greatest rivals were Dublin. However, Cork generally pushed us to the pin of our collar. I gave a talk once at the Jurys sportstar of the year awards in Cork: talk about meeting the enemies. Niall Cahalane was in the audience. He was probably the most difficult player I ever marked. I told the crowd that Niall had such a love of the Kerry jersey that he used to collect bits and pieces of my Kerry jersey by marking me so closely all through the years.

'In my time, Cork and Kerry players always enjoyed an intense but generally good-natured rivalry. To fully understand the rivalry in my playing days, we had to look to Ambrose O'Donovan. His farm in Gneeveguilla straddled the Cork–Kerry border. He is a lovely guy, but when we played Cork it was like he was transformed like Lou Ferrigno into the Incredible Hulk. He had an absolute hatred of losing to Cork. His attitude was if we beat them in the Munster final that would keep them quiet for 12 months. When Kerry lose to Cork in the Munster championship, the Cork fans will stay in Kenmare all night. When Cork lose, they drive straight through Kenmare at 5.30 that evening as fast as they can.'

TOP OF THE POPS

Back in 1979 the Buggles raced to number 1 with the song 'Video Killed the Radio Star'. Spillane sees a parallel for the game he loves so well.

'I think video is killing a generation of sports stars because it is encouraging negativity and focusing on curtailing the opposition from playing their game. I long for the innocent days of Gaelic football when one team beat the other team by scoring more than them. To achieve this I propose as a first step all match video tapes should be destroyed. Instead of worrying about the opposition, coaches should revert to the basic philosophy of sport: trying to score more than the opposition. Unfortunately, it sounds like a pipe dream in this cynical day and age.

'We are even importing the language of rugby into Gaelic games. When I was playing, I never heard anyone talking about "taking hits", but today players speak that language all the time.'

Spillane believes that Kerry's rivalry with Cork did ultimately cloud O'Dwyer's judgement.

'Nowadays players have diet plans and schedules for the gym. In our time, when we won the All-Ireland in September we weren't seen again until March or April. Micko did have a problem with what were termed "the fatties" on the team who put on weight, like John Egan and the Bomber. He would bring them back earlier for extra training. He would always have a few rabbits or hares to set the pace for them. The interesting thing, though, was that there never was a complaint from Egan or Liston.

'Dwyer's final year with Kerry came in 1989 after three successive defeats to Cork in Munster finals. That year he thought he could get one last hurrah out of the team. It is probably the six-million-dollar question for a player or a manager coming to the end of their career: is there one last kick in the team? That year Dwyer felt the only way he could eke out one last title from us was if he had us all really, really fit. He had us training at a little all-weather track in the Kerins O'Rahilly pitch in Tralee. We ran and we ran and we ran. It is one of the rare mistakes he made. Unfortunately, all of our energy was left on the training field and when it came to games we had nothing left in the tank.'

31

WHEN ALL BESIDE A VIGIL KEEP

Sligo v. Galway

Sunt lacrimae rerum.
(There are tears in the nature of things.)
– *The Aeneid,* Virgil

Sligo's most famous son, William Butler Yeats, was preoccupied with the notion of tragedy. For Yeats, life is essentially a struggle with destiny. The real antagonist we all face is fate. We struggle as we get caught in its net. The harder we struggle to get out if it the more we get enmeshed in it. Applying the Yeatsian concept to sport the tragedy is that the best team will not always win because of the fickle hand of fate intervening via a poor referee's decision, the weather or the oppressive weight of history, which turns a talented team into an inhibited one and prevents them from achieving their true potential. Each game is determined by the tiniest psychological edge, by sniggering fate – by the sneer of the GAA gods who determine the rub of the green. Had Yeats been musing in his Sligo home in August 1993 he would surely have had a wonderful case study in tragedy in the sad state of Connacht football following Mayo's tame capitulation to Cork in the All-Ireland football semi-final. The word 'nadir' was coined for a banquet of incompetence like this. To outsiders, Connacht football had become nothing more than a joke. It seemed a miracle of some kind was needed to transform the situation. A little miracle for Sligo football would finally come in 2007.

That year Eamonn O'Hara produced the defining image of the football championship in the Connacht final against Galway. He took a pass from David Kelly 50 yards from the Galway goal. With the defence trailing desperately in his wake, he made over 30 yards before unleashing a rocket of a shot to the roof of the net. A 32-year famine had come to an end for Sligo.

'We said before the game, it is not about heroes today, it's not about a fella getting ten or 12 points on the board or about personal vendettas. It's all about working hard for the Sligo team, putting your neck on the line – fellas did that and it's what it took. We hadn't done that completely in over 30 years.'

O'Hara first played senior football for Sligo in 1993 in a challenge match against Mayo when he was just 17 years of age and found himself marking the vastly experienced John Finn. The next year was to bring the low point of his career.

'I was playing against Mayo in the Connacht championship in midfield and thought that I was doing OK, but I was substituted after 20 minutes. Somebody had to be made a scapegoat and I was the choice. The management probably thought that they were protecting me, but it was a long, lonely walk off the pitch. I learned from it, though, and promised that I would never let myself down again by ever having to be taken off in a match.'

At the time, playing for Sligo had very little glamour.

'We were playing in front of small crowds and in not very

glamorous venues. I suppose the best illustration of it was when we went down to play Kilkenny in a league match. When we got off the bus, there were about eight thousand people there and we thought that was great. What we hadn't realised was that the Kilkenny hurlers were playing first and by the time we ran onto the pitch there were about two people in the stand.'

MOVING ON UP

The arrival of Mickey Moran was a catalyst in the upturn in the county's fortunes.

'We started to do well in the league in '97, '98 and '99. We beat Kerry in the league in '97 in Kerry and we also beat Dublin in Markievicz Park, which was great. We were always capable of creating a shock. The bigger the team, the more we liked it and the better we played.'

For O'Hara, 2000 was a turning point; in fact, for the team as a whole.

'We beat Mayo in the Connacht championship by three points in Markievicz Park. It was a huge relief to finally beat one of the big teams in Connacht. We kind of lost the run of ourselves before playing Galway in the Connacht semi-final, thinking we were about to make a breakthrough. Galway were on fire that day and we failed to get a single score in the first half. Everything they tried, even the most outlandish, came off. Niall Finnegan got a point from such an acute angle that it defied the laws of physics. We lost the game in the end by 18 points. A lot of fingers were pointed at me after the game. I learned a valuable lesson that day. After the game against Mayo, I had been treated like a hero, so I discovered that there's only six inches between a pat on the back and a kick in the ass.'

Criticism is not something that bothers O'Hara unduly, though his intense will to win does not always endear him to some, who confuse it with arrogance. His lack of interest in playing in the Tommy Murphy Cup was not popular with the GAA authorities but reflected his disinterest in being second best.

'People are very quick to judge you. The odd time you might hear people talking about you and saying, "He's a right f**ker." I was not there to entertain people, and I am the way I am. If people don't like me, it doesn't bother me. I kept my head straight through talking with friends and getting away from the hustle and bustle on the family farm.'

O'Hara had the opportunity to showcase his competitive spirit to the nation when he played for Ireland in the Compromise Rules. O'Hara used the whole International Rules experience as a personal research project.

'I was mixing and sharing rooms with players who had won All-Irelands or experienced great success. I saw myself as a messenger who would relay what I learned to the Sligo team. The big players on the Irish team were all winners. In Sligo we went out to play games in hope. These guys went out in expectation. Our mentality was that we were happy with a good performance. This attitude came from the county board, from managers, from the general public and from friends, and it did seep into our consciousness, which led to "Ah well, sure we never expected too much" syndrome. It was because of our attitude that we had never been good enough to win anything. What was different about Sligo in 2007 was that our attitude was no longer about doing well but about winning and doing whatever it took to get a title at last.'

O'Hara plays down the significance of his own goal in the Connacht final.

'If we had taken all the chances we had in the game, my goal would have had no importance. It was not about me, it was about winning the Nestor Cup at last. To beat Mayo or Roscommon was always sweet, but to win a Connacht title by beating Galway was special because we had all watched them winning two All-Irelands a few short years beforehand. Rivalries are good because they bring out the best of teams because the fans are going crazy to get the bragging rights. I think the Galway rivalry in those years was the main one for us. Later on, when Mayo became kings of Connacht, they were the ones we wanted to knock off their perch, but we weren't able to do it.'

32

THE LIMERICK LEADERS v.
THE CLARE CHAMPIONS

Limerick v. Clare

'Snow is falling all around ...'

These lyrics from Shakin' Stevens' classic Christmas song took on a new significance for Clare and Limerick fans in Cusack Park in Ennis in March 2019, as the old rivals warmed up the crowd with a red-blooded league clash. So bad were the conditions that one of the umpires, nicknamed 'Frosty the Snowman' by one fan, fell over on the slippery ground at one point.

Limerick's rivalry with near neighbours Clare can be traced back to the genesis of the GAA itself. However, in the mid-1990s it would go up a few notches. Limerick struck first blood.

Gary Kirby first came to prominence in 1984, winning an All-Ireland minor medal with Limerick and taking his first senior medal with Partickswell. Three years later he helped Limerick to an All-Ireland under-21 title and captained the Irish under-21 shinty team. In 1986 he made his senior debut for Limerick, and in 1991 he won the first of his four All-Stars. In 2009 he was chosen at centre half-forward on the Munster team of the previous 25 years and he ranks among the greatest hurlers never to have won an All-Ireland senior medal. The high point of his hurling career came in the Munster final in 1994. 'My greatest and fondest memory would have to be looking down on the Thurles field, seeing it full with Limerick people waving their green and white, and as captain lifting the Munster Cup after we beat Clare', he says. 'There was a huge sense of excitement because it just meant so much to the fans because hurling means so much to Limerick. Although we had won the match, the significance of the occasion didn't sink in for a while.'

The match added another chapter to Clare's script of hurt. Clare were trounced by Limerick in the Munster final. The scale of the defeat came as no surprise to Ger Loughnane, his face mottling in anger at the memory.

'I knew we were going to be eaten alive that day. On the morning of the game all our players were as unsure and as nervous as could be. I wanted to say something but as a selector I didn't because I didn't want to impose on the manager Len Gaynor's domain. The pace of the training coming up to the Munster final wasn't fast enough. One night I was in the dugout watching the training and was horrified at the pace because everything seemed to be moving in slow motion. I jumped up on the dugout and hit my head off the roof and lifted the galvanise off it. Martin Flanagan, the caretaker in Cusack Park, asked, "What's wrong with you?" I barked back, "Can't you see the f**king training that's going on here. We'll be destroyed in the Munster final." He said, "Ah, take it easy." He often spoke to me about it afterwards. Sure enough Limerick devoured us in the Munster final.'

REWRITING THE SCRIPT

After the defeat, the hurling world in Clare and beyond was largely unmoved when Ger Loughnane took over as Clare manager. Loughnane had an uncanny ability to turn the most unlikely scenario into a motivational ploy.

'Morale was at an all-time low when we took over in September '94. Clare had been hammered in two consecutive Munster finals. Partly to build up morale we went for a weekend to Kerry at the end of the following March just before the real hurling began. We had four training sessions and a match against Kerry and a bit of fun as well. We found a corner in a small pub in Killarney on the Saturday night. Everyone was drinking away and eventually a sing-song started. A night like that is so enlightening because you see another side to people's personalities. Dalo and Fergal Hegarty are brilliant singers. At about one o'clock in the morning I was pressganged into singing a song. They all expected me to sing a silly song but I had just done a song with the kids in school, 'The Band Played Waltzing Matilda'. I'd heard it sung by Ralph McTell and I knew the air of it but it wasn't for the quality of the song I chose it but because of the message I wanted to get across.

'I started the song, and coming to the end I stopped and said, "Now, listen carefully to the next bit. These lines are about ye coming home for the last two years after the Munster final, but it'll never happen again.

And the band played Waltzing Matilda
When they carried us down the gangway.
Nobody cheered.
They just stood there and stared and turned their faces away.

'Then I said, "Do you recognise that situation? That's never going to happen again." You could hear a pin drop. They never forgot it. It had such an effect on them. You could see the goosepimples rising. It happened by fluke, but it was a defining moment for us.'

DALY TASKS

In 1995, the last time Clare had won the Munster final Éamon de Valera had just been elected Taoiseach for the first time (that was back in 1932). During a game, communication is almost impossible on the field because of the noise. Ger Loughnane had to rely on his players for leadership on the field. While his famous speeches and innate media skills might have seemed to be his obvious credentials, Loughnane chose Anthony Daly as captain for his ability in the dressing-room, given his flair to help players cope with frustration and disappointment. 'Dalo' was adept at deflecting any anger by giving his teammates a chance to air their complaints.

Never was Daly's role more clearly illustrated than the Munster final in '95, although he plays down his own importance.

'Everybody in Clare was convinced that we had no chance of winning that game because two weeks before we had played Galway in a challenge match in Shannon and we bombed. On the day of the final we stopped in the hotel in Cashel for a cup of tea. We were on the way into Thurles and just when we came to the bridge the place was crowded with supporters wearing the Limerick colours. A few of them shouted at us, "What a waste of time." They were sure they were going back to the All-Ireland final. Straight away, I said, "We'll show ye whether it's a waste of time or not." Some of the lads afterwards said it made a difference. I'm not so sure.'

However, Ger Loughnane has no such doubts.

'Nobody in Clare thought we would win that game after we lost so badly to Galway. It was on a glorious, sunny day and the previous day had been the very same. When we were inside in the dressing-room I noticed that some of our players were sunburnt and I said, "What the f**k were ye doing? Two weeks before the Munster final and ye come here sunburnt." Clare were disastrous. Most of the crowd that were there went home at half-time, thinking we hadn't a chance in the Munster final. When the team came into the dressing-room I gave them a fierce lambasting. We trained very well after that.

'As everybody got off the bus for the Munster final, there wasn't a word. As the players went out of the dressing-room I said to Pat Fitzgerald, "If Clare don't win today, we're never going to win anything." I was sure we were going to win. Everything was just right. The rest is history, but the incident on the bus showed Daly's sharpness of mind. Top marks to him for picking it up. It set the tone for the match. A small thing like that can make a big difference.'

One memory from his playing days gives Anthony Daly the most contentment.

'It was great going to the schools after we won the All-Ireland in 1995, just to witness the magic, the awe and the wonder, but to me the most special part was meeting the older people. I remember meeting my brother's father-in-law crying in Thurles after we won. He could remember back to '55 and the catalogue of Clare's heartbreaks. At the time I was so wound up and drained from games that I didn't fully appreciate it till later.'

Jamesie O'Connor came to that realisation earlier.

'People were in euphoria after we won the Munster final. Sixty-three years is a long wait. People couldn't believe it actually was happening. I remember towards the end of the game, as people started climbing in towards the pitch, thinking, "Jesus, get off the pitch or he'll abandon it!" I thought some catastrophe was in store for us.

'With that win, a massive weight was lifted off the county. Clare people had travelled to so many Munster finals – minor, under-21 and senior – and always came home with their tails between their legs. I had the cup the next week and I brought it to Don Ryan, who lived just around the corner from my parents' shop in Ennis, who was a diehard Clare fan. He had been the first fan to every match for years and years. I said that he might like to take a look. He just broke down in tears and I said, "I will call back later." That's what it meant to the guy.'

NOT GREAT EXPECTATIONS

In the '95 Munster final Loughnane felt himself quiver with the excitement of a hound on the scent of a fox. Even when one major disappointment followed another, hope and dreams always lived side by side in Clare. In '95 Loughnane's team was poised to react hungrily to a disappointing first half of the year.

'I think that after the league final in 1995, 90 per cent of Clare followers felt *That is it, we can't take any more trouncings.* You couldn't blame them. Although we hadn't been trounced on the scoreboard, in hurling terms we were. Coming out after the game, one supporter said, "Kilkenny were a different class." This massacre came on the back of major defeats in the two previous years. When I spoke about us winning the Munster final, none of the fans believed me.

'Before the team went out on the pitch I did something I never did before. I held up a Clare jersey before the players. I reminded them of all the disappointments of those who had worn the Clare jersey down the years and all the heartbreak the Clare fans had experienced, but that would be cast away by five o'clock that evening.

'We were out on the pitch first, but when Limerick came onto the pitch you could feel the whole place shaking. It was as loud a cheer as I ever heard. I was standing at the end of the tunnel and as Limerick's Steve McDonagh was coming out something inside me said, "Will I flatten him?" It would have been an absolutely crazy thing to do. I wanted something to show them that although they had all the noise from the supporters, by God we were going to take them on that day.'

In his distinctive soft-spoken manner, Seánie McMahon plays down all talk of his greatness, but when prompted reflects on his day of days.

'Personally the memory that will stand out was when we won the first Munster final in 1995. I never dreamt of All-Irelands, just the Munster final, and I remember when we won I just went down on my knees and said, "Thank you, God." It was such a relief. There were lots of tears shed – but for once Clare people were crying tears of joy. It brought a huge uplifting for Clare people.'

For Loughnane, the best-laid plans finally came to fruition.

'We started off at a lightning pace. At half-time we knew the chance was there. That gave the players confidence as well. In the second half we took over completely, but there was always the fear that something would happen because something had always happened before. Even with five minutes to go we were still afraid that we'd be hit by a thunderbolt from the sky.

'When the final whistle blew it was such a relief. The hoodoo had been broken. It had nothing to do with beating Limerick. We were incredulous. It only really struck home when Dalo said in his victory speech "We'll go to Croke Park in our thousands." I thought, "Jesus, we're going to Croke Park." This was fantasy stuff. We had talked a lot about winning the Munster final, but when it happened we couldn't actually believe it. Even when we saw the cup we were wondering if we were dreaming and would it be gone when we woke up in the morning. There wasn't a huge sense of excitement because we just weren't prepared for it. Although we had won the match, the significance of the occasion hadn't sunk in.'

SHANNONSIDERS STRIKE BACK

In 1996 the tide would swing back in Limerick's favour. In that year their main priority was to win the All-Ireland. Clare had to be dethroned for that to happen. The wounds of Limerick's defeat by Clare the previous year had not healed, but as Gary Kirby recalls the defeat to Offaly had certainly not healed either.

'The 1994 All-Ireland hurling final was one of the most dramatic matches in the history of the game. Limerick outplayed Offaly throughout the match and with just minutes remaining had an apparently unassailable five-points lead. Then Offaly's Johnny Dooley scored a goal from a free. Within a minute, Pat O'Connor had a second goal. Limerick floundered, while Offaly players suddenly looked as if they could score points at will.'

Kirby had won a National League medal in 1992, when Limerick made a dramatic comeback against Tipperary to snatch a one-point victory in injury time. What was it like to be on the opposite end of the experience?

'It's a feeling I wouldn't wish on anyone. With seven minutes to go, I felt I would be going up to be presented with the Liam McCarthy Cup. Then, all of a sudden, it was gone. Something happened in the last five minutes. You can't analyse it. It was a huge disappointment.'

Two years later, Limerick again won the Munster final after snatching victory from All-Ireland champions Clare in the final minutes of the semi-final. Limerick went all the way to the All-Ireland final again that year, but it was to be Liam Griffin's Wexford that claimed the title.

The match itself was a personal disappointment for Kirby.

'I got a broken finger in the first five minutes. I remember going over towards the Cusack Stand to take a free from near midfield. I was trying to stop the bleeding before I took it, but as I took the free I felt a searing pain go up my hand.'

Kirby, though, did take a crumb of comfort from beating Clare that year.

'Let's just say it was sweet to beat them because of what they had done the year before and because they had done what we had failed to do and won the All-Ireland. Our fans enjoyed beating Clare in 1996.'

A HUMBLING EXPERIENCE
Though Loughnane's motivational qualities were undoubtedly extraordinary, there was never a likelihood that he could indefinitely rescue his team from the consequences of their deficiencies. In '96 he could not save his team from a blunted appetite. Clare would once again re-acquaint themselves with the emotional turmoil that passes for a losing team's thinking processes.

'For any team who wins an All-Ireland, the following year is always a very difficult challenge. To get back into the same physical shape is hard enough, but the real problem is to get back the same mental shape. To get the same hunger back was impossible, especially in Clare, where the celebrations were extended and everybody was feeling so satisfied. You can be starving for ages, but then you get a big meal and you forget what it was like to be starving. I would say the same hunger wasn't there.

'I knew things weren't right. Six or seven weeks before we played Limerick we played Laois in a challenge match and struggled to beat them. We probably trained as many times in the period January to June as we had the previous year, but all of us weren't pushing ourselves the same way. The glow of the previous year was dazzling us. We were still in the comfort zone from winning the All-Ireland final and we didn't have that same fight. In the Munster championship, Clare pulled three points clear; five minutes from the finish it looked as if we might triumph again, but Limerick came with a late surge to get four points in an amazing finale.

'That game was one of the great days. I went to Limerick that morning, around about eleven o'clock, to have a look at the pitch, just as the hawkers were setting up their stands. It was a lovely sunny morning and even though there were only about 100 people there you could feel the atmosphere. You just felt this was going to be something else. When we came in later, there was just a river of people in white shirts and in the Clare and Limerick colours, in a kind of shimmer of heat.

'In Limerick the crowd is right in by the sideline, so there was a brilliant atmosphere. The game was very even throughout. It was tough and hard, but there was no rancour. With about six or seven minutes to go, we seemed to lose all our energy. That was epitomised by Liam Doyle. Barry Foley came on as a sub and scored two points off him. At one stage Liam had the ball in his hand but let it fall and Foley popped it over the bar.

'Near the end, when we were two points up, I met a Limerick selector, Liam Lenihan, and he said, "Jesus, if we beat ye it will be total robbery." I said, "Ye are going to beat us." I just felt that the tide had totally turned against us. Then they got level and Ciarán Carey scored the point that is now gone into folklore. It was the sort of wonderful score that deserved to win a game. It was a brilliant day and that match will always stand out as one of the great hurling clashes for me.'

Loughnane's unflinching ambition would nullify that reverse, but as he lights the lamp of memory and looks back on the game with affection, there was a post-match incident which left a slightly bitter taste. It was only afterwards that he saw that the rivalry between both counties was more intense than he had appreciated.

'I went into the Limerick dressing-room afterwards to sincerely congratulate the team on their victory. It had been a terrific occasion and a wonderful game and even though we were beaten I felt enlivened.

'It wasn't the usual atmosphere after a team wins the Munster semi-final. I didn't get the warmest reception. They were talking about bones having to be picked out there that day – whatever that meant. They seemed to have the attitude that the record had been set straight after '95. I had a totally different attitude going out of the Limerick dressing-room to that coming into it. My own mind was firmly set that we would really set the record straight the next year.

'When I got back into the Clare dressing-room all the top GAA journalists were there from the main newspapers, standing around waiting for something dramatic. Although nothing was said there was a feeling there that this was the end of the road for the Clare team, which seemed to reflect what the journalists were thinking: we were a flash in the pan and came for a year and now we were gone. They were just waiting for the epitaph.

'Unusually for him, Dalo got sucked into the atmosphere that these journalists had created by their presence. He said that he had the time of his life and if he never did anything else in his career he would cherish the experience and he thanked everyone. It was up to me to respond. I said we would have a meeting the following week to discuss what happened that day. It was a total anti-climax for the journalists, but I wasn't going to show my hand in front of them.

'The following week we had a meeting in the Clare Inn. I told the players to enjoy the summer and not to resent who won the championship because we would get our chance again the following year. After what happened in the Limerick dressing-room I was determined we would come back again. The players had picked up the vibes from the Limerick team and wanted to get revenge. Ideally in '97 we would have beaten Limerick, Cork, Kilkenny and Tipperary, but maybe it was better to beat Tipperary twice than Limerick once!

'I went to the All-Ireland final that September. In normal circumstances I would have been passionately shouting for Limerick, but when the final whistle went I, and at least three Clare players, instinctively jumped up with joy. It wasn't because we had a great love for Wexford! It was just a reaction to the atmosphere in the Limerick dressing-room after the Munster semi-final.'

Although he would not get the chance to cross swords with Limerick in 1997, nonetheless, as only he could, Loughnane somehow managed to fan the flames still further between the two counties.

HARSH WORDS

As he grew into the job, probing the Clare manager was at times like trying to trespass behind forbidden gates. Yet when he wanted to, Loughnane left no room for ambiguity. After the 1997 All-Ireland final he clashed publicly with Limerick legend Eamonn Cregan on *The Sunday Game*. In May 2019, when Anthony Daly was asked to select his highlight of 40 years of *The Sunday Game*, he chose Loughnane's response that night.

Following Cregan's analysis Loughnane began his response with the comment, 'After that ten-minute whinge from Eamonn Cregan.' He then launched into an attack on Cregan. Given the intensity of Loughnane's comments, it seemed to outside observers that there must have been some history between them.

'I played with and against him. I always thought he was a fantastic player. He was so competitive. He had a poisonous will to win, which so few players have, to go with the great skill he had.

'That was why it was such a disappointment when he came to train the Clare team in 1983. He'd have known the top three or four players, but he never made a great effort to get to know the rest. He had no plan in training or matches. There was nothing you could say he did that brought on Clare hurling. Worst of all was that after a while the players started to treat him as a joke. He had a rule whereby training started at seven and if you were one minute late you did one lap of the field, if you were two minutes late you did two laps and so on. There was one player in particular, Declan Coote, a very talented individual who could have been a really great player if he was handled properly but he never achieved his potential. He'd come to training at a quarter to seven and would stay deliberately in the dressing-room until a quarter past seven and then he'd come on the pitch and say, "Eamonn 10, 15 or 20?" He'd start off his 15 laps of the pitch at near walking pace and by the time he was finished the training session was nearly over. Everybody saw that system was stupid, except Cregan.

'There was one specific incident where I lost all respect for him as a coach. We got to a league final against Limerick and were getting hammered at half-time. Everybody was crying out for some instruction as to what was going wrong and what we could do to turn things around. All he did was go ballistic and launch into a tirade which went way over everybody's head about how bad we were. There was no diagnosis of our problems nor prescription – which is what I think good coaching is all about in that situation. You were just looking at him and thinking, "Would you ever shut up?"

'Never once during a game did he ever give a direction that would change the way a match was going. He never showed any of the characteristics of a good coach in Clare. Maybe he showed them somewhere else. I'd no regard for him as a coach. I'd have way more regard for Justin McCarthy. I'd have a thousand times more regard for Len Gaynor. He was exactly the wrong one to come on and criticise Clare, considering he had no success here. There is always a suspicion that if you do not have success somewhere and somebody else comes on and has success there, you may have a chip on your shoulder.'

Indeed, in more recent years Galway fans would hurl that accusation back at Loughnane. In 1997, though, there was no holding back the Clare manager.

'I was inside in the hotel that night listening to Cregan and I was thinking back to that day in Thurles and those training sessions in Cusack Park, and here was the same man criticising Clare after they beat Tipperary in an All-Ireland final. Who would ever have thought that possible when he was in charge? I was standing beside Ger Canning, who is a really smart guy, and he sensed that the crowd was aghast. He looked me straight in the eye and said, "That's terrible, isn't it?" I replied, "Pay no heed. That's only Cregan." I knew we were going live on air in a few minutes and I waited till we did and then I let fly!'

To some people without the same emotional entanglement in the issue, Loughnane ought not to have launched such an attack in such a forum. Does he have any regrets about it?

'If I have a regret it is that I didn't go further. I think it was totally small-minded of him. What he said didn't seem to me to be a fair judgement of the game. It was never going to be a 2-24 to 1-25 game. Given the two teams involved, you were always going to get a tense, bruising encounter. If you want an open match, go to a league game.

'We had a function at the end of the year. As part of the ceremony segment they showed five minutes of highlights of the final. At the end, when the speeches were over, they left on the last 20 minutes. I was talking to Marty Morrissey and after a while I noticed there was nobody else talking. Everyone was sitting down, glued to their seats, watching the end of the match. It just showed how tense the game was. Yet Cregan could find nothing good about it. A few years later I really felt I should have torn into him much more strongly that night.'

33

NO LOVE LOST

Carlow v. Laois

For many fans, true happiness is an occasional summer lightning thing.

No sociologist can ignore the power of Gaelic games in Ireland to harness the communal values of loyalty, self-discipline and sacrifice, and all for the glory of the parish and the county. They epitomise the importance of respect for place – including where a team stands with its rivals – memorably captured in Anthony Daly, the captain of the Clare hurling team, and his victory speech in 1997 when the Banner County emerged from decades in the wilderness to claim their second Munster title: 'We are no longer the Whipping Boys of Munster.'

In the great scheme of things Gaelic games may seem a peripheral pursuit. But to those within the games they are the great scheme of things, a world strangely obsessed with trying to make one team score more than another. At its core the GAA is about identity. It is part of who we are. Fr. Harry Bohan captures this so economically and so evocatively: 'That's what we had, Mass and the match.'

Each year fuels a new chapter in the GAA rivalries. Carlow were one of the stories of the 2018 Gaelic football championship. Such was their progress that they were chasing their first Leinster semi-final win since 1994 when they played Laois. After scoring from every shot against Kildare, they were less clinical against Laois and Turlough O'Brien's defensive counter-attacking strategy was not enough for Carlow on this occasion. Having met twice in the league earlier in the year, the rivalry between the counties was fermenting nicely.

A few weeks after the Leinster semi-final a Carlow fan was driving home from a night in the pub. He was pulled in by a guard. The guard said, 'I'm going to have to get you to blow into the bag.'

The driver pulled out a card from his pocket which read, 'Asthmatic. Don't take breath samples.'

The garda said, 'I'm going to have to take a sample of your blood.'

He took out a card from his pocket, 'Haemophiliac. Don't take blood samples.'

The garda said, 'I'm going to have to take a urine sample.'

The motorist took out another card from his pocket. This one read, 'Member of Carlow supporters' club. Don't take the p**s.'

Needless to say, this story was told by a Laois fan. In retaliation Carlow fans, hard-edged and quietly condemning, tell the story of when Laois went crashing out of the championship a few weeks later and the then Laois manager John Sugrue rang Jim Gavin and asked, 'What's the recipe for winning an All-Ireland final?' Gavin told him, 'You get the following drill: get loads of cones, placing them carefully around the field, loads of balls, have the players soloing around the cones, doing one-twos, side-steps, swerves and kicking the ball over the bar.'

After a few weeks, Gavin was surprised that Sugrue hadn't rung him to thank him for his brilliant advice, so he rang him and asked him how well they'd got on.

'Not great,' Sugrue replied. 'The cones beat us by six points.'

34

KILDARE KINGPINS

Kildare v. Dublin

In recent years uncertainty, like a clenched fist, pummelled Kildare fans. The cause? Dublin.

In the 2015 Leinster semi-final Dublin put Kildare to the sword with Bernard Brogan and Diarmuid Connolly scoring 4-06 between them, as Dublin won 5-18 to 0-14. Four years earlier at the same stage of the competition it took a late free from Brogan, after a controversial decision by referee Cormac Reilly, to secure a victory for the Dubs by the narrowest of margins. In the 2009 Leinster final Brogan scored 0-07 from play and Jason Sherlock and Barry Cahill chipped in goals to give the Dubs a 2-15 to 0-18 victory in an evenly matched contest over their neighbours. Mick O'Dwyer's two terms as Kildare manager had raised the rivalry to a new level, as he led the county from the exile of hurt to the joy of belonging.

THE EARLEY YEARS
In the early 1990s O'Dwyer turned the Kildare team into big box office and led them to a Leinster final in 1992, where they

really put it up to Dublin until a brilliant goal from the pride of Finglas, Keith Barr, secured a 1-13 to 0-10 victory for the Dubs. O'Dwyer would have to wait for his second incarnation as Kildare manager to exact revenge, but when he did it would be sweet for Kildare – although it would bring unexpected grief to one of his former Kerry stars.

When I asked the late Dermot Earley which of his son's games for the Lilywhites he had most enjoyed, he immediately went for Saturday, 12 August 2000.

'It was the Leinster final replay. The Dubs were on fire in the first half and led by 0-11 to 0-5. Pat Spillane was writing Kildare's obituary. But 90 seconds into the second half Dermot got a goal back and then Tadhg Fennin got an equalising goal. The pendulum swung completely in Kildare's direction and Willie McCreery was mighty in midfield. Any Kildare fan who was there that day will never forget it. Kildare ran out comfortable winners by 2-11 to 0-12. It was a great day for the Lilywhites and another proud moment for a Dad of one of the players. It was like a moment of grace, but a moment of grace that is granted only rarely.'

UNFORGETTABLE
This was a match that Pat Spillane will never be able to erase from his memory.

'There was the only time I had reservations about Mick O'Dwyer's methods. I remember meeting him after Kildare's second drawn game in the epic trilogy with Meath in 1997. As usual the Kildare forwards had been generally kicking the ball everywhere but between the posts. He told me that he had brought the Kildare team in for extra training that night and that Pat McCarthy had them down to the Curragh and that he was going to "run the sh*t* out of them". I thought to myself that they should be doing the extra training somewhere with goalposts and loads of footballs and they should be practising getting the ball between the posts.'

O'Dwyer brought the glory days back to Kildare, taking them to a Leinster title after a 42-year-gap. The 2000 Leinster final is seared in Spillane's memory.

'One of the games I got into most serious trouble for as an analyst came in 2000. It was the day of the Leinster senior football replay. Dublin led by 0-11 to 0-5 at half-time and had swept aside the Kildare challenge in the second quarter, scoring seven points without reply, playing some thrilling football. Kildare brought on two subs at half time, two of their "imports", Karl O'Dwyer and Brian Murphy. I was in jocose mood and said Karl couldn't get on the Kerry team and Brian wouldn't have got on the Cork junior team. Within 90 seconds of the re-start the picture had changed dramatically, as Kildare got a two-goal blitz and Dublin collapsed and only scored a single point in the second half. Yet again I was left looking silly and fully expected to eat humble pie, but there was much more in store.

'All hell broke loose. To my mind, it was completely over the top. I was making just a few tongue-in-cheek observations, as is my wont, and had not intended to be taken too seriously, but it seemed to be the end of the world to people in Kildare. There was a huge sign outside Monasterevin to the effect that Spillane was a goat. I was driving through Kildare for the next few weeks on wet Monday mornings with sunglasses in case anyone recognised me. It was just ridiculous.

'The most sinister reaction was apparent when I was shown a letter in RTÉ from one of the most influential GAA officials in Kildare demanding that an apology would be issued and that I would be dropped as an analyst by RTÉ otherwise he would ensure that the GAA would not renew their contract with RTÉ.

As the contract negotiations for the right to the GAA games were imminent the powers that be in RTÉ were genuinely very worried about this threat.

'You have to hand it to Mick O'Dwyer. He brought Kildare to life. You might not describe them as a sleeping giant, but they were a sleeping something and he woke them up. While he was in charge, he made the Dublin–Kildare rivalry big box office and brought great joy to Kildare fans and brought great enjoyment to neutrals. Those Kildare v. Dublin games had a show-business quality about them and that rivalry was wonderful for the GAA and the television audience.'

35

FERMANAGH'S FOES

Club Rivalry in Fermanagh

It was a tableau of agony.

Fermanagh people have specialised for a long time in applying balms to wounded spirits. In the past, not even the eating and drinking establishments around Enniskillen had made more bearable the pain of real body blows like the disappointing defeat in the 2014 Ulster championship to Antrim – losses in Ulster as regular as the leaves falling and scattering in the breeze in autumn. Of course, there were reasons for that defeat. But failure that day was no less painful a memory for being readily explained, especially in a county where thrilling images were less frequent than bleak recollections for fans wearing world-weary smiles.

As part of their quest to finally drink from the keg of glory they have brought in some high-profile managers from outside the county to help them finally cross the Rubicon. Pat Spillane poses an intriguing question.

'Do you have to win an All-Ireland to be a top manager? If that is not the case there are a number of contenders in that category. First up is John Maughan, famous for always wearing his shorts on the sideline. There is a general rule of thumb that I believe carries a fair amount of weight that teachers, priests, army men and guards do not in the long run make great managers because they are used to getting their own way; are disciplinarians; like the sound of their own voice and are not the greatest of communicators. I was a teacher myself and I know I would not make it as a manager for those reasons. Maughan did an excellent job with Clare to win a famous Munster title in 1992 and a good job with Mayo.

'He made his mark as a manager, as an army man, by being a strict disciplinarian and a fitness fanatic, and that is not criticising those two qualities, but the problem with getting teams so fit and disciplined is that they can only get you so far. They will get you over many fences but not the final ones. It is interesting that he failed at the second last hurdle with Clare and at the last hurdle in the case of Mayo.

'His man-management skills were not the best. They were shown up badly when he managed Fermanagh – which was an unmitigated disaster.'

Maughan's tenure disappeared like morning fog touched by the warmth of the sun. He concedes his reputation was a factor in Fermanagh.

'I have a name for being a disciplinarian and there was a concerted effort on the part of a few players to get rid of me. A meeting was called and I agreed to stay on for another year, but on the journey home I changed my mind because I knew things were not right and stepped down.'

The Erne County is not the most hospitable environment for the GAA. One fan joked, 'Half the county is made up of water and the other half is made up of Protestants!'

PETER'S GREATNESS

One vignette which illustrates the character of Peter McGinnity, the man and the footballer, comes from a Railway Cup semi-final against Connacht in Ballybay with the kind of wind that seemed to peel the flesh off your bones and come back for the marrow. The gale blew from one goal to the other, so that one team had a distinct advantage. Connacht won the toss and elected to play with the wind and led by 2-12 to 0-2 at half-time. In the second half McGinnity took control of the game and scored two goals and orchestrated a gallant Ulster fightback. Connacht managed only one point in the second half but that was their winning margin at the end.

In 1988 McGinnity played his last senior game for Fermanagh after a 19-year career with the county which began when he was 17. He won four Railway Cup medals. In 1982 he became the first Fermanagh player to win an All-Star, being selected at right half-forward. He jokes, 'I'm not a great man for individual awards but I dare anybody try and take it from me!'

While the focus of this book is on intercounty rivalries Peter gives a snapshot of club rivalries in Fermanagh, which are illustrative of the intensity of rivalries in club football throughout the country.

'No matter how high you go, there is something special about playing for your own parish or village, the people you grew up with, the true fans whose life is football, and the kick you get out of achieving something with your parish – that's the heart of the GAA.

'I was playing for my club, Roslea Shamrocks, and marking Paddy Reilly from Teemore Shamrocks. Paddy's brother Barney and I played for Fermanagh under-21s. We came up the ranks together and I always had great time for him. In one club match the ball went up between Paddy and myself and a kind of ruck developed. I snatched the ball as Paddy came charging in to give Barney some "assistance". Happily for me, but not for Paddy, in the melee and confusion Barney struck his own brother instead of me. It still sticks in my memory, as I was heading up the field with the ball before Barney started chasing me, saying "Sorry, Paddy" as his brother lay stretched out on the ground!'

36

BLACK CATS AND YELLOW BELLIES

Kilkenny v. Wexford

As only he can, Liam Griffin captures the essence of the Kilkenny–Wexford rivalry. 'It is bullfighting by a different standard.'

Wexford academic Professor Kevin Whelan captures the intensity of the feeling between the counties. He shares the anecdote that when a Wexford fan sees a car in front of them with a Kilkenny registration their immediate instinct is to overtake them – even if there is a dangerous bend ahead.

After he retired from playing, Martin Quigley immediately took charge of piloting Wexford's fortunes. Quigley was replaced as Wexford manager by Christy Keogh. Among Keogh's innovations was to enlist the services of Cyril Farrell to assist the team in their preparations for the Leinster championship, particularly the clash with old rivals Kilkenny. The move did not have the desired impact, as Kilkenny inflicted a heavy defeat on the Slaneysiders. How does Quigley react to the criticism that was aired at the time that instead of rallying Wexford Farrell's mere presence inspired Kilkenny?

'I wouldn't pay any heed to that sort of talk. Anyone who

thinks that Kilkenny need Cyril Farrell's involvement to be fully motivated to beat Wexford in the championship knows nothing about hurling – and Wexford's great rivalry with Kilkenny hurling in particular. Kilkenny had a strong team and beat us badly. I don't think it would have made much difference who was managing us that particular year. The one thing that Cyril's involvement did achieve was to dramatically heighten the expectations within the county. Not for the first time, though, they were to be cruelly dashed.'

A TONY AWARD

Tony Doran played for Wexford from 1967 to 1984, winning an All-Ireland with the county in 1968. One of his biggest admirers was the late Mick Dunne, former Gaelic games correspondent with RTÉ.

'Although Tony had the good fortune to win an All-Ireland early on in his career, he and that Wexford team were unlucky in many ways. Having said that, they beat old rivals Kilkenny in a Leinster final by 17 points in the 1970s and that made up for a lot of disappointments. Wexford played well in the 1976 All-Ireland final but they lost to Cork by four points.

'The problem for great players like Tony Doran was that it was so difficult for them to be seen in Croke Park on All-Ireland final day because every year they had to face the most formidable opposition of all in the Leinster championship: Kilkenny, who have to be seen as the aristocrats of hurling. True to form after "loaning" their Leinster crown to Wexford for two years, as they would have seen it, Kilkenny were back in '78 and went on to win the All-Ireland in 1979 against an emerging Galway side.

'I know Tony would feel that the All-Ireland that really got away from Wexford was in 1974, even though they lost to Kilkenny at the Leinster final stage. Wexford were going toe to toe with them but had to play the entire second half with only 14 players after Phil Wilson was sent off. Yet true to form Wexford hurled out of their skins and it took Eddie Keher to characteristically win it for Kilkenny by a point with the last puck of the game. What made the defeat so galling was that Kilkenny beat Galway and Limerick very comprehensively in the All-Ireland semi-final and All-Ireland final respectively.

'Unlike today there was no second chance for teams like Wexford because there was no backdoor system then. Also, back then the only games people saw live on television were the All-Ireland semi-finals and finals, which meant that the national audience were deprived of the opportunity to see the wonderful players Wexford had, like the Quigley brothers and Doran.'

Eddie Keher captures the mutual respect that traditionally underlines the Wexford–Kilkenny rivalry when he generously acknowledges the contribution of Doran.

'Tony was one of the greats of the game. He really announced his arrival on the national stage when he scored two great goals in the 1968 All-Ireland final. The fact that they beat Tipperary, who had defeated Wexford in 1965, added to the sense of occasion. Yet it says so much for Tony that he saw the highlight of his career as when he won the 1989 All-Ireland club championship with Buffers Alley at the tender age of 42, when they beat a gallant O'Donovan Rossa from Belfast in the final. It shows that the pride of the parish is everything and that is why the GAA is so special.'

A MISUNDERSTANDING

Late afternoon sunlight suddenly shone into the sitting room and illuminated a long bar of green carpet, as Mick Dunne was anxious to correct the record for me about an occasion when Keher attracted the ire of Wexford fans.

'For a perfectionist like Keher routine is everything. You have to get the little things right. A famous incident occurred in the 1974 Leinster hurling final with the sides tied. With seconds to go Kilkenny's legendary corner-forward had an opponent tread on his foot and his lace was broken. Almost immediately Kilkenny were awarded a free. As a meticulous player Keher knew he wouldn't be able to score with the lace not attended to, so he bent down and tied it. The Wexford fans thought he was engaged in gamesmanship, running up the clock, and let him know with a chorus of booing, but Keher kept his concentration and slotted the sliotar between the posts to win the match.'

DAVY'S DERBY

After Wexford came back from eight points down to beat their old rivals in the league in March 2019 Davy Fitzgerald showed the rivalry still runs deep.

'OK, we beat Kilkenny by seven points today. What way do you think [Brian Cody] is going to be next door? He's going to be chomping at the bit to go for it in June. He's going to be absolutely coming with everything. I'm really excited by that prospect. Being a hurling manager involved with a team like Wexford, you want Kilkenny coming at you 110 per cent. Listen, the Leinster championship against Kilkenny will be special.'

It was.

Micheál Ó Muircheartaigh claims that there are two Christmas Days every year: one is on 25 December, and the second is the day of the Munster hurling final. In 2019 Christmas came early for Limerick when they won the Munster final. That same day, though, Wexford were enjoying a 'cool Yule' when they beat their bitter rivals Kilkenny to win their first Leinster title in 15 years. A Wexford fan did his own play on Marty Morrissey's famous quote: 'There won't be a strawberry picked in Wexford this week.'

37

AN ACT OF TREASON

Roscommon v. Mayo

We age as the rest of the world watches, but we are always the last to know. In the 1970s when I was a boy I saw the great Kerry–Dublin rivalry unfold. In the 1980s a fierce rivalry emerged between Galway and Tipperary. Over an epic series of four games the Meath–Dublin rivalry reached its zenith in 1991. In the noughties, there was a thrilling new chapter in the age-old rivalry between Kilkenny and Cork, as the nation watched a new and ferocious rivalry emerge between Tyrone and Armagh. Indeed, in the late '70s and early '80s I was very engaged by a rivalry that developed between Armagh and my beloved Roscommon.

For Cardinal Newman 'to be perfect was to have changed often'. The logic of institutions is that to live well is not to change at all. Yet the GAA is, like buttermilk, not quite what it used to be. Irish society is changing rapidly and the GAA is struggling to keep up in many areas. Many of its rivalries, though, remain refreshingly constant.

The 2012 Connacht club final had a unique pairing when two

Roscommon teams, St Brigid's and Ballaghaderreen, contested. For historical reasons Ballaghaderreen take part in the Mayo championship.

Dermot Flanagan is all too keenly aware of this. His early years were spent on the Mayo side of Ballaghaderreen. 'So split is the town between Roscommon and Mayo that I joke that even the marital bed could come under pressure when the two counties meet in the Connacht championship.'

Roscommon fans have not always appreciated this fact when Ballaghaderreen players go on to play for Mayo, despite the fact that they were born in Roscommon. The 2011 Connacht final saw both counties contest a tight affair, played in almost Artic conditions in the Hyde. In John Mullane parlance, it was 'a day you wouldn't even throw out a milk bottle'. Whenever Mayo's All-Star forward, the Ballaghaderreen-born Andy Moran, touched the ball a lone Roscommon fan, so thin that his shoulders looked like a coat hanger, approaching the shores of middle age, who had a way of presenting all his opinions as well-established facts, full of certainties that had a sinuous power, was heard to boom out, 'Traitor, Traitor, Traitor!' He was clearly uneasy, with the type of sensation that swept over him just before an electric storm broke and lightning ripped through the sky. His fears were justified as Mayo won.

DAVID BRADY GETS IT WRONG

In 2019, Mayo began the championship with renewed confidence, fresh from their National League win and because James Horan was back as manager. First up in their Castlebar home were old rivals Roscommon. David Brady confidently predicted a 12-point victory for Mayo. Then came one of those moments that can derange the emotional life, when the Rossies ambushed them, as they did in 1986. The misery enveloping the county afterwards was palpable. Joe Brolly described it as 'the disaster of disasters'. He went on to describe them as 'the nation's favourite tragic comedy unfolding again' and that it was 'more enthralling watching them losing than watching any other county winning'.

38

EVERYBODY NEEDS GOOD NEIGHBOURS

Cavan v. Monaghan

In the world of Gaelic games every day may not be good but there is something good in every day.

Monaghan 'enjoy' a great rivalry on the football field with Cavan and their fans are never slow to invoke the stereotypical image of Cavan people revealed in stories like the Cavan footballer who gave his wife lipstick for Christmas every year so that at least he could get half of it back.

One story they tell in this context is about the Pope. He had a very, very unusual blood type. The doctors could only find one person in the whole world who had the same blood type, Paddy O'Reilly, the Cavan footballer. So Paddy donated a pint of blood and the Pope recovered. As a gesture of goodwill the Pope sent Paddy on £20,000. The Pope got ill four times in successive years after that and each time he got a pint of Paddy's blood and each time he sent Paddy £20,000. The sixth time he got Paddy's blood the Pope sent him only a holy medal. Paddy was devastated and rang the Vatican to ask why he'd got no money this time. The Pope's secretary took the call and answered, 'Well, Paddy, you have to understand he has a lot of Cavan blood in him at this stage!'

That may be why Monaghan fans say that when the Cavan football team went on a short holiday the hotel they stayed at put their Gideon Bibles on chains.

For their part Cavan fans counter with this story.

A young boy's parents were being divorced. The judge asked him, 'Would you like to live with your father?'

'No, he beats me.'

'So, you would like to live with your mother?'

'No, she beats me.'

'Well, who would you like to live with?'

'The Monaghan football team – they can beat nobody!'

PURE POETRY

It is among the oldest rivalries in Ulster football, and perhaps the bitterest. To paraphrase Monaghan's greatest poet, Patrick Kavanagh, Cavan have tended to weave a snare that Monaghan might rue. There is mutual reciprocity when it comes to that sentiment.

Those in the know suggest that the origins of the animosity can be traced back to Cavan's narrow win in the 1915 Ulster final. Eoin O'Duffy was the godfather of football in the Farney county, and he did not take the defeat well. He was an IRA commander during the War of Independence and became the first commissioner of An Garda Síochána, but is probably most remembered as the founder of the right-wing Blueshirt movement and he fought on General Franco's side in the Spanish Civil War. At an Ulster council meeting following that 1915 defeat, O'Duffy complained of crowd encroachments, a disallowed goal and requested or demanded, depending on which version of events is to be believed, that the match be replayed. Decisions are taken by those in the room and, as there was nobody from Cavan present, a replay was ordered. Cavan appealed to Central council, won the appeal and kept their title.

A defeat to Monaghan in 1917 led to Cavan appealing because their bitter rivals had been 'late fielding'. They got nowhere, but star of the 1947 team John Wilson told the story that Cavan had grown so fed up of Monaghan that they proposed setting up a fifth province – to be known as Tara – where they would compete against Meath, Westmeath, Louth and Longford. They were denied the opportunity by, in their eyes, 'short-sighted GAA administrators'.

Patrick Kavanagh regaled Charlie Haughey once about how Cavan and Monaghan met in the 1930s. Cavan were winning so handily at half-time that the team sat down on the pitch at the break, smoking cigarettes. Their full-back took things to a whole new level, stretching out for a siesta. The Monaghan players were a tad annoyed and felt badly disrespected. Charlie Haughey suggested that they should have rubbed it in by smoking cigars and drinking champagne and eating strawberries.

'Why would they need strawberries?' asked a puzzled Kavanagh.

From his throne of authority Charlie rolled his eyes in frustration before growling, 'Everybody knows strawberries add flavour to champagne.' (Richard Gere makes the same claim in *Pretty Woman*.) When he told me that story, Charlie nodded his head vigorously, in full agreement with himself.

DRIVEN TO DISTRACTION

The last word goes to Monaghan's Nudie Hughes. He spoke to me about playing against the Breffini men in the Ulster final in 1988. 'Damien O'Reilly was marking me and I turned to him at one stage and said, "Jaysus, there's an awful lot of people up on the hill. How many people would you say is up there?"

'He looked up to make his guess and the ball came between us and I caught it without any obstruction and stuck it over the bar. He was taken off me immediately.'

39

LOVELY LEITRIM

Leitrim v. Roscommon

It is said that Lester Piggott could identify every horse he had ever ridden even when it was walking away from him in a rainstorm. Packy McGarty has a comparable instinct for Leitrim football. Born in Mohill in 1933, Packy's senior intercounty career began in 1949 and finished in 1971, when he was 39. He played in six senior Connacht finals without winning one of them and reached the National League semi-final in the spring of 1959. The closest he came to glory was when Galway beat Leitrim by 2-10 to 1-11 in the 1958 Connacht final. Although there was no question that McGarty was the star, Leitrim had other good players at the time, like Cathal Flynn at corner-forward. Football dominated Packy's life from an early age.

'Football was all you had. Every evening as a boy I'd go with my friends to see the men training. We'd be hoping that the ball would go over the bar and we'd be fighting just to get a kick of it. As kids we hadn't footballs, just a sock with grass in it. You'd be listening to a match on a Sunday, which was the highlight of the week because my father had 15 shillings a week to keep a family of five of us. I remember working for three shillings a week.'

McGarty won a third Railway Cup medal as a sub in 1967. He would have needed a trophy cabinet if the plethora of individual awards that we have today existed in his playing days. Leitrim's rivalry with near neighbours Roscommon was always a big deal for him. McGarty was a great thinker about the game and there was one occasion when Leitrim reaped the reward for this.

'George Geraghty of Roscommon was an All-Ireland colleges champion high-jumper. I vividly remember the first time I ever saw him play. He was selected for my club, Sean McDermotts, at midfield. Although I wasn't a big man, I loved running for the ball and jumping and could reach a fair height. I was on the 40 that day and I went up for the ball once and had my hand on it, but somebody soared in like a bird and took it off me. It was my own teammate, George. I knew we were playing Roscommon the following Sunday in the Connacht championship and we would be in big trouble because they had both George and Gerry O'Malley at midfield.

'The thing about Gerry was that if he had been blessed with a great shot he would have beaten you on his own. He'd catch everything and solo through the entire defence, but his kick would as easily go wide as it could go over the bar. That's why I would always have picked him at centre half-back.

'That whole week I spent thinking about how we would stop George because I knew we wouldn't be able to stop O'Malley, no matter what plan we came up with. At half-time we were leading Roscommon by eight points to three and we had been playing with a bit of a breeze. Twenty minutes into the second half it was 8-8 and George and O'Malley were lording it at midfield. I decided to go to centrefield because we weren't in the game. I switched out on George because Gerry was like an octopus. I had a plan in my mind. As the ball was cleared out,

George was winning everything by running up and catching it, so I would back into him and stop him running but when the ball was about to drop I'd sprint out and catch it. We won by 11 points to nine. The next morning the headline in the paper was "Super Switch by Leitrim Wins Game" The thing was, Leitrim didn't know a thing about it! I told George later that the biggest mistake he ever made was playing for Sean McDermotts the week before because I knew his form.

'I saw Pat Donnellan of Galway doing the same to Mick O'Connell once in an All-Ireland final and Mick didn't like it! It was effective, but it wasn't dirty.'

Roscommon got the best out of McGarty, even when he could not shake the doubt that was drilling deeper into his heart.

'I always tried to give my best when I played for Leitrim, but when you are playing your nearest neighbours the stakes are much higher and that is why we in Leitrim remember the years like 1994 when we beat Roscommon in the championship.'

THE GREATEST DAY

Leitrim's first-ever All-Star Mickey Quinn was central to the county's success in 1994, when in one of the greatest Cinderella stories in the history of the GAA Leitrim won only their second Connacht title. The clock stopped, as magic and wonder replaced reality.

'Roscommon had been the biggest bogey team for us. We had great battles with them in previous years, but no matter what we threw at them they always seemed to have the upper hand. That spring, though, we relegated Roscommon from our division in the National League in Carrick-on-Shannon. We knew then we could beat them and we did in the Connacht championship. In previous years, we should have beat them but that year they should have beat us!'

40

TALES FROM THE BACKING OF THE BUS

Sligo v. Roscommon

The great French philosopher Jean-Jacques Rousseau spoke of a 'social contract'. Gaelic games is a world of a uniquely Irish social contract. We give our teams all our support. In return they give us everything on and sometimes off the field. As an example, in 2011–12, when the Vita Cortex factory workers were on strike, one of the county's most iconic hurlers, Jimmy Barry-Murphy, visited them to offer his support. It was a potent symbol of the radical solidarity between the team and the community. In Connacht football, local rivalries are very important.

The ultimate test of a player in any sport is that they have the power to make the pulse skip a beat whenever they are in full flight. Once they get the ball a buzz of expectancy goes around the ground. For an entire generation the defining image of Sligo football was the penetrating runs of Eamonn O'Hara. In full flight he lit up the pitch like a flash of forked lightning, thrilling and, from the opposition's point of view, frightening.

O'Hara has been described as Gaelic football's answer to martial-artist Chuck Norris. He had the opportunity to showcase his competitive spirit to the nation when he played for Ireland in the Compromise Rules. His eyes twinkled at the memory of the challenge.

'I had been doing the training sessions for a number of years but was cut from the final panel when Colm O'Rourke was in charge, which surprised a lot of people. I think Colm had his mind made up before the trial games, but he won the series and you can't argue with success. When Brian McEniff took charge, though, I was selected and going to Australia was the experience of a lifetime. We won the series, which was great – though losing at home the next year, especially with the violence that marred the spectacle, was a disappointment.'

One of the talking points of the 2013 championship was Eamonn O'Hara's severe criticism of his former Sligo manager, Kevin Walsh, on *The Sunday Game*. Suffice to say he did not hold back after an initial pause; it was like a comedian calming the crowd before delivering the punchline.

O'Hara is much more tongue-in-cheek about the rivalry between his native Sligo and Roscommon. He has a riddle that perfectly captures the great love Sligo fans have for their near neighbours.

Q: What is big and yellow and goes b-b-b-beep?'

A: 'The Roscommon bus backing into the garage in June, having gone out of the championship typically early.'

PART V

When Two Tribes Go to War

Fans of Gaelic games are passionate, partisan and protective: often embattled but always loyal. They have an ancient form of competitive instinct and have enemies everywhere – with a rotating cast of characters.

Some rivalries can be really intense for brief periods and are generally mired in controversy. Such rivalries get the GAA nation talking and generally generate great media coverage. They are the type of rivalries that even provoke heated debate on *Liveline*. It would not be accurate to describe them as 'one hit wonders' because generally there are way more than just one hit!

This section celebrates some of the rivalries that drove fans' excitement into frenzied empathy with each other and into an exalted form of hatred for the enemy. Pain at this level is both a tranquiliser and an enforcer.

41

WATERFORD'S WINNING STREAK

Waterford v. Cork

In Brian Corcorcan's 2006 book *Every Single Ball* he ignited a new controversy between Cork and Waterford when he described two posters put up in the Cork dressing-room, one outlining Cork's world, the other Waterford's: 'Losing; Fighting; Blaming others; Playing for oneself, not the team; Relying on luck; Bringing others down to their level.'

The Waterford GAA secretary Seamus Grant was prompted to remark in response, 'We were very upset down here about his comments ... I know several people who said they would not read the book if they got it for nothing. It caused a lot of anger.'

The animosity quickly faded and two of their three games in 2007 were classics. It is telling that in their 11 championship games between 2002 and 2010 Cork's five points win in the '05 All-Ireland quarter-final was the highest winning margin. Who will ever forget the 2004 Munster final? Thunderbolt City when, despite having John Mullane sent off, the Déise won 3-16 to 1-21.

This was a new and thrilling rivalry in the noughties, with a lopsided tradition. Before they played in '02, the counties had met 50 times in the championship. Cork had won 39, Waterford just eight. When Waterford won their first Munster title in 1938, they defeated Cork on the way, their first win against them in 19 contests. Cork and Waterford had a meaningful rivalry between 1957 and 1967, when Waterford had their greatest team, but Cork then restored normal service of total dominance.

In the noughties, games between both counties were inextricably bound to drama. Think of Ken McGrath coming off the bench to hit the winning point in '02; John Mullane's three goals in '03; Paul Flynn's stunning goal in '04; Brian Corcoran's incredible drop-shot winner in the '05 All-Ireland quarter-final; Donal Óg Cusack stopping Ken McGrath's late free going over the bar in '06; Eoin McGrath going man for man with Donal Óg Cusack in '07; and perhaps the end of an era in 2010, with Tony Browne scoring the equalising goal in the 74th minute of the drawn Munster final and Dan Shanahan scoring the winning goal late in extra-time of the replay in characteristic high-octane contests.

There was even an interesting subplot. Cork royalty Gerald McCarthy and Justin McCarthy coached Waterford teams against Cork. When Gerald returned to manage Cork against Justin in three games in '07, the rivalry increased even more.

Jimmy Magee watched the rivalry unfold with relish.

'Rivalries add an extra spark to the GAA because both fans and the media love them. It was wonderful to see Waterford arrive as a serious power in hurling in the noughties and this new rivalry with Cork was a breath of fresh air to the GAA. I loved what Waterford brought to the table, and they had a unique marriage of skill and great characters like John Mullane. Of course, Cork too have this wonderful tradition of great, skilful hurlers and they had some very big personalities of their own. They produced some breathtaking games which really got the heart pumping.

'Both of them won Munster titles, but my one regret is that Waterford did not go on to win an All-Ireland, whereas Cork did. We saw in the '90s what happens when new blood comes, as it did then – with Offaly, Clare and Wexford winning five All-Irelands between them. The surge of energy it gave everyone, it would have electrified everyone again if Waterford had gone on to win an All-Ireland.'

A Liam McCarthy Cup would prove elusive for Waterford. Babs Keating has a firm view on the reasons for their failure to go all the way.

'I would say the Waterford team of the noughties was very unlucky. Waterford had three massive players – Tony Browne, Ken McGrath and Paul Flynn. On the crucial games they never got the three of them to play well on the one day. If you take 2004, Paul Flynn got 13 points in the All-Ireland semi-final against Kilkenny. If he had got any help at all they would have won, but neither Browne nor McGrath backed him up properly. Ken McGrath let them down badly against Cork in 2006 in my opinion. That was their undoing. They were so dependent on those three. They were like the Waterford team of the late '50s and '60s. They were just short of two or three players.'

BREWING UP A STORM

In July 2019 Waterford and Cork appeared to have reached a new rapprochement when Donal Óg Cusack and Derek McGrath had a bonding session on *The Sunday Game*. Donal Óg said that criticism of the rehearsed defensive styles of Davy Fitz and Derek McGrath – dressed up in charges of 'disrespecting the traditions of the game' – is 'part of the last remnants of British culture on these islands'. He added, 'The British, they founded a lot of games, but they struggled to accept and adapt to the wider influences in their games. What I mean is the long ball to John Bull, Jack Charlton-type spirit. I'm delighted the modern player has moved on.'

Derek McGrath criticised *Sunday Game* panellists for their ignorance of his style of play as Waterford manager, that 'what would be espoused and pontificated from these seats I'm sitting in now looked like a public forum of self-indulgence'.

Not everyone in Waterford agreed. Ken McGrath – a panellist on the live programme earlier that day – tweeted: 'Absolute nonsense, egos gone out of control.' Limerick's Ollie Moran tweeted that Donal Óg and Derek had 'wasted ten minutes of *The Sunday Game* pontificating about hurling philosophies and ideologies. Joe Public would prefer if you just raved about the exhibition of skill and manliness that we saw today.' Another viewer tweeted that this was Donal Óg 'blaming the Black and Tans for lads not liking the sweeper system.'

42

IN THE LYONS' DEN

Dublin v. Armagh

On every side in the orchards the apple trees were bending over with heavy fruit.

In the early noughties, Armagh and Dublin enjoyed a decent rivalry. Pat Spillane believes that to some extent the rivalry was fuelled by the media because they both had high-profile managers.

'Much of the credit for Armagh's success in the noughties goes to Joe Kernan. Joe is a larger-than-life individual and a great raconteur. He is a bit like Páidí [Ó Sé] in many ways, including the fact that they both possessed very underestimated footballing brains. As Joe is such a gregarious character, there is a danger of missing his inner strength and brilliance. He has a superb record at club level with Crossmaglen. He was the final piece in the jigsaw that was needed to bring an All-Ireland to Armagh. To me it seemed he had inherited an Armagh team close to the end of the line. He reinvigorated them and got what looked like a tired team at the end of its road back on the track to ultimate glory. I like the way they seemed to play with a lot more joy in subsequent years and they put in an awesome performance in the Ulster final in 2004, while on the same day the so-called aristocrats, Kerry, were completely uninspiring in the Munster final.

'One thing I like about Joe is that he was one of the managers, like Anthony Daly, Mickey Harte, John O'Mahony, Micko, Páidí and Seán Boylan, who were not running along the sidelines wearing earpieces. I am always intrigued when I see managers with earpieces. Who are they talking to? It is all part of a fad and it highlights a problem we have in Gaelic football today – style over substance. Wearing an earpiece is a sign that you have an extra edge. I always think part of the ruination of Gaelic football came when the PE teacher came on the scene as coach and manager. At the time there was a few bob floating around for coaching and they had to be seen to bring something extra to the mix to earn their fee, so they brought in cones and introduced drills, which was the first step in complicating the game.

'I go back to Mick O'Dwyer's training with us. For the first half-hour the forwards just kicked balls into the goal and the backs caught them and kicked them back out to us. The key skills were there in that exercise.

'Joe was the manager when Armagh played an Ulster final in Croke Park in 2004. What did not surprise me was that there was nothing for the players in Croke Park, not even a cup of tea after the game. I have been down this road myself many a time during my playing days. I can recall going to play in games to open so-called "state of the art" stadia like Páirc Uí Chaoimh only to discover that the dressing-rooms would at best be suitable for a team of pygmies, or to discover that there was no toilet roll in the players' toilets. I can still remember after winning the All-Ireland in 1984 trying to get a drink with Ger Lynch and my brother Tom in Croke Park only to be told, "Sorry, VIPs only."

DJ Carey has a similar story about trying to use one of the lifts in Croke Park and being greeted with the words "This is a lift for VIPs only."

'In the GAA there is a very definite hierarchy when it comes to big games. At the top of the list are the VIPs. Then just underneath them come the corporate people and sponsors. Then come the officials of all sorts. Supporters come a distant fourth and a very distant fourth at that.'

A DIET FOR SUCCESS?
Spillane enjoyed a close friendship with the former Dublin manager, Tommy Lyons.

'The same critics who were throwing bouquets at Tommy in 2002 were swinging cleavers the following year. Some of the criticism was of such persistence and hostility it might have made Richard Nixon wince. After Dublin lost to Laois and Armagh in 2003, Tommy's fall from grace is reflected in the comment of one former Dublin player: "The only way Tommy Lyons can get up again is with Viagra."

'Tommy led Kilmacud Crokes to an All-Ireland. He also took Offaly to a league and Leinster title, playing a very attractive brand of football. At the time the secret of Offaly's success was supposed to be the Nutron diet. Whatever happened to the Nutron diet?

'He came to the Dublin job with ambition you could sharpen knives on. To be a good manager you need to be such an optimist that you believe that when your shoes wear out you will be back on your feet. He seemed like a man who could inspire a donkey to win the Derby. In his first year his optimism was justified when Dublin won the Leinster title.'

A one-point defeat to Armagh in the All-Ireland semi-final would put a halt to Lyons' gallop. Dublin were a 'nearly team' in 2002 and were unlucky to lose against Armagh. There is a very thin line between laughter and loss. Who will ever forget Ray Cosgrove's free coming off the post at the end? The problem is that, as we say in Roscommon, nearly never bulled a cow. The Emperor Napoleon used to ask his aspiring generals whether they were lucky. Sporting champions need their fair share of luck. The weather and the toss of a coin can make a huge difference, dictating surfaces, ends and directions. The wind is arbitrary, the sun has no favourites, the rain like the tide waits for no one. The best prepared manager can't prevent his star player pulling his hamstring or breaking his leg or missing an easy free, and hopes of All-Ireland glory can vanish in an instant.

Pat Spillane believes that to some extent Dublin's form that year was something of a mirage.

'Dublin fans looked back at 2002 as a golden era. It must also have been the year they all bought rose-tinted spectacles because Dublin were heavily reliant on the goals of Ray Cosgrove. Their problem was that they had too many forwards who wouldn't get a kick in a stampede.'

The following year saw Armagh dumping the Dubs out of the championship for the second consecutive year. There was controversy afterwards, as Pat Spillane recalls.

'Tommy's reaction to the defeat against Armagh in 2003 did him no favours with his players. He came out in front of the media and had a go at his own player, Stephen Cluxton, who had been sent off. Tommy's critics will say that he hung Cluxton out to dry and humiliated him, and that he broke the golden rule because he had spoken out about a player outside the dressing-room. Tommy will maintain otherwise. He would say that if Cluxton deserved to be sent off he should have been, and he hadn't seen the video evidence when he gave his now infamous interview to Jim Carney. I thought it was a good interview, but I genuinely don't think Tommy hung Cluxton out to dry. When you interview a losing manager immediately after such a big game, when the stakes are so high, he isn't thinking rationally. Instead he's wounded and emotional and you can't expect a detached, clinical analysis with total objectivity.

'One thing always puzzled me about that affair. Before the sending off, Dublin were in the ascendancy and they seemed likely to win, but after the sending off the wheels came off the Dublin wagon. Afterwards Tommy was vilified. Cluxton got away scot free in terms of public criticism, even though his sending off cost Dublin in all probability an All-Ireland appearance. Yet Cluxton became the victim and Tommy Lyons the villain.'

Spillane believes that Lyons was treated unfairly.

'It was totally unfair to make Tommy the scapegoat for all of the problems of Dublin football. The level of personal criticism of Tommy was way over the top. He was not the only one in that situation. Joe Brolly was very, very critical of Mickey Moran before and after Derry's defeat by Tyrone around that time. I know Moran rang the powers that be in RTÉ and complained about the nature of the criticism that was levelled at him. I can understand that because he made the valid point that he was watching it on the television with his 15-year-old daughter. That is tough on anyone in that position.'

Spillane believes that the fallout from 2003 was very detrimental to Lyons in '04, when they lost to Westmeath in the Leinster championship.

'Tommy did get three lucky breaks in the draw for the back-door games – with London, Leitrim and Longford respectively, which gave them the opportunity for gentle rehabilitation. They were also lucky to draw Roscommon – though if Roscommon had shown more composure in front of goal they would have beaten them.

'I met Tommy the Saturday night after they lost to Westmeath, in Jury's Hotel. They had just beaten London. Tommy was far more relaxed. The great thing was that the "olé, olé brigade" didn't arrive at the match. Tommy in particular, and the team in general, got a great welcome. The Dublin players were in the bar as well. I don't enjoy that sort of a situation too much because I don't like to get too close to players in case it compromises my objectivity and colours my opinion. I would like to think that if I was watching my brother playing in a match I would call it as I saw it without fear or favour. That's why I'm wary of seeing the players at too close quarters.

'That night I had gone out to get advance copies of the Sunday papers. I had written a sympathetic article about Tommy in my column, but I hadn't written the headline. I nearly fell off my chair when I read it. "Jackeens like Jack-asses!" To compound my discomfort, the Dublin midfielder Darren Homan asked me what I had written about them in my column. That was the moment I decided to sprint out of the bar! I only stopped to tell Tommy Lyons's wife, Noreen, that I had not written the headline for my column.

'The following night on *The Sunday Game* I asked Colm O'Rourke to clarify comments he had made within minutes of Dublin's defeat to Westmeath when he was perceived as calling for Tommy's resignation. Colm clearly explained that if he had been in the same position he would have resigned immediately after the loss to Westmeath, anticipating the inevitable backlash and mindful of the strain it was going to put on Tommy's family. Tommy rang me the next morning to tell me that he had got 25 texts telling him that I had put Colm O'Rourke on the spot. Yet another reminder, not that I needed one, that television is all about perception.

'Some of the production team on the programme were

concerned afterwards that I had put Colm on the spot, but I think Colm was glad to put his position on the record because he felt he had been accused in the wrong. Tommy Lyons was very appreciative of his clarification. I said to him, "You have one enemy to cross off your list."'

In his incarnations as Kerry and Westmeath manager, Páidí Ó Sé was keeping a close eye on the developing Dublin–Armagh rivalry at the time.

'When I was growing up in Kerry, the old people talked about people who had "old" money and those who had "new" money. It took me a long time to understand what they meant. But the Armagh rivalry with the Dubs grabbed people's attention for that reason. Outside Dublin, and probably Tyrone, everyone was shouting for the team who were "new" money and what made it all the sweeter was that it was this crowd who were winning.'

43

THE BIG APPLE

Cavan v. Kerry

In 1947 to shamelessly steal from New York's own Paul Simon, the country fixed its gaze onto the Big Apple and GAA fans at home and abroad were captivated by the rivalry between Cavan and Kerry.

Right half-back on that Cavan team was the late John Wilson, who went on to become Tánaiste in the Irish government in the 1980s. He spoke with me about what is arguably the most iconic match in the long history of the GAA.

'The final was held in New York as a gesture by the GAA of goodwill to the Irish people in America. Once it was announced it aroused great interest in every county. To get there was a great prize in itself. The teams left Cobh together for a six-day trip on the SS *Mauritania* to New York, after getting our vaccinations against smallpox, which were compulsory at the time. The fact that we were playing the aristocrats of football, Kerry, added to the occasion for us, but the fact that it was the first final played abroad gave it a much more exotic quality, so it really grabbed the public imagination.'

For Cavan, the trip to New York was particularly welcome because in previous years they had experienced many bitter disappointments.

John Wilson explained: 'Initially most of our team would taste the bitter pill of defeat in three All-Ireland finals before getting his hands on the ultimate prize. We lost to Kerry in 1937, Roscommon in 1943 [after a replay] and Cork in 1945. The replay against Roscommon was mired in controversy because of our frustration with some of the refereeing decisions.

'What I remember most was the mayhem at the end. First Cavan's Joe Stafford was sent off after having a go at Owensie Hoare. We got a point but Barney Culley didn't agree and put the umpire into the net with a box. Big Tom O'Reilly, our captain, came in to remonstrate and T.P. O'Reilly threw the referee in the air. After that game the GAA came down on us like a ton of bricks and imposed heavy suspensions on some of our greatest players. We felt there was an injustice done. The trip to New York was a great adventure for us all, but we were there on a mission – redemption. We knew this was history in the making and that we would write our names into GAA immortality if we won. We wanted to show everybody at home as much as in New York that we were top-class footballers. From the outside, it might have looked like this was a holiday, or "a jolly", as some people call these trips, but we were there on a serious mission, which was to reclaim our reputation and it was going to take a great team to stop us. We knew Kerry would be good but they were going to have to be very, very good to beat us.'

Joe Keohane offered an interesting perspective.

'Despite the hype at home, in fact the game was poorly publicised and advertised in New York, and this was reflected in the fact that only 34,491 attended. The pitch was too small and rock hard. In fact, the surface had a crucial bearing on the outcome because Eddie Dowling was on fire that day and scored one of the goals that put Kerry in the lead and seemingly on course for victory, but he was knocked out cold when he fell on the ground and had to be carried off. This was the turning point of the game. I suppose because the final was played in New York it gave an extra edge to our rivalry with Cavan in those years because of its historical significance.'

44

MAKING OMELETTES

Meath v. Tyrone

The Meath–Tyrone All-Ireland semi-final in 1996 was, to use a classic GAA euphemism, 'a robust affair'. The Meath team were criticised for their aggressive treatment of Peter Canavan and some of the Tyrone players. Discretion precludes me from naming the very earnest Meath legend who afterwards apologised in a team meeting for losing his man momentarily in the match. One of his colleagues had the dressing-room in stitches – though not the player in question – when he quipped, 'Not to worry. The only reason you couldn't see him was that you had your boot on his throat at the time.'

After the All-Ireland semi-final, two irate Tyrone fans were loud in their condemnation of the Meath team, particularly of their alleged ill-treatment of Peter Canavan. A Meath fan made an interesting and revealing slip of the tongue in response: 'You can't make an omelette without breaking legs.'

It is fair to say that match lingered long in the memory for fans and defines their rivalry. Pat Spillane has reason to remember the game clearly.

'Colm O'Rourke and I were analysing that match that night for *The Sunday Game*. There was an incident when I found myself in that very rare position for me of not knowing what to say. John McDermott knocked over Peter Canavan. The more you looked at it, the more you could find a reason to argue vehemently that he did it deliberately, but equally you could claim with the same conviction that it was an accident. An even more controversial incident occurred when Martin O'Connell was alleged to have stamped on Brian Dooher when he was on the ground. I could not be sure of O'Connell's intent, so I gave him the benefit of the doubt.

'There were a lot of calls into the programme about the incident and the producer decided Colm and I should discuss it. The problem was that we were watching the incident on a small monitor and were a little bit further away than usual, and I wasn't fully sure so I was very wishy-washy and gave the benefit of the doubt to O'Connell. Being wishy-washy is not something I make a habit of. Colm was not very critical of his former teammate. Afterwards most people said that's all they would expect from O'Rourke when it came to Meath but that I had chickened out.'

Spillane has a counterbalancing memory.

'Fast-forward to the Leinster semi-final in 2004, when a Meath player stamped on a Laois player. In the analysis afterwards O'Rourke, without any prompting, said immediately that the unsavoury episode was a "disgrace to the Meath jersey". Everyone would agree that Colm is a top-class analyst, but he went up still further in many people's eyes on the foot of that refreshingly honest comment.'

So how then does Spillane see the Meath team's tactics against Tyrone?

'A lot of players have the attitude of never going for a 50–50 ball unless they're 80–20 sure of winning it. Meath players never had that problem.'

TOUGHER THAN THE REST

Former Meath star Bernard Flynn agrees, but with a caveat.

'Under Seán we were not going to back down. We played Laois in the 1991 Leinster final. I was marking Tommy Smyth, who was a brother-in-law of my best man and business partner Mick Dempsey. We were close, but once the game was on there was no place for sentiment. Leo Turley got this great point under the Hogan Stand into the Hill 16 goal to put them two up early on. Tommy did this little jig and said in my face, "We have ye now, youse hoors ya." I wasn't getting the ball, so I slipped out to centre-forward, got this ball, dished off to Jinxy [David Beggy] and he got the goal that changed the match. I ran back in, went straight up to Tommy's face and said, "You're not f**king laughing now, you hoor ya!" He thumped me and got put off. The rumour was I spat in his face. But I was right up in his face.

'In all my time in a Meath dressing-room Boylan never once told us to hit anyone. He never had to. He didn't have to tell Mick Lyons what to do, or Joe Cassells, or Colm O'Rourke, or Liam Harnan. Looking back, I wished Seán had curbed that physicality a bit. There were games where we seemed more interested in the man than the ball and it cost us All-Irelands. I think especially of the '91 final against Down. We spent the first 40 minutes trying to soften Mickey Linden and those lads before we started playing football. By then we were playing catch-up.'

Flynn has an interesting take on the Tyrone manager.

'I'm a big admirer of Mickey Harte, but I was taken aback when he wrote in his book about Seán Cavanagh's inability to start against Cork in the 2009 All-Ireland semi-final. Cavanagh nearly single-handedly won Tyrone the 2008 All-Ireland. Boylan wouldn't dream of criticising one of his players in public like that.'

45

HIGHS AND LOWS

Cork v. Mayo

The Mayo fan was medium-sized and wiry, bouncing on his toes, full of get-up and go as he almost raced out of Croke Park. He had a shaven head and a scar on the side of his face. He looked like someone from a photo in a war crimes tribunal. He carried the sorrow of a generation who live in a unique world of half hope, half agony.

When Cork beat Mayo by 2-12 to 0-12 in the 1999 All-Ireland semi-final, the one consolation for the Westerners was that at least it was nothing as bad as the humiliation in 1993, when in the All-Ireland semi-final the Leesiders trounced Mayo.

Having won an All-Star the previous year, T.J. Kilgallon would wear his Mayo jersey for the last time in 1993.

'Jack O'Shea's appointment as manager generated a lot of enthusiasm in the county. We won the Connacht final. I was brought on as a sub that day and felt I had made a good contribution. I was fuming when I wasn't chosen in the starting team against Cork in the All-Ireland semi-final and felt like not turning up on the day. On the Thursday before the game my quad muscle went astray. I was asked at half-time if I was OK to go on and I replied that I would give it a go, but understandably they decided not to risk me. The last ten minutes of that match was probably the low point of Mayo football, as we stopped playing and Cork stuffed us by 5-15 to 0-10. Although I was only 32, I had a lot of mileage on the clock and retired.'

In 1992 when Mayo football seemed to be in disarray during the former Dublin player Brian McDonald's controversial tenure as county trainer, former star player Willie McGee was recruited in a campaign to take corrective action.

'I felt at the time that Jack O'Shea was the man to bring some good days back to the county. Some people close to the top in Mayo football had the same view and I was asked by the chairman of the county board, Christy Loftus, to raise the funds from the friends of Mayo in Dublin and to personally approach Jacko to take on the Mayo job. To be fair to him, I think that given the travel involved he deserved to be properly looked after.'

It was hoped that Jack O'Shea's appointment as manager would revive Mayo's fortunes, but it was not to be, as Dermot Flanagan found out at first hand.

'We were very lucky to beat Roscommon in the Connacht final in 1993. I picked up a cruciate ligament injury and had to decide whether to retire or have surgery, knowing that it might not be a success.'

Peter Ford saw the demolition job up close and personal.

'I was a sub in '93 and didn't really play. Jacko was very enthusiastic, but people were expecting miracles. They thought he had some kind of a secret ingredient from playing under Mick O'Dwyer, but there is no magic formula in Kerry or anywhere else. Cork hammered us in the All-Ireland semi-final and I retired.'

The rivalry between Cork and Mayo came to a head in 1989 when the counties served up one of the best All-Ireland finals in years, with Cork winning by 0-17 to 1-11.

CLOSE-RUN AFFAIR

A broken leg had caused Kevin McStay to miss the Connacht championship triumph in 1988.

'In '89 I was struggling to get my form back to where it had been. [He had been an All-Star in 1985.] I knew that when there were selection meetings there was discussion about my name. I was trying really hard and John O'Mahony [the team manager] gave me great support. In the championship that year we got into the habit of winning tight matches in the last ten minutes. Johnno was always harping on about the last ten minutes and we felt we could really plough it. We felt we were invincible. In the All-Ireland semi-final we gave a very un-Mayo-like performance when we wore Tyrone down. We thought we had a great chance, going into the final.

'We were millimetres from winning the All-Ireland in '89. We hit the post twice and the ball bounced back into play. They hit the post twice, but each time the ball went over the bar. One of their players double hopped the ball and scored a point, but the ref, Paddy Collins, who was normally an excellent referee, missed it. After scoring the goal, Anthony [Finnerty] got another chance, but the late John Kerins got a touch to it. The umpire backed away because he was afraid the ball was going to hit him. He missed John's touch and, instead of giving us a 45, he flagged it wide. Our freetaker, Michael Fitzmaurice, was on fire that day and hadn't missed a placed ball, including a 45. If we had got a point at that stage it would have been a big help to us. Cork were a more experienced team than us, having contested the All-Ireland final the previous two years, but they were very brittle at that stage of the game. As a forward I could see their nerves in the way the backs were shouting at each other, but we allowed them to settle rather than keep them on the ropes.'

Martin Carney had been through big games for Mayo but had never experienced anything like this.

'This time things were a bit different. Up to then Mayo had always been a rollercoaster, from one extreme to the other. We were either fully up or completely down, but John O'Mahony kept things grounded. We won the Connacht title again in 1989, when Liam McHale literally owned the ball and gave one of the great individual displays. We also had Seán Maher in the side, who was a very under-rated player, and he gave us that enforcer rather than a creator presence we badly needed. Anthony Finnerty famously described Jimmy Burke's goal that year as "the push-over goal". It kind of bounced off him.

'For a county that had not won an All-Ireland final for so long there was such an outpouring of goodwill and an incredible longing to win. Johnno tried to control it as best he could, but a lot of local interests were looking for a slice of the action. When we scored the goal, I can recall looking down the Cork bench and seeing the sense of shock. They were as brittle as us in a different way, but John Cleary and Michael McCarthy took over and they deservedly won. Although we lost, the team was feted. There was plenty of back-slapping, which created its own problems. The team was distracted the next year and the opportunity to build on the advances of 1989 was lost.'

AN ICONIC MOMENT

Some players have their careers defined in moments. Willie Joe Padden is such a player. In the All-Ireland semi-final in 1989 against Tyrone he was forced to the sideline with a dangerous cut to his head. In one of the most iconic images in the history of the GAA he later returned to the fray, covered in blood, his head wrapped in a bandage, his shirt splattered in blood.

'Everybody had written us off before the match. I got an injury. I'm not too sure which Tyrone player it was. He was going for a ball and he hit his knee off my head and I got a few stiches in it. You don't mind getting a few things like that, as long as you win the game. It was our first experience of getting to a final after all our endeavours from the previous years. From our point of view, and from the spectators' points of view, it was a great period because we were basking in the build-up to the final, especially being in our first All-Ireland for so long.

'The '89 All-Ireland was one of the more open ones. Unfortunately, Jimmy Burke, our full-forward, got injured and he had to go off. That really took the wind out of our sails because he was in there as a target-man and did that job very well. We were forced to re-jig the team. Having said that, when we took the lead in the second half we looked as if we were in the driving seat but we got another injury and had to re-jig the team again. I think it was that that cost us the game rather than a lack of concentration. We were just as well prepared as Cork, so it certainly wasn't a lack of fitness. We didn't press home our initiative, so we didn't get the extra couple of points up to have the cushion there for the end of the game. Cork rallied and pipped us in the end.'

The disappointment for Padden was heightened because he knew there were not many chances left for him to win a coveted All-Ireland medal.

'It's all right playing in an All-Ireland final, but if you don't win no one is going to say who the runners-up were in ten years' time, if they're asked the question. I remember thinking at the time, "Am I going to get the chance to stand in Croke Park again and have another go at winning an All-Ireland?" Sadly, it was not to be.'

SO NEAR AND YET SO FAR

T.J. Kilgallon believes the '89 All-Ireland is yet another case of what might have been for Mayo.

'After Anthony Finnerty got the goal, we were in the driving seat because, having lost the previous two years, they were starting to doubt themselves, but in the last ten minutes we went into disarray and let them off the hook. They finished strongly and got the final three points.

'There were 10,000 people waiting for us when we flew back to Knock. It was awfully moving. There was a real party atmosphere and we went on the beer for three or four days to kill the pain. There was none of the back-stabbing you normally have after a defeat. It was almost a mini-celebration, and Mayo people were proud of us for getting there and playing well. There was a feeling that we needed to do a tour of the county as a political move as much as anything else. I went back to work on the Wednesday, though, because for me it was over and done with – but not achieved.'

Peter Ford's enduring memory of the All-Ireland final is not the most obvious one.

'There was a picture of me in the paper next day with tears in my eyes, but my abiding memory will always be the Cork captain Dinny Allen's speech when he was presented with the cup. He came out with a load of bollocks. He spent nearly all his speech lacerating the media. I couldn't believe that after winning the All-Ireland that was all that was on his mind. If we had won, it would have been a very different story.'

46

KING HENRY

Kilkenny v. Clare

The Kilkenny–Clare rivalry heated up again on 31 July 2004 in the All-Ireland quarter-final replay. Kilkenny won 1-11 to 0-9, but nobody was talking about the score.

On the previous Sunday the two teams had drawn. The ending was mired in controversy. One person equipped to give a 'neutral' view of the incident is Pat Spillane, who had a professional interest in the game as the then presenter of *The Sunday Game*.

'The chaos and confusion after the Kilkenny–Clare All-Ireland hurling quarter-final in 2004 was another GAA fiasco. After the match was drawn, the teams were exchanging jerseys and the crowd was leaving Croke Park when an announcement was made over the public address system that extra-time would be played. Mass head-scratching took place. There would be extra time. No, there would not. Nobody knew what was happening. Players, team management, match commentators, fans, the national television audience were completely in the dark. GAA officials were spotted running around like headless chickens. Eventually another announcement was made that a replay would take place. The shambles was captured live on television. What was the problem? The *clár an lae* said there would be extra time.'

Temperatures rose dramatically in the replay over a controversial incident. Again, Spillane found himself having to try and make sense of it for the national television audience.

'I actually think violent incidents are much more isolated now than they were in the past. The big difference is that there is so much media exposure, whether local or national, that nothing is missed and many are magnified. Of course we cannot condone them, but they are symptomatic of what is happening in society, particularly among the young, where there is a creeping aggressiveness surfacing and they are much more likely to engage in confrontation.

'On *The Sunday Game* we set the agenda for the debate on the Henry Shefflin incident by showing for the first time the footage of the blow which could have seriously damaged Henry's eye. When we got the clip that day, our analysts Tomás Mulcahy and Larry O'Gorman watched it and watched it again and again. I do not have the expertise to judge but they felt that the Clare player who clashed with Henry, Gerry Quinn, had two hands on his hurley when the incident took place, but Tomás said that under a dropping ball a defender's reaction is to put up one hand to catch the ball. The problem in this situation is that it is impossible to adjudicate on intent. I have learned this from personal experience.'

EQUAL JUSTICE?

Not for the first time the issue was raised about apparent double standards, as Spillane explains.

'In the Shefflin case the Clare hurling family came out strongly against the media treatment of Gerry Quinn and claimed it was an accident. I understand that they felt aggrieved that Quinn got such unfavourable press comment and that they contrasted that with the situation in 2002 after the All-Ireland hurling semi-final when Quinn's arm was broken by a Waterford player. Yet the Waterford player in question was never named. The GAA launched an investigation into the incident. Surprise, surprise nobody saw anything but the whole country knew who the Waterford player was.

'Notwithstanding the Clare criticism I believe that *The Sunday Game* was right to address the issue and I do not believe it was trial by media. We would have abdicated our responsibilities to the viewer had we not tackled the story head-on because it was the main topic on people's minds that day and we had to deal with it.

'I did have a problem with the reaction of the Cork county board to our coverage of the melee that erupted after the Cork–Laois minor football quarter-final around the same time. A Cork mentor had been clearly caught on camera striking a Laois mentor, who did not retaliate. Yet far from apologising for the incident, the powers that be in Cork were quick off the blocks to lambast us for not showing the whole incident. We showed all we had. This was a classic case of shooting the messenger. The scene spoke for itself. The cameras do not lie. The Cork county board would have been better employed investigating the conduct of their mentors and players rather than attacking RTÉ.'

47

THE FAITHFUL

Offaly v. Kerry

Outside the county nobody gave Offaly a chance of winning the 1982 All-Ireland football final. Had they asked the most famous son of Offaly, Barack Obama, if they could win, he would have answered "Yes, we can."

Pat Spillane gets a little squeamish at the memory of that game.

'In 1982 Kerry planned a trip to Bali in the Far East to celebrate what we had expected to be our five-in-a-row. After sensationally losing the final to Offaly one of the lads said that the only Bali we would be going to was Ballybunion! Another said, "It won't even be the Canaries this year. All we'll get is the Seagulls."'

Spillane is keen to pay tribute to Longford native Eugene McGee, whose sudden death in May 2019 in the immediate aftermath of his son's wedding shocked the GAA world. He instantly joined the elite of the GAA Immortals when like a runway beacon showing a pilot the correct path he master-minded perhaps the most famous All-Ireland win in history.

'Offaly manager Eugene McGee must take a lot of the credit for that. His Offaly team asked a lot of questions of us in the All-Ireland semi-final in 1980 and the final in '81. Of course, McGee's decision to send on Séamus Darby with just a few minutes to go seems the greatest substitution in the history of the GAA, as he sensationally got the winning goal. Trust me, nobody in Kerry will ever forget it!

'As a manager McGee first came to prominence in club management in the 1970s with UCD. But it is that 1982 All-Ireland win that has immortalised him. The first half was open and it was a very good game of football. During the second half it started raining fairly heavily and the game deteriorated a good bit. Kerry dominated for a long time and Offaly were lucky enough to stay with us. Martin Furlong's penalty save from the normally lethal Mike Sheehy was very important. If we had scored that, I don't think they would have come back. The rest is history. They were four points down and got two frees to put them two points behind. Then a long ball came to Séamus Darby and he banged it into the net. All Croke Park went wild, but there was still a minute and a half left in the game and they had to hold on with all their might.'

Páidí Ó Sé recalled his memories of the game for me.

'It was a massive disappointment to lose in '82 and a memory that has never left me because we were minutes away from immortality. We had plenty of chances to win the game, but we became too defensive when we went four points up and this allowed Offaly back into the game. People say if Jimmy Deenihan was in there, the famous Séamus Darby goal wouldn't have got in and they were right. Jimmy knew how to "put manners" on anyone. I think it was a bigger deal for our supporters than for us. I think we were the better team but the result said otherwise.'

THE TRILOGY

The game itself was the third instalment of a rivalry between the two counties which began in a thrilling All-Ireland semi-final in 1980. In a match played at a ferocious pace that generated a feast of scores Kerry came out on top by 4-15 to 4-10. An astounding statistic from the game is that all of Offaly's scores came from just two players, Gerry Carroll, who got 2-1, and the extraordinary genius of Matt Connor, who scored 2-9.

The second instalment came in 1981 in a tight match in the All-Ireland final. The Kingdom won their four-in-a-row because of the goal of the year, which saw six Kerry players handling the ball in a sweeping move which culminated in Jack O'Shea unleashing a rocket of a shot.

48

THE LYNCH MOB

Cavan v. Cork

You can choose what you desire but you are not free to choose your desires. In the world of Gaelic games, your rivalries choose you.

One test of fame is a person's ability to define an era. The Beatles did it in the 1960s; Princess Diana did it in the 1980s. And for Cork fans, Jack Lynch did it for generations on the playing fields and in the political field. We expect a lot of our heroes. A lot of the time they disappoint us. Occasionally, as in Jack Lynch, they were even better than we expected for Lee-siders. For Lynch, the fascination with Gaelic games arrived like talking, too early to remember.

Johnny Giles once said, 'The team with the least ifs, buts and ands always wins the championship.' There is a lesson for everyone there. Jack Lynch learned that lesson very early.

The sun was shining on suburban Dublin, a little low in the sky, like the first days of autumn but it was still as warm as summer. Jack Lynch won five All-Ireland hurling medals with Cork. He also won an All-Ireland football medal. His football career left him with one happy memory from the 1945 All-Ireland football final.

'Cavan were one of the superpowers in Gaelic football at the time and from the Cork fans' perspective our new rivalry with them had captured the attention of people in Cork and indeed around the rest of the country. As many people inside the county and further abroad saw us as basically a hurling county and Cavan as a serious football force there was a bit of an edge to this game for the footballing community in Cork. We wanted to change the perception about us and were determined to beat Cavan. When we beat them, we felt we achieved more than winning a match. We had changed the perception of Cork outside the county, but much more importantly inside it.'

The rivalry began in 1943 when the sides met for the first time in the championship, with Cavan beating Cork by 1-8 to 1-7 in the All-Ireland semi-final. Cork would atone in 1945 by beating Cavan 2-5 to 0-7 in the All-Ireland final. In 1949 Cavan would wrestle back supremacy with a 1-9 to 2-3 victory over Cork in the All-Ireland semi-final. Cavan also emerged victorious over Cork, coming from behind in a thrilling All-Ireland semi-final in 1952 to win 0-10 to 2-3.

49

MIGHTY MULLINALAGHTA

Mullinalaghta St Columba's v. Kilmacud Crokes

It was one of those moments that can derange the emotional life – the fulfilment of an ancient dream. People felt it before they saw it – like eager first-time parents waiting for their child's first words.

There was a presence in the air, like a shuddering or a tense moment in a film.

Close your eyes and the years roll back. Great hurling and football matches refuse to be undramatic. If the form-book suggests predictability, there is almost always a sub-plot to send the blood pressure into orbit.

People who witness miracles, even minor ones of the sporting variety, are wont to carry around forever afterwards a potent cocktail of reminiscence, and any Gaelic football fan who wants to avoid a long monologue on the 2018 Leinster club final better steer miles clear of Longford.

Gaelic games are the ultimate virtual reality because they can take you anywhere you want to go. Contrary to real life, sport offers us a state of being that is so rewarding one does it for no other reason than to be a part of it. Such feelings are among the most intense, most memorable experiences one can get in this life. There are moments that stand out from the mundanity of everyday as shining beacons.

While rivalries are at the core of the GAA another great charm of the games is that they provide a platform for David to take on and sometimes slay Goliath. In February 2019, the Carlow hurlers shocked Galway by drawing with them in the league. Galway had won the All-Ireland less than 18 months earlier. However, while this book was being written a real fairy-tale emerged, which sums up the magic of the GAA.

Christmas came early for GAA romantics in December 2018 when Mullinalaghta St Columba's team completed one of the most remarkable stories in the history of Gaelic football by winning the Leinster football championship title and beating the famed Kilmacud Crokes in a perfectly constructed rollercoaster. They are the first-ever Longford team to win the Leinster title. That night thousands of stars twinkled brightly in triumph and a slice of gleaming moon hung low in the Longford sky, giving a silvery sheen to the dark Shannon waters.

Mullinalaghta's name, Mullach na Leachta, means 'Hill of the Standing Stones' and is derived from a hill which was the original site of the local church that dates back to 1839. There are just 447 people living in this half-parish in County Longford and the other part of the parish is Gowna, which is in County Cavan.

The Mullinalaghta GAA membership is just 155, in contrast to Kilmacud's 4,800 members. Dogged determination delivers resources beyond logic. This win is an incredible tale on many levels, not least the fact that Mullinalaghta were not even rated as a team to ever win a Leinster title. They have done the unthinkable, something nobody believed they could do – except themselves, with their self-belief. To dream the impossible dream and make it a reality is what mighty Mullinalaghta have taught us all.

Some sporting moments transcend the realm of sport itself and assume a significance in terms of the human spirit that no mere sporting victory ever could. This match was one of them.

One small step for GAA rivalries. One giant step for Mullinalaghta.

50

WHO FEARS TO SPEAK OF '98?

Waterford v. Clare

It was a masterpiece of emotional manipulation.

There has never been a year like 1998 in hurling terms. Waterford and Clare would find themselves cast as enemies. Waterford had already played a surprisingly significant part in Ger Loughnane's managerial career.

In 1991 Len Gaynor was appointed as Clare manager. The following year Loughnane was appointed as one of his selectors. As he was manager of the under-21 team that season, and because there was an overlap of players like Anthony Daly and Brian Lohan on both teams he was a natural choice to assist Gaynor. In 1992 his under-21 team qualified for the Munster final against Waterford. Waterford were powered by Tony Browne, Fergal Hartley, Johnny Brenner and Paul Flynn, and in a superb final emerged victorious 0-17 to 1-12. They went on to beat Offaly in a replay in the All-Ireland final. The Waterford defeat was to prove to be at once a formative and a bruising experience for Loughnane and would shape his subsequent relationship with the county board.

'There was such a furore over Clare losing the under-21 final that people never wanted me in charge of a Clare team of any kind again. Clare imagined they had a super under-21 team because they had been in the minor final in '89 and were beaten by Offaly. People assumed that there was an automatic correlation between minor and under-21, but that doesn't always happen. The reality was that we had a very average team and very few of them went on to make it at senior level. I had introduced this new system in training of moving the ball really fast, which I later used with the senior team, and had explained to the county board that it would take three years of this type of training to make proper players out of those lads.

'We beat Limerick and Tipperary playing beautiful hurling but were beaten by a superb Waterford team. What really annoyed me about the county board's attitude was they were only interested in winning. The fact that we were producing great hurling didn't matter. They didn't care if we kicked the ball as long as we won. What did it matter if we won an under-21 title or not, as long as these players were developing and could make it on to the senior team?

'That experience did teach me a valuable lesson. Up to that Munster final I always felt that the best place to observe what was happening on the pitch was to stand in the one place and keep a close eye on proceedings, but after that match I decided that the best thing was for me to move around and force more life into the players.'

Loughnane was given the sack as coach of the under-21 team and senior selector in the one night.

'The county board meeting came a night or two after the Munster under-21 final. They went absolutely ballistic! I was totally to blame for losing the under-21 final. While some of the criticism was sincerely motivated, the main thrust came from a small clique who wanted to put their own man in charge because they saw their opportunity for the following year. A lot of people at the meeting had their own agendas. They wanted more players from their clubs on the team or people from their backroom teams on the management team. The real sickener was that 17 of our panel were still eligible to play under-21 the following year and they had a great future if they were "minded" properly. The next year the Clare under-21s were trounced by Limerick. Seánie McMahon was left on the sideline for that game, while players with a fraction of his talent were playing. That whole episode left me with a complete distrust of the Clare county board.'

Typically, Loughnane did not take his dismissal lying down.

'I went to the next meeting of the county board and stood right up in front of the lot of them and faced them all down. I especially stared at the ones who were chiefly responsible for my dismissal. I said, "At your last meeting you were all complaining about me. Stand up now and I'll answer any question ye have to ask me." Nobody stood up.'

CONTROVERSY

Like a wasps' nest Loughnane is glued by something so powerful that it withstands the storms that whirl outside in layers of sturdy filaments woven into the fabric of his life. But, like the nest, if anybody probes too closely about the events of 1998 the memories fly out and sting him: disappointment, sadness and above all a sense of injustice. The Colin Lynch saga and the controversy about the Munster final replay have been the source of much speculation. On this subject he is so keenly alert that you worry about your next remark.

'There was a brilliant article in the *Clare Champion* by Joe Keane in which he spoke about Ernest Hemingway. After the publication of his book about bull fighting, *Death in the After-noon*, he was asked by an interviewer what he thought about bull fighting as a sport. He replied, "One has to be in with the bulls to know." It is amazing so many people spoke with such certainty about the Colin Lynch affair without knowing all of the facts and circumstances.'

How did such an atmosphere build up? Time does not stand still for reflections when the clash of the ash is at its fiercest, but the seeds for the extraordinary scenes that day had been sown the previous week. There are major hazards in deciding to ration commitment according to assessments of the opposition. Clare paid the price for that lapse in the first game.

'We had made a savage effort against Cork in the previous game and we always found it very difficult to raise our game the next day after a heroic effort. Every team does. It was the second year of the backdoor system, so there was always a safety net there. There was no real rivalry between Clare and Waterford. There was nothing there to give us the edge against them. All of us went down there with the nearest thing to a casual attitude in my time as Clare manager. The same drive wasn't there.'

RISING TEMPERATURES
From the beginning it was clear that Waterford's attitude was anything but casual.

'Whenever we played in Thurles, the Clare supporters were always given tickets for one part of the ground and we sat in the dugout in front of them. If we had sat in front of the rival supporters that could have been the recipe for all kinds of nasti-ness. When we went out against Waterford, the first thing we noticed was that all the Waterford subs and officials were in our dugout. We said nothing and went into the other dugout.

'Even though we were leading all through the game, Paul

Flynn got a late goal and then he had a chance to win the game from a long way out, but he put the ball wide. A few incidents had happened. P.J. O'Connell was sent off but there was a photo published the following day which showed Fergal Hartley giving him a ferocious tackle just before. Yet it was O'Connell alone who got sent to the line.'

SLEDGING

Fame can be a mixed blessing. One of the inevitable products of success is that there is increased interest in a new celebrity's private life. GAA players are not insulated from this trend, and from time to time they suffer the slings and arrows of the rumour mill. Generally, the bigger the name the more outrageous the rumour.

After their second All-Ireland in '97 a few of the Clare players became the subject of salacious gossip. Even before the rumour monger's paradise that is social media they were by no means the first or last GAA players to suffer in this way, as Loughnane acknowledges.

'When the players came back into the dressing-room I had never seen them so agitated and I asked what was wrong. They were fuming.

'One of the rumours doing the rounds at the time was that one of our players was beating his wife. Anyone who knows anything about his character would have known immediately how scurrilous and far off the mark it was and wouldn't have entertained it for a second. One of the Waterford players had shouted at the player in question, across the pitch, that he was a wife-beater. A lot of our players heard it. The player himself said nothing but it was the other players who were incensed. If anything triggered our players' huge response the following day, it was that.'

If the entire Clare squad were galvanised by the wife-beating comments, Loughnane was livid with the poor showing of his team. Understanding the ambushes of the mind his team had capitulated to, he was determined to reverse the pattern in the replay. His eyes drove through his players like two steel nails.

'On the bus back all I was thinking of was our performance – which was brutal. At training on Tuesday night the riot act was read! Mike O'Halloran was missing that night and when he came back the next night he said, "I hear the paint was falling off the goalposts!"

'In retrospect there was no need for me to have said anything. The players were so pumped up about what had been said to one of their own. I was angry with myself as much as with the players that none of us had picked up what was happening on the pitch and taken steps to correct it.

'The first step was to get all the players together the following night. I didn't go into the dressing-room. I stood out on the field. They knew that there was something up. I think Mike Mac did a lap or two with them and then I called them in to the midfield and I laid into them about backing down. I said Munster championships and All-Irelands weren't worth a damn. I didn't care about anything the following Sunday except we weren't going to be intimidated. Then I moved on about ten yards and laid into them about the next point. That was the pattern. I moved forward ten yards for every point till they all ended up in the net with me standing outside looking in at them, delivering a lecture about what was going to happen the following Sunday.

'I picked on every player who had backed down. Seánie, Brian Lohan and Colin Lynch got special attention first. Whenever I wanted to attack, I started with the strongest players. Seánie got a ferocious lecture, Lohan 40 times worse and Lynch as bad as the two of them put together for having backed down. I told them they could dump their medals because anyone who backed down from a challenge didn't deserve any respect. The next day we were not going to back down.

'We then adjourned to the Sherwood Hotel. Our planning committee, Tony [Considine], Mike [McNamara] and I went through where we had gone wrong the first day. Tony pointed out to me about the dugout. Mike said that there were too many people in the dressing-room before the game, with subs and officials. I said we'll get them out, but we have to do it in a way that they would still feel involved. So we decided we would get them to secure the dugout. It was like a military operation!

'In the meantime, Tony was to fire a few broadsides in *The Examiner* about Gerald McCarthy's behaviour on the field so that everyone, especially the referee, was aware of it for the following Sunday.

'The players weren't allowed to train. They would be about to go training when I'd deliver another lecture about the way we were going to play and then take them back into the dressing-room so that by the Sunday they were itching to play. The only training was psychological.

'Ninety-nine out of a hundred people will argue it was over the top. I didn't care whether it cost us the All-Ireland. We weren't going to be a team that backed down. I did emphasise that I didn't want any wildness, but everyone was prepared to give their life for Clare to win.

'On the day of the replay we went to Cashel for a puckout before the game as usual. The players were untypically quiet. I was as sour as I could be with them. The message was being delivered loud and clear. This was the day to deliver.'

Loughnane was fingered as a catalyst for the undeniable drama that unfolded in the replay.

'We went out onto the field and there was a photo published in the *Clare Champion* of me really putting it up to Colin Lynch before the game. All I was saying to him was that he had really let himself down the first day with the way he hurled, that he was a much better player than Tony Browne, and luckily enough he had one more chance to prove it. There were other players I had also singled out to deliver a similar message to, like Alan Markham, who had allowed themselves to be pushed around by Waterford the first day and that was never, ever going to happen again.

'When Jamesie came out with a broken hurl after a clash between himself and Brian Greene you could really sense the tension. There was a warning for all the officials to stay in the dugout but Tony Considine wasn't in the dugout. Just as he was about to throw in the ball the referee spotted that Tony wasn't in the dugout and walked over to put him back. In the meantime, the four players in the centrefield were jostling and waiting for the ball to be thrown in. By the time the ball was thrown in Lynch had let fly three or four times, but the only one he actually hit was Ollie Baker! He hit him on the heel.

'The first ball that went down was between Alan Markham and Stephen Frampton and both of them pulled a mile above the ball. I thought, "Oh, f**k." I said to Tony Considine, "It's lucky we're up for this one, otherwise they'd devour us." Waterford had caught Clare totally by surprise; collectively our players weren't able to react to it. They were ready for anything the second day.'

Sport is agony and ecstasy. It does not lend itself to grey areas. The next development would spiral crazily out of control.

'For the first five minutes the pulling was absolutely fero-cious. Then we had the [Brian] Lohan and [Micheál] White incident. Out of the corner of my eye I saw Colin Lynch and Tony Browne flaking each other. Who started it? That is a different story. I honestly don't know.

'A hurley is a dangerous weapon. If a player wants to use a hurley to inflict damage, he can do so. To the onlooker, pulling seems vicious, but in reality it's just like sword-fighting. If you strike somebody, it is always on a part of the body that is least vulnerable. If Lynch wanted to injure Browne he could have done so easily.

'Pat O'Connor, the well-known referee, was a linesman on the day. He saw what happened and put up the flag. Lohan and White were sent off. The noise from the crowd was unreal. There was total chaos in front of the Clare goal. My immediate concern was to sort out the defence now that Lohan was gone. I wanted Brian Quinn to stay on Paul Flynn and let Frank [Lohan] cover behind him.

'Meanwhile Pat O'Connor had gone to the referee, Willie Barrett, and reported the incident between Lynch and Tony Browne. Willie Barrett booked both of them.

'After that the whole thing settled down and Clare completely outhurled them and demolished Waterford. About five minutes before the end of the game I said to Gerald McCarthy, "Sure the game is over now." We chatted away for three or four minutes. He said, "Oh, ye're by far the better team." There was no anger at all.

'Dalo got the cup and we went into the dressing-room. Pat Joe Ryan, the chairman of Waterford county board, came in and said, "Ye're the best team I ever saw in my life. Ye're hurling is way better than anybody else's. I hope ye go on now and win the All-Ireland." There was no more about it.

'I do admit it was a warlike atmosphere against Waterford. It was the same on both sides. Clare went into the game like never before. It was a day to kill or be killed. The players weren't thinking about winning an All-Ireland. It was about putting Waterford down. If we had won an All-Ireland by coming in the backdoor, after allowing Waterford to intimidate us in the Munster final replay, it would have been useless. I freely admit putting down Waterford was absolutely vital. There were always hard physical exchanges in the Munster championship but when it was over players shook hands and it was forgotten about.

'In normal circumstances we'd have loved to have seen Waterford winning the All-Ireland. Nobody remembers Daly's speech afterwards, nor the cup coming into the dressing-room. We often remember the glow of satisfaction we got from having downed Waterford.'

IN THE EYE OF THE STORM

Ger Loughnane dominated 1998 along with the many controversies that dogged his team: the clashes with officialdom, the rows with referees, as well as the unprecedented media attention. Things really ignited after the Munster final replay against Waterford, where the intense aggression began even before the match started. The man at the centre of the storm was referee Willie Barrett.

'The criticism of my performance did get to me and I wasn't appointed to any other intercounty games that year. I got letters from people who were very angry. I stopped answering the phone for a while. My wife started taking the calls and she got the brunt of it. Someone said to me once that it was nice to have your picture in the paper but I saw my picture every day 12 or 13 days in a row and it didn't add to me, I can assure you. It did affect me and I didn't know at that stage if I would have the confidence to referee a big game again. My daughter was in

France at the time, and I felt under siege, so I brought the family to France until things settled down a bit.'

THE LYNCH MOB

The day after the replay there was a bit of a ripple about the physical exchanges in the papers but nothing extraordinary. The temperature rose dramatically on Monday evening after the *Sportscall* programme on RTÉ radio. It was clear from very early on that one Clare player was being singled out for special attention, with comments like 'the Vinnie Jones of hurling' and 'I'd love to see him tested for steroids'.

It was not long before Loughnane was brought into centre stage. 'What you saw for the first three minutes was like what you'd see on the Ormeau Road. It was orchestrated violence … "and if he's in charge of schoolchildren in Clare" …'

Loughnane was well used to, and more than able for, comments about his tactics, but the repeated implication that he was unfit to be a teacher or in charge of children crossed a new line for him.

'The *Sportscall* programme after the Munster final was totally scandalous, totally one-sided. Two solicitors approached me with the tape of the programme and said they'd take on the case for nothing to sue RTÉ, but I said I didn't want it to go that route. They kept saying to me, "But you will win hands down." After that programme the media focus on us became crazy.

'The following Sunday Tony Browne played the match of his life. This was the man who had been nearly killed by Clare seven days before!'

As the week went on the controversy developed a momentum of its own. Amid the hysteria there were the occasional dissenting voices. However, behind the scenes judgement was being passed.

The bigger issues were apparently ignored, in Loughnane's eyes.

'I didn't realise there had been anything afoot. We went back training on the Thursday night. I'd been at the Galway races on the Wednesday and, looking back, there were rumblings that there was trouble ahead but I didn't pick up on them. It had been non-stop in the papers. One headline posed the question: "Is this Space Age Hurling?" Were Clare trying to take hurling on to a new plain? It was total rubbish.'

Loughnane's gut instinct was telling him to brace himself for trouble. The chill of doubt that had settled over his spirit back then soon became shattering reality.

'The first inkling I got was after the All-Ireland quarter-final when Robert Frost, chairman of the Clare county board, had overheard a conversation that Lynch would get a three months suspension. I dismissed it at first, but with all the clamour that was going on I began to wonder. The next thing we got the letter that Lynch was to appear before the Munster council.'

THE BOOK OF EVIDENCE

We prefer to play hopscotch in a familiar minefield. Loughnane was used to investing all his energies into battles on the field now he was finding himself concentrating most of his energies to an off the field battle.

As if the Clare camp did not have enough reason to feel sore the temperature really rose on Sunday, 26 July. The chairman of the Clare county board, Robert Frost, attended the Waterford versus Galway All-Ireland quarter-final at Croke Park. He was in the VIP section of the Hogan Stand. There were three clergymen seated immediately behind him. He overheard their conversation. The Munster final replay of the previous Sunday was the main topic of conversation between them. The immediate response to this conversation was the depiction of Loughnane and his players, the famous line that: 'The Clare team were tinkers, Loughnane was a tramp and the Clare team must be on drugs.' Loughnane knew the stakes had been massively increased.

'The really significant part of the discussion on Sunday, 26 July, was that it took place two days before the meeting (scheduled for Tuesday, 28 July) of the Munster council to make a decision on the referee's report and one of the priests stated:

'Seamus Gardiner (a reference to Father Seamus Gardiner PRO of the Munster council) has told me that he had been speaking with Donie Nealon (Secretary to the Munster council) and that the Munster council were going to get Ger Loughnane up on the Stand and suspend Colin Lynch for three months.

'On hearing this Robert Frost stood up and challenged the three priests about what they had been saying and what they had said and being embarrassed about having to do so in public, he then left. Of course, questions were immediately raised: how could three outsiders know Lynch's fate two days before the meeting to adjudicate on his "crime"? How could this possibly reflect proper procedures? Could justice be served in this way?'

Loughnane believes that Clare made a fundamental tactical error in all of this controversy.

'At a meeting of the Munster council Waterford proposed having an investigation into the events of the match. Their proposal got no seconder. Clare should have seconded it to ensure there was a full, fair and open investigation.'

Instead the Clare county board went down the legal avenue, seeking a pre-emptive strike against the Munster council taking disciplinary action. With the benefit of hindsight Loughnane identifies a better strategy.

'Pat Fitzgerald said the only way was to get a court injunction against the Munster council. If Colin Lynch was brought before them, the only question they would ask him was, "Did you strike Tony Browne?" The context and the question of provocation would not be considered.

'The council's verdict still wasn't announced, but essentially Clare's case was that Colin Lynch shouldn't be called in front of them in the first place. It all became very technical then. The court case was on the Friday before the All-Ireland semi-final against Offaly. I didn't think it had much chance of succeeding because the courts were not going to get involved in the rules of the GAA. I wasn't a bit surprised when it was thrown out.'

FAMILY TIES

The previous year a string of top-class performances had provided a convincing assertion of Colin Lynch's right to be considered as one of the radiant stars in the hurling firmament. His loss to the team in '98 cannot be overestimated. The media attention on Lynch came at an extremely inappropriate and unfortunate time for all his family. They had suffered two serious bereavements over two months when his uncle's wife and his grandmother passed away. He was unable to attend the meeting of the Munster council on 7 August because that evening his grandmother suffered a serious setback and was dying. Loughnane takes up the story.

'The Lynches are a very close family. Colin was very close to his grandmother. We had been waiting all day for the verdict from the courts. That night when we got to the Limerick Inn there was an incredible atmosphere. There were 120 Clare people there to show their support. There were camera crews and media. I was interviewed and Marty Morrissey misunderstood a comment I made about Colin's grandmother's condition. He thought that she was dead when she was very, very close to death. We were in the back-room waiting all night. At one stage I got a call. It was Colin Lynch's aunt. She said, "Do you know that Marty Morrissey has just announced on the television that Colin's grandmother is dead?" I apologised profusely to her for the distress the inaccuracy had caused the family. I tore out and saw Maurice Reidy, a senior producer in RTÉ, was there. I said, "Where is Marty Morrissey?" Lucky for him he was gone. I'd have nearly killed him. When he discovered his mistake, he went to the hospital to apologise to the Lynch family.'

Ironically Loughnane would find himself at the other end of such a story in 2011 when he had leukaemia and a national newspaper erroneously reported that he had died – to the great distress of his family.

Given his role on *The Sunday Game* in 1998 Pat Spillane had the opportunity to speak to Reidy about the experience.

'Maurice had covered many big sporting occasions before but he told me he has never experienced anything like that. You could cut the tension with a knife. The atmosphere was getting more frenzied by the second, as they waited for Loughnane to appear. They knew there would be fireworks. Two things struck Maurice about his performance. He never used any bad language and he never repeated himself. Given the toxic atmosphere and the emotional intensity, not to mention the pressure he was under personally, Maurice thought his self-control was remarkable.'

Privately Loughnane was silently seething.

'We sat there until twelve o'clock but there was no way we were going to be let in to speak on Colin's behalf. The Munster council knew from previous experience that if I was let in there would be a serious confrontation. We decided to go home. We heard on the way out that Colin had indeed got a three months suspension. There were still Clare people in the foyer. The rumour was that the Munster council went out through the window to escape them.'

Alex Ferguson would always defend his players regardless. Loughnane was cast in the same mould. The solidarity that had been so assiduously nurtured in the team over four years could evaporate in a flash by a moment's carelessness.

'Everybody on the team appreciated that no matter whether Lynch was wrong or right he was going to be defended and that was important.

'Colin Lynch was a very good underage hurler and footballer. I regarded him as a great hurler at under-21 level. When Len Gaynor took charge, he didn't seem to take to him and he never featured while Len was here. When we took over, we brought him on to the panel straight away. He then got glandular fever, which took a lot out of him and he missed over a year's hurling.

'He was as professional as Jamesie in his preparation, which is the ultimate compliment. He never said a huge amount but was a strong character in the dressing-room. He had great leadership qualities. He was outstanding in '97 and against Cork in '98. Although he had a bad game in the Munster final that year, he completely outhurled Tony Browne in the replay. He was outstanding the second day against Tipperary in 1999. I was going to be loyal to him because he had given so much for Clare.

'I have no regrets because the players knew that I would go to any lengths to defend any player on the panel – until they were proven guilty. If he was seen by the referee or the linesman, or if there was video evidence that was fine. They would deserve to be suspended. But I think that nobody deserves to be suspended unless there's evidence. You can't suspend someone on the basis that somebody in the crowd saw something. That was the basis on which I fought the case.

The only reaction that mattered to me was that of the players. Anybody else was only an outsider.

'We had a policy in the Clare team that we would never complain after what happened in a game. We never made an issue out of it at the time, but the most serious injury inflicted on a Clare player came in the Munster championship against Limerick in 1996. Ollie Baker's eye socket was smashed very, very seriously with about five minutes to go in the match. We lost our way after Ollie went off. It showed how crucial he was to the team. He was able to make the difference at vital times. Likewise, in 1999 we lost the Munster final when he went off injured.

'It was premeditated because the Limerick player in question had warned him beforehand that he was going to do it. It was the sort of injury that could end a career. It could also have been very damaging for him professionally because it could have stopped Ollie from getting a position in the guards. Yet nothing was said about that. Action should have been taken against the player involved. You'd have to be blind not to see it. This is not sour grapes about losing that match. I never said anything about it afterwards. I don't have a problem with justice but I do have a problem with selective justice. The video evidence was used selectively in '98.

'It was fair game for the media to lacerate me, I give it and I take it, but what I objected to was that Colin Lynch, who had no contact with the media whatsoever, did not get the opportunity for a fair trial, with the verdict already announced before the meeting to discuss it.'

Loughnane's summation of the Colin Lynch saga is said with a sideways grimace. What is certain is that he feels his team were wronged. 'The problem was that there was no evidence either from the video or from the referee's report.'

DESTINY'S CHILD

Having such an unseemly public squabble leaves a legacy of bitterness which would take a long time to heal. Loughnane finds it hard to make sense of it all.

'It is very hard to describe the atmosphere that prevailed in the '98 Munster final replay. I've often tried to figure out why the players reacted the way they did. My comments were part of it, but I think the big thing was what the players said among themselves. It was like going to war. You just didn't care what was going to happen to yourself individually. All that mattered was that you were going to fight for the players beside you. You were going out with a tunnel vision; you were going to give of everything you had to put them down. Once we got to Thurles you could feel the hostility in the air. I still can't rationalise what happened and why Waterford felt the same way. It was a two-edged sword.

'Pat Fitzgerald had told me it was raining outside so I told the players to put on their tracksuits till the match started. Many of them didn't want to put them on. They said there was no need and some of them didn't. Somebody handed me a wet suit to put on but it was soon on its way, flying through the air. We were going into battle and this was no place for any creature comforts for me.

'It was a day when there was really no need for any words in the dressing-room. I held up the county jersey again and told the players that they had sh*t on it the first day and anyone who was going to allow that to happen again should stay in the dressing-room and tog in. The jambs of the door nearly went flying with them on the way out. They hit the field like an absolute tornado that day, but the fact that they were wearing tracksuits aroused suspicion. I learned afterwards that when he saw them wearing them a prominent GAA journalist in the press box asked, "What's the bastard done now?"

'In the drawn game one of the Waterford mentors stood in front of our dugout. It was total and utter intimidation. Wherever we walked, he walked in front of us so that we couldn't see what was happening properly. The second day we detailed Mike Mac to mark him. The plan beforehand was if a row broke out he was to "look after" him; Tony would "look after" the other selectors, and I would "look after" Gerald McCarthy. It was every man for himself after that.

'Before we went out on the pitch I stared right into each player's eyes. It was the only time I ever understood how soldiers could go out into battle and not be afraid of dying. The cup meant nothing. This was personal. Waterford were not going to be allowed to humiliate some of our players the way they had done the previous Sunday. We wanted to put them down. I admit completely it was war without bullets.'

THE RESTORATION OF FAITH

Loughnane's faith in the system was restored by a meeting on 11 November that year with the GAC (Games Administration Committee).

'The Munster council had made a complaint about us to the GAC about my Clare FM interview. There were rumours that the Munster council were going to take Clare FM and I to court.

'Robert Frost, Pat Fitzgerald and I had no inhibitions about travelling up. Unlike any of the meetings from earlier that year we made no serious preparation for it. Luckily in their wisdom the GAC excluded the Munster council representatives. The chairman was John Greene from Longford and the others included Brian McEniff, the former Donegal manager, and Seamus Howlin, later chairman of the Wexford county board. Basically, they were people we never met before.

'At the start of the meeting things were very tense. Initially they were unusually aggressive. They tried to deal with the interview in an overall context but we said no, and insisted they take it step by step. After we eyed each other up, gradually the meeting settled down and the level of confrontation decreased. We began to realise that this was not like a Munster council meeting because the outcome wasn't decided before we went in.

'I knew they were hearing our side of the story for the first time and they were taken aback with some of the detail we presented. From time to time there were long pauses as they absorbed what we said. We spent three hours in discussion until they were left with nothing to say. They could see that we had a grievance. Coming out, I wasn't thinking about their verdict. I was just happy that at last we had met with people who were prepared to listen to what we had to say.

'We had to wait until 22 December to hear the GAC's verdict. The Munster council got the same letter. People with a suspicious mind might think that the reason that they left it till three days before Christmas was that they didn't want their decision to get any publicity!

'They did express their disappointment that we hadn't pursued our grievance through the proper GAA channels. I completely understand that. However, the really significant part of their letter was their admission that "we acknowledge that there have been some inconsistencies in the manner in which disciplinary matters have been dealt with by the Munster council and that Clare may have perceived grievances". I don't want to be like Albert Reynolds after the beef tribunal and talk about "a total vindication" but here was a top-level committee of the GAA investigating another powerful organ of the GAA and rapping the Munster council on the knuckles in relation to inconsistency in applying discipline over the course of the Munster championship. To my knowledge this is the first time something like that happened.

'The letter is couched in the most diplomatic language, but there is no ambiguity about the meaning. Whatever the means we used, there is no doubt they were saying that we had a legitimate reason to believe that proper procedures were not deployed in the case of Clare that summer. We weren't looking for publicity about the verdict. We were satisfied that at last we had got a fair hearing and had got fair play.

'I'm convinced that the Colin Lynch debacle was the catalyst for the change that took place in the GAA's disciplinary procedures, when disciplinary measures were taken out of the hands of the provincial councils and put in the hands of the GAC. The Munster council were hoist by their own petard. They had made the complaint about us, but the result was that their powers were curtailed.'

Given the emotional rollercoaster that was '98 Loughnane might be expected to be bitter, but surprisingly this is the chapter of his life that furnishes his most nostalgic reminiscences.

'It was a year never to be forgotten. I wouldn't swap it for anything. It was the experience of a lifetime. It was a test of yourself. Could you not alone survive but triumph over all adversity? A year like that strangely was as enjoyable as the previous year when we won the All-Ireland. I know a lot of people who didn't go through such an experience would find that strange, but there is a certain satisfaction from having survived it. I wouldn't change anything about 1998, despite all its controversies, with those games against Waterford. The rivalry between the two counties on the day of the replay was like nothing I had ever seen before or since, but it faded afterwards.'

CHANGING THE SOCIAL ORDER

Some officials on the Clare county board never forgave Ger Loughnane for not living down to their expectations. He knew that if the Clare team was to triumph he would not only have to win hurling matches, he would need to end the *ancien regime* – off the field as much as on it.

The Clare that Loughnane grew up in was a very stratified society, with a layered social fabric. Irish people often delude ourselves by pretending that unlike the British we do not have a class system. That is not true because we have something much more subtle. In rural Ireland there was a very definite social hierarchy in every parish which kept everybody in their pre-ordained niche. The only way to break free from your appointed status was to move out.

Loughnane offers a sociological perspective: 'Once the English domination went in the 1920s a new order was needed to keep people in their place. That only crumbled in the late 1960s, when free education was introduced. Young people started to go to university and to mix with people from other counties and to see they were as good as anybody else. The revolution started from down below. Our parents' generation were afraid of authority. Nowadays younger people do not have the hang-ups that other generations had. With that came greater confidence.

'Hurling was between the big three, the rich farming lands of Tipperary, Cork and Kilkenny. The view was that when it really came down to it you could never beat those and so what you did was try and become kingpins in your small pool. This created all kinds of feuds in the county and very little commit-ment to the county team. Players wanted to get the jersey but they had no real commitment to it. That was a huge impediment to Clare and when they had good teams usually internal feuds stopped them making the breakthrough. They blamed referees, drinking, pitches and anything else they could think of. The reality was it was the fault of the divisions within the team that brought about their disruption. Once you understand that, you can understand how to remedy it.

'It all came down to self-belief. Our All-Ireland-winning team were not overawed by anyone or anything. In fact, far from being overawed they were all anxious to prove themselves and to show exactly what they could do. We had so many of those – I suppose you could call them leaders: Anthony Daly, Brian Lohan, Davy Fitzgerald, Seánie McMahon, Ollie Baker, Jamesie O'Connor. You could go on and on. Far from shirking the challenge, they were going to embrace it. The bigger the challenge, the better they were going to perform, and that was actually the crucial difference between the team I played on and the team I managed. The change that took place in the Clare team was a reflection of a lot of changes that had taken place in society.'

In Clare hurling, the hierarchy was very clearly defined.

'I was there as a player when the county board blocked every-thing that would have been a step to progress. They considered the team not even secondary but tertiary. They were the most important. There was no doubt about that. They weren't sure what was the second most important thing, but the players were way down the line. That was the mentality that was there for years and years. It was not just the case in Clare. It was the same in a lot of counties and is still the same in some counties where the eminence of the county board is more important than anything else.

'After a Clare match the hotel would be full to the rafters with county board officers of all types, like those who were on various committees. They were willing to provide meals for players but never for their wives or girlfriends. Most players wouldn't go in for a meal for that reason, though the wives of the officials were always brought in for meals. Players would have expenses but rarely would they get the full amount. The county board always found some pretext to dock them.

'When I was playing there was no such thing as swapping jerseys. When the practice did become commonplace there was uproar from the county board. It didn't matter whether you won a game or not. The officers came in and checked off each jersey on their list to ensure nobody slipped one away. When you've just lost a big game this is not the sort of thing you want to see happening. They also made a big deal out of socks. If you lost your socks you had to replace them yourself. It was at that ridiculous level.

'I can't say I was ever badly treated. I got on with the people I was with. No matter how difficult an officer was, they knew that I wasn't going to be subdued. That's the way life was and you just accepted it.

'Worst of all was that the county board only appointed selectors they could dominate, intimidate and keep control of. The selectors were usually as afraid of the county board as the players were. The county board wanted to control and dominate everything. If they did it in a way that was best for the county team I wouldn't have minded, but it was their pettiness that destroyed morale on the Clare team. They were just watching their own careers and everybody else suffered because of that.'

THE SOUND OF SILENCE

The Waterford–Clare rivalry would make occasional rallies in subsequent years. The spat of the year in 2013 was between Ger Loughnane and John Mullane. That January Mullane announced his retirement from the Waterford team. After Waterford lost to Kilkenny in the championship Loughnane appeared to blame Mullane for the defeat by retiring and for 'letting his county down'. Asked on Newstalk's *Off the Ball* about Loughnane's remarks Mullane appeared to be the bigger man when he replied, 'He's entitled to his own opinion. But I'm not going to comment on that.' However, he couldn't resist saying, 'I think if you're dealing with ignorant people, the only way you can deal with it is to ignore it.'

Loughnane looks back on Clare's rivalries with undisguised affection.

'From a personal perspective I owe a lot to the rivalry with the teams in Munster. They stopped me from achieving my goals as a player and because of that I pushed myself and my team to beat them as a manager, and those times we did were very sweet moments. That is the real magic of the great GAA rivalries. Long may their magic continue.'

CONCLUSION

In Thomas More's classic satirical novel *Utopia*, the common good – as opposed to partisan advantage – is the overriding concern; the human family is called to serve one another's best interests. With empowerment as the prevailing dynamic, winning and losing are transcended. *Utopia* was a clarion call to live in ever more radically relational and interdependent ways, and to enter a vast weblike network of relationships, dynamic processes and organic inter-connections. But real life marches to a different drum than the one in More's Utopian creation.

Competition permeates all walks of life. As the anecdote tells us, two cardinals were bemoaning the drop of vocations. One, a Jesuit, remarked, 'It will be a shame if in the next fifty years or so if we have no more Jesuits. It would be a tragedy and a huge loss to the Church.'

His colleague, a Benedictine, said, 'Nonsense. The Church managed for 1,500 years without any Jesuits. It will do so again. Now if there were to be no more Benedictines that would be a crisis.'

For fans of Gaelic games when the world is weighing us down too much and our way forward is obscured by confusion our team is a ray of light to beam peace into our stressful lives and focus us forward with renewed hope in our hearts.

Our rivals, though, are a target for all our pent-up feelings of disgruntlement. They are a beacon and a curse: a source of despair and hope, of darkness and light. They hover in our hearts, whether in the bad defeats when we feel the cold breath of doom on our backs and our stomachs are twisted into raw knots of anxiety, or the heady victories, when a thrilling tingle tumbles down our spines. We open ourselves to them like a flower to the sun.

There is no reason to suspect that their status is under threat in any shape or form, as they are so integral to Gaelic games. Here we are all prisoners 'of our own device', to allude to the phrasing of those well-known writers on the GAA identity, the Eagles in 'Hotel California'.

You can check out your GAA rivalries any time you like.

But you can never leave.

ACKNOWLEDGEMENTS

It is a massive honour for me to have Ireland's greatest living writer Donal Ryan write the foreword. Donal's genius with the pen is only eclipsed by his greatness as a man.

I also wish to express my profound gratitude to John O'Mahony, Cyril Farrell, Brian Corcorcan, Tom Parsons, Michael Duignan, Michael Darragh MacAuley and the crown prince of hurling full-backs Brian Lohan for their help.

Special thanks to the wonderful Nicole Owens for sharing her story so generously with me.

Thanks to Simon Hess, Campbell Brown and all at Black & White for their help.

In May 2019 we lost Eugene McGee. I had experienced his kindness at first hand. He will always be remembered as a giant of the GAA, but I will also think of him as a champion of rural Ireland and as a quiet but effective campaigner for those with special needs.

Joe Barry has been much in my thoughts because of the loss of his beloved wife Siobhán.

Congratulations to John and Marie Reynolds on their Golden Jubilee this year. Meanwhile their son John is contributing to the betterment of society through his work for those who need a hand up.

Thanks to the doyen of Ballygar, Michael Nolan, for his generous support of my books.

My gratitude to Lauren Fallon for being such a discerning reader and my ongoing thanks to her father Noel for his sustained support.

Shannonside's Kevin McDermott has always been of very great assistance and I really appreciate it.

A Donegal star in the making, Ruadhán Starkey was born this year to his proud parents, Eibhlin and Brendan. May the homes of Donegal sing his praises in years to come. Thanks to Ali, Emily and Robbie Henshaw for their assistance, and congratulations to them on their outstanding achievement with their awesome fundraising CD with the iconic Sharon Shannon for the South Westmeath Hospice, *The Secret Sessions.*

My good friend Gareth O'Callaghan has gone through a challenging couple of years. One of the most uplifting moments of the year came when he announced his engagement to the wonderful Paula just before Valentine's Day. May they both discover that love changes everything and that ultimately all you need is love and may the sparkling sunshine in your souls continue to shine.

Marie Maher has played the game of life with grace and grit this year. May she only experience good things in the coming years.

Michael Daly's star has risen still further in the literary firmament this year. May it continue to do so.

Lisa Dobey got married in June. I hope that she will forever surf on waves of love and happiness.

ACKNOWLEDGEMENTS

Katy Dobey has had a momentous year. I hope she will be happy as long as the sea is bound to wash up on the sand.

Malachy Thompson has found a new role this year. I hope he will find happiness and satisfaction in his new ministry.

Monika Herok achieved her life ambition this year. People are people and everything counts and may she always feel in Heaven and enjoy the silence with her personal Jesus.

Monaghan's biggest fan, Gerardine Heaphey, graduated with distinction this year. I hope the best is yet to come for her.

Lydia Greene has had a significant year in career terms. May the sun shine on her in this new position.

Dave O'Connell is the personification of the old adage that 'the West is best'. I am very grateful for his ongoing support of my books.

Judith McAdam has had a Masterful year. May the road rise to meet her in the future.

Ace camogie player Karen O'Donovan has taken on a new leadership role and brought her customary dedication and commitment to the task.

Former Roscommon footballer Róisín Ní Dhonncha has also been upwardly mobile this year. May she continue to represent the Rossies with distinction.